Without a Parachute

DAVID FENNARIO

McClelland and Stewart Limited

<u>The Canadian Publishers</u>
McClelland and Stewart Limited
25 Hollinger Road, Toronto
Printed and bound in Canada

TO BETTY ANN

THANK YOU
SALLY AND RICHARD
FOR THE CONFIDENCE

Feeling ill with the flu. I'm working in the cosmetics stock room department of the St. James Simpson's warehouse, surrounded with the smell of a thousand different perfumes all around me. Mr. Forget, the chief boss, is a tiny man with a dwarfish voice. The freight trains go by the back windows and I remember. We will live in beauty some day. And I'm listening to a girl singing on the radio but I'm listening to her draw in her breath and I can almost see her lungs expanding releasing the air that comes out of her mouth as music. On my lunch hour. The working conditions here are infinitely better than at Ribkoff's - no hasslings, just do your work. Nearly all the people play cards after eating in the cafeteria. I didn't want to appear odd by sitting by myself and staring into space so I came back downstairs to write my journal. Yeah the cafeteria reminded me of the Don Jail in T.O. Long tables of card players slapping down those hearts and diamonds. I'm sitting on top of a large box in back of the stock room wondering how long I'll be working here, wondering what 1970 holds for me, and the world. I think I'm predicting correctly when I say that this is going to be the roughest winter of a lot of people's lives. The people here have the impression that I'm a very quiet guy. (I can remember when airplanes were strange things and people looked up at them when they passed by.)

The West End is the area in Montreal that stretches from Atwater to Peel Street, from St. Antoine to the canal. It's commonly known to hot shot social workers and Montreal Star reporters as "Little Burgundy". I think maybe Dick MacDonald may have invented the term, 'cause none of the families I know in the area ever use it.

The West End is like an old whore that still retains some of her youthful beauty. The weather reflects her passing moods: on a rainy November afternoon she's getting up from a bad drunk and on a sunny April morning she's waking up with a good loving man in her bed, plenty of good wine in the kitchen, food in the fridge and great prospects of easy scores in the future. She speaks like a honky tonk piano. A salty old doll with a laugh like a passing freight train. She tattooes herself with wild flowers in May and in December puts on a snowwhite overcoat over her rags.

Sailor Rick, just out of the Navy, dropped in on us last night. Standing at the front door, blue tuque on his head, sporting a heavy rum-stained beard, a Halifax seabag slung over his shoulder with a thousand stories in his head to tell me. "I'm not getting smarter every year, Dave," he said, "I'm just getting less stupid." He's been working as a diver in the Navy for the last three years and he had some pretty gruesome tales to tell about fishing dead men out of lakes and shit like that. He stayed until ten o'clock rapping with us in the living room than left to go to his sister's house in the Point for the night. "I'm going out west, Dave, to Vancouver where I heard they have jobs for divers, but first I wanna check out on my younger sister who was beaten up and raped about a month ago and I'd like to find out who was responsible." Judging from the light flashing in his eyes when he said this there'll be murder if the guys are found.

And I was thinking of old Joe Coté this morning at work. Wondering if the old guzzler is still alive and getting drunk daily at the Empire Tavern. Seventy-seven years old, a veteran rounder who can remember when there were dinosaurs on St. Antoine Street. I'll have to drop in the bar soon and find out how he's doing.

In the Gazette there was an article on welfare stating that the number of welfare recipients was up from 26 to 28,000 this year. It is expected that this winter the number will rise over the "danger point" of 30,000. Danger for whom may I ask?

2

December 15, 1969   Sunday

   Bought a gas balloon for Elizabeth today and I really
looked a sight carrying it through Place Bonaventure while
wearing my shades and greasy-looking leather jacket. People
laughed to see a guy looking like a Hell's Angel carrying a
gaily coloured balloon bobbing in mid air on the end of a
string. And I laughed with them. On the way home down
St. Antoine Street some guy across the street yelled out
to me above the traffic. I looked in his direction and
thought it was Joe Coté calling me so I yelled "Hey Joe"
and the little man came running over. It wasn't Joe but
some drunken old Irish Newfie who bummed me for a
quarter. "Hey c'm here," he said and I moved closer to
him. "Bend over I wanna tell you something." I did so
and then the old fucker gave me a big wet kiss on the cheek
and went away laughing. Well, so did I as I walked away
holding my gas balloon.

December 20, 1969   Saturday

   A confused apathetic day with so many things to do and
nothing done. Went about downtown for a few hours looking at the Christmas shoppers and stopped off at Ribkoff's
to talk with the guys, Mike, Andy, Butch and Pat, all West
End boys, and paid Rolly the four bucks I owed him. Big
city Dave Fennario blues have got me. I am frightened of
the many things that have to be done. Liz is lying in bed
and she's called out to ask me if I want her to talk to me.
Pearl, our little cat, keeps jumping on my lap as I sit at my
desk writing this. It is twelve-thirty at night and we have
just come back from watching three movies at the Vogue
on Charlebois Street in the Point. The long walk home
through that whole vast slum area was very depressing for
me. Where do these people get the strength to keep on
living in the face of such despair and hopelessness. The
whole area stinks of broken dreams and insanity. Little
taverns hugging the corners of the street. Factory chim-
neys, match-box houses, solitary street lamps. Second-

hand, everything is second-hand, including their lives. We sell our love and hopes cheaply down here. I always shudder when I pass over the black waters of the canal my Uncle Gus drowned himself in, I feel like I'm jumping a hurdle my uncle didn't get over.

Decay and death. These houses were built a long time ago by our great-grandfathers. The plumbers, plasterers, brick-layers, carpenters, tinsmiths, house painters and architects of the 1880's. All gone to the grave one way or the other. Ate their suppers, drank their beer, made love to their wives, fed their children, smoked their pipes, enjoyed their summer nights and Christmas festivities. With little triumphs and many tragedies lived out their days of hard work and small pleasures.

December 26, 1969   Friday

I keep writing because I don't feel like sleeping. It's one o'clock in the morning. The electric hum of the fridge is the only sound in the house. Liz is asleep with Pearl. I have no gods nor do I talk with dead men. I kiss my children's hands and work for good harvests.

January 13, 1970   Tuesday

I've got that old blue feeling like I want to break up all the furniture and punch the walls. My Aunt Irene's husband Sonny used to do it whenever he was on a bad drunk. Put his foot through the T.V. and smash up all the beds and bureaus while his wife and children huddled together in a corner screaming. I was only about five when I overheard my parents in the kitchen talking at the breakfast table about my Uncle Sonny, and I remember how puzzled I was with the idea of Sonny busting up his own furniture. Why would he break up something that belonged to him? I asked my parents about this, but they didn't understand it either. "He drinks too much - that's all," said my old man. So many of the old vices are masqueraded today in clinical terminology.

4

I pinched a half-dozen of aspasia soap from the stock room today for Liz. They cost 98 cents a bar - strictly for the Upper Westmount trade. I stuffed them down behind my shirt just before the bell rang. I got a little nervous when one of the bars slipped down my pant's leg while I was walking down the stairs. Billy Sullivan saw me pick it up and he threw me a smile and a wink. Coming home I said to Liz at the front door, "Well Liz, for the first time in your life you're gonna get to use real soap." "Oh boy," she said with her face all lit up like a rainbow. "This stuff smells good enough to eat."

January 14, 1970   Wednesday

Just took a whiff of Pear's Soap and was transported back to bourgeois Great Britain red coats tin soldier 1890. Yeah the scent of Pear's Soap is the essence of the polite Edwardian Era. Of ladies with their perfumed hair and fragile faces, porcelain nerves and glass hearts. Old dowagers with blacklace fans. I once saw a photo of a London street scene circa 1900 and one of the advertisements on the double-decker bus parked by the curb was for Pear's soap. A solidly middle-class commodity also used by the more impoverished of the aristocracy. The coarsest of soaps, if any at all, was used by the badly washed working class of this time. Clay pipes, heavy brogues, cloth caps, wide braces, thick working pants and beer-stained moustaches. My grandfather, an Edwardian workman, reminded me as a child irresistibly of a strong, quiet, slow-moving work-horse. A beast that could be violent on rare occasions when it was prodded beyond its tremendous endurance. Endurance, that is the key word in the character of my grandfather, the Edwardian worker.

January 18, 1970   Sunday

Got a card from Sailor Rick postmarked Edmonton, Alberta. Gonna mail him a few lines and find out what's happening.

Delinquent Dave, the fourteen-year-old kid who broke into our basement with his brother last fall, was down this afternoon telling me about his troubles with his mother. Very bold kid and a real thief, he keeps kidding me that he's gonna rob my cowhide boots out on the porch. I told him I'd kick his ass all the way down Coursol Street if he did. He respects me because I didn't put the cops onto him and his brother last fall. Instead I grabbed a hold of him on the street when I saw him wearing my sweater, grabbed him by the neck and said, "Look, man that's my sweater you're wearing. I know it was you and your brother who broke into my place. So what am I going to do? I'm too old to fight you. I could get my brother who is your age to beat the shit out of you. I grew up in this area and I don't like to phone the cops. Look if you have to steal, why do you have to steal from your own people? Why don't you go up to Westmount for fuck's sake." Ever since then Dave has been visiting me regularly and I like to think I've had some kind of good influence on him. At least he's not in Shawbridge like his brother. The boys have a really sad story to tell. They don't have a father and their mother is a drunken old whore who sleeps with all the men in the taverns. She's always going berserk and tossing her kids out in the street. A lot of the families here in the West End know all about the Cleaver family situation and they take turns feeding the boys and finding them places to stay. Short of a revolution, I can very easily forecast Dave's life. Drink, jail and death. So cruel to be doomed at such an early age.

January 22, 1970   Thursday

I went up the hill this evening and called on Charly. He was studying for an exam so I only stayed a few minutes. I then went up on Lincoln Street to Stu's but he wasn't home so I cut over to Sir George to see if I could spot anyone there. Had to talk to someone. I hit the jackpot in the cafeteria, three people I knew were sitting at a table, Stu, Barry and Robin. I walked up behind Robin leaned over and surprised her with a kiss. "Absolute strangers are always coming up and kissing this girl," I said to the other people at the table. They all smiled except for the dude Robin was with, he never took his eyes off the table the whole time I was talking with her. Seemed pissed off at my familiarity with Robin. Fuck him anyhow! I've known and loved the girl for years. I invited Stu down to our place where we swopped stories for two hours in the living room. A very clever guy with an unusual personality that I haven't puzzled out yet. He's so complexly intelligent that I feel like an oaf beside him. I've got more balls than brains. Clumsy, a plodding beast. A land-locked bird that flies on rare occasions under special conditions. The tongue-tied son of a house painter afraid of dying alone. Yeah I'm not the naked boy I was five years ago.

January 27, 1970   Tuesday

Received a letter today from an associate of Betty Ann's, a social worker by the name of Linda Smart. The McGill College of Social Work has their students doing some silly thing about studying the different communities on the island. Linda asked me, because of my familiarity with the back streets, whether I would condescend to speak with the group that is doing missionary work in the Point. Betty Ann is in the habit of fobbing such people off on me. Well what I'm gonna say to them ought to raise their educated blood pressure a few points - You wanna know all about the back streets, girls? Well lose your jobs and move on down here for a couple of years, scrounging your daily meals. Consider yourself graduated when you've managed to con your way on to the Welfare Rolls. It would also help if you took a crash course on how to dish up Kraft Dinner and hamburger a hundred different ways. I have very little patience with these Westmount types coming down the hill in droves to start community projects for the "poor".

Years ago when I saw my Uncle Art laid out in the
funeral parlour, I turned and said to my father, "He looks
like he's wearing a mask." "They did a good job," answered my father, standing by the cheap coffin. "You
should have seen how wasted his face was in the hospital.
At least now he looks human." His mouth was drawn
down in a thin line right to the jaw bones, seeming to
express eternal anger at his sad death. Nine years ago the
doctors had told him that if he didn't quit drinking he
would be dead in five years. He made his choice. The
day before he was hospitalized he paid our family a visit
carrying the usual gallon of alcool under his arm. Although I was only eleven I was immediately struck by
the strange quiet look upon his face. A look that I haven't
seen before or since on any other human being. Custom-
arily my uncle would walk in, give all the kids a quarter
and a hug and then sit down in the dining room with
my old man to drink and talk. My Uncle Art was a
bachelor and every Saturday afternoon he would visit
one of his brother's families, and my old man was his favourite. Generally all the kids would run down the hall to
greet my uncle, but that day we sat where we were, puzzled by his sad appearance. "Come on into the living room,
Jim," said my uncle, "I want to talk to you." The door
was closed. "What's happening, Ma?" we asked. But she
only said, "Mind your own business." We all sensed that
something terrible was wrong, but we didn't know what.
Later on I learnt that during the hour my uncle and
father were together in the living room, my uncle told my
old man that he only had a few months to live and would
be hospitalized the next day. After talking over the funeral arrangements they came out and sat with us in the
dining room drinking from the gallon of alcool and orange
juice kept under the table. I was always asking my uncle,
who was the most educated of the family, questions about
history and I began asking him that afternoon about Robin
Hood and what state his body must be in after lying for
long centuries under the forest trees. "Dust," said my
uncle very coolly downing another glass of alcool. "You

hush up, David," said my mother wishing I hadn't brought
up such a morbid topic. "Don't bother the boy, Peggy,"
said my uncle, "It's alright." I loved the man and I still
treasure his memory. My old man says I'm a lot like him.
When he found out I was learning how to play a harmonica
he said, "Your Uncle Art used to play one too," He was
the most sensitive and gentle of all my father's brothers.
Fond of singing, of children and old fellowship. He had a
favourite song that he could never remember. Every time
he came down to my father's holiday parties, friends and
relatives would request him to sing it, but he could never
find the tune. "It's a real old one," he'd say, "as old as
the hills." And all his old pals would be sitting around
trying to guess what it was. This happened every time
they got together and I grew to expect it. Even, sometimes, I'd join in on the game of what song it was and give
unheard of suggestions very shyly into my uncle's ear.

Coming home from the library, three young boys
with wind-red faces half-covered with hockey tuques
brightened up the long cold wait for the bus with their
joyful chatter of their day's events. Like young sparrows
discussing their first solo flights.

February 5, 1970   Thursday

What ya looking at out the window, Pearl? Something in the night that interests you? Perhaps he is hallu-
cinating and thinks he's seeing a twenty-foot pigeon
strutting down Coursol Street saying, "HERE KITTY
KITTY KITTY". King Pigeon out to get Pearl for all the
birds he's murdered out in the backyard. If pigeons really
grew that big, Montreal would need not only a special
snow removal crew but also a shit removal crew. Dirty
birds those pigeons with no respect for their betters.
King Edward, who has been standing in Phillips Square for
the last sixty years, must really hate their guts. He takes
swipes at them with his sceptre late at night when there's
no one around to witness his unroyal behaviour. I know
'cause I saw him do it once when I was crossing the square
in the wee hours of the morning on the way home after

getting thrown out of a bar. He blushed when he saw me looking and quickly pulled himself back into his usual kingly stance. "I saw you do that," I yelled, "and I'm gonna report you to the S.P.C.A.! " A very hollow, brassy voice boomed out the words "Fuck you! " in an Oxford English accent. "Such language from a king," I said indignantly as I stomped out of the square into the arms of some dudes with long white coats who quietly insisted that I get into their ambulance.

February 7, 1970   Saturday

The freight train is always getting on the wrong track and wrecking itself like a perverse child wantonly destroying his birthday gifts. Dark thoughts coloured by despair. Snap - into a suicide grave like my Uncle Gus welcoming the canal water as he sank into it, gulping it down into his lungs like a half-suffocated man sucking in the fresh air. Yeah, Uncle Gus, the causes of your untimely death are still functioning, still killing good men like yourself. Your death is one of the statistics. One less working man to give welfare to. They pray for our deaths, now that they have machines to do the work we were once needed for. They would rid the earth of all back street rat-people if it were in their power. We are fighting to avenge your death, Gus, we are fighting to build a world in which suicide can play no part, a world in which no man will suffer any unnecessary indignities. Every family has had its casualties and some of them have had more than their share. The people are gathering, the common suffering is breaking down the walls that formerly divided each man in his own interests. It can only be a matter of time before any class of men with common interests organize amongst themselves to rid their lives of the evils combined against their happiness.

Liz just piped up and said, "You know David what I
feel like? I wish you would sing a few songs." "La, laa,
l-a-a-a," I replied and she broke into laughter. I love her so
I gave her a few verses of "Good morning Mr. Railroad
Man" in a flat, uninspired bass that she thought was beautiful. Then a bravado chorus of "Sweet Jenny Lee" after
pulling the plug out of the refrigerator which makes one
hell of a buzzing racket. "It's so peaceful now," said Liz.
Twelve o'clock at night. People get together. That's all
I've ever really talked about, that's all I ever really wanted
people to do since I was a little boy. I'm not as blue tonight as I could have been if I had allowed myself to wal-
low in my usual fears like a spoiled child shitting himself.
We have lived in fear for so long that it has become a way
of life for us. Well, fuck that bullshit from now on, if I
can help it.

The streets in the area are gnarled with traffic this
evening because a small factory on St. Antoine Street is
on fire. Nearly half of the West End is out on the sidewalks gaping at it, especially the kids responsible for it.
The frequency of fires in the area is something else.
Spooky old Liz, imaginative as ever, thought the whole
block was burning down and ran out of the house with
her most prized possessions in her arms, her sheepskin
coat and Pearl. I had a good laugh at her nervousness
when I came home and assured her that everything was
under control. Since the Coloniale Street blaze she's been
very sensitive about fires. Natural disasters are the least
of my worries. The powerful hum of the pump truck
across the street is vibrating through the room as I sit
writing this. R-r-r-r-r-m-m-mmm. At the age of three I
witnessed a great fire on Canning Street. The water that
had been hosed on the flames cascading down the long
staircase like Niagara Falls. I was more impressed by the
great mass of people bunched in the street than I was

with the actual fire. "Wouldn't it be nice," I thought, "if people had parties together on the streets like this every night."

February 11, 1970   Wednesday

Rolling cigarettes, singing Hank Williams songs and adding to my 1967 journal. Our lives are so lonely. Breaking windows as I pass along to gain attention. Yes who do you love, stranger? Did you kill ants in sport as a child? Did you ever dream that your mother was getting on a bus and leaving you lost in the big city? Were you ever lost? Don't we know all this? Then why are we strangers? Do people ever get together at all? Jack the Ripper is hiding behind every door we open, posing as a friend. Will he be in my house when I get home tonight? Will I be able to reason with him? Will the people come quickly if I call them? Yes, David Fennario, the circus is coming to town but you can't afford to go, nor is Charlie Chaplin's daughter ever going to fall in love with you. An avalance of insurmountable problems is about to bury you, flick and struggle as you will.

The seemingly long distances between each person alive today are only illusionary. We are all looking through the telescope the wrong way.

February 15, 1970   Sunday

Yes, everybody showed up last night, including Jackie who did a hilarious spoof on Johnny Cash in pantomime. Also did Billy the Kid picking his nose with a six shooter. I entertained the group by telling them about the funniest score I had ever heard about - Long John's attempt to B & E the office of the Vancouver Aquarium. Long John and his partner went out there late one night and were diligently stripping the door off its hinges when a sudden distant barking sound drew away their attention. Off through the moonlit fields they could see two bounding police dogs followed close behind by two puffing

security guards with pistols drawn coming right for them.
"In no way," Long John told me, "did we feel like trying
to outrun those fuckin' wolf hounds so we scrambled up
onto the roof figuring we could jump off the other side.
My buddy got to the edge first and I expected he'd jump
right off but instead he turns around and says, "Hey wait
a minute, John, there's a pool of water there. "Fuck the
fish you idiot! " I yelled. "Dive! " And that's just what I
was gonna do when I saw a big white sign over the pool
saying "NARVOO THE KILLER WHALE". Needless to
say the guys decided to take the dogs and in the process
got themselves a little mangled about the legs in their get
away. "But what's a few bites from some mangy dogs
after escaping from a whale," said Long John philosophi-
cally. "Can you imagine how puzzled the caretakers
would have been the next day if Long John hadn't read
the sign?" I said to Charly. "There's old Narvoo lying on
the surface of the water refusing all offers of food and
constantly burping up shoes, buttons, burglar tools."

I also told the group the old story of the stroll I in-
advertently took through the Lincoln Tunnel back in 1963,
following the directions of a traffic cop who must have
assumed I had a car when I asked him how to get out of
New York City. That I didn't succumb to the deadly gasoline fumes in that two mile long no pedestrian tunnel
must constitute some kind of minor miracle. I think I
owe my life to the fact that I was very early conditioned
to the heavy pollution of the St. Antoine Street area.
Fresh air was more likely to kill me. It was only years
afterwards that I discovered why the passing drivers looked
so stunned and beeped their horns when they spotted me
inching along the narrow foot-square edge that lines both
sides of the tunnel. "Fuck," I remember thinking to myself at the time, "They ought to put decent sidewalks in
here. Somebody could get killed." I silently cursed the
heavy transport trucks wheezing by, creating winds that
almost sucked me into the traffic while tossing up suffo-
cating clouds of dust. The terrifying predicament I had
placed myself in failed to impress me, it only served to
strengthen the poor opinion I already had of New York
City's public facilities. I compared the lack of sidewalks
in the Lincoln Tunnel to the shocking absence of free
toilets in Grand Central Station. Inconveniences like this

were the norm in New York City as far as I was concerned.

February 17, 1970   Tuesday

     Yeah, the train pulled into the station, I had my suit-
case in my hand. The Delaware and Hudson express going
down to New York City and I'm sixteen years old with
two hundred and fifty dollars in my pocket. A post card
is dropped into the mailbox. "Dear Ma. I can't explain
why I'm leaving the only home I ever knew. Maybe I'll
be back." There's a friend to see me off and he shakes my
hand twice, the second time with the realization that I
might not be back. We get our pictures taken together in
the 4 for 25 cents photo booths a half-hour before departure. My adolescent face peers out at me from the mirror,
thin, worried and pale; my mouth, childlike in its fullness
destroys my boyish attempt to project maturity and I
shove my photo into my back pocket. Larry, my friend,
with his more certain identity, is pleased with his picture
for the camera recorded faithfully his own image of himself, the confident hard smile, the hooded rough eyes, all
practised at home in the back streets.
     Let us dig holes in our cellars to bury our scars in. Our
impaired vision of the whole corrupts our love making.
Richard Nixon has no balls.

February 19, 1970   Thursday

     Yeah, that down home back street funky rock'n roll
beat really moves me. Jazz just does nothing for me. Jazz
is a pot high, for users, for relaxed people who don't give
a damn and can afford not to. Rock is the loud and angry
voice of the people crashing through the empty façade which
remains of bourgeois culture. Rock'n Roll is the music
or our Revolution and great compositions in this art form
are already arising. Yeah, Rock'n Roll summer night
dances at the Pavillion on the Boardwalk, open air dances
sponsored by the city. Hundreds of tough greaser kids

14

with their combed back D.A.'s, motorcycle boots and rolled up shirt sleeves. Flashing knives and the twang of zip guns signalled the end of the last dance and the rumble spilled over onto Wellington Street and stopped all the uptown traffic. French and English battling it out that long ago summer night of 1961. Violence, uncurbed, rang in the air like a thunder storm. The current had been short circuited and the electricity flowed where it pleased. I believe that mob battle was the last classic rumble Pt. St. Charles ever had. New ideals of the back street youths were already forming and gang fights in masses were becoming history, stories to be told to younger brothers of those valorous battles when the streets were really tough, when the Highway Snakes roamed the dark alleyways skirmishing with the Golden Eagles their neighbourhood rivals. The Snakes finally did in the Eagles one night by burning down their club house, by spilling gasoline all over it and throwing a torch on the roof. I saw the whole thing, at the age of ten, from behind a backalley fence. The Eagles really got their feathers dusted when they poured out of the flaming shack into a gauntlet of chain swinging Snakes. It was a bad beating and the Eagles never got over it. The Snakes reigned supreme until they in turn were crushed by the cops. One night half-a-dozen Snakes managed to ride some rented horses off the mountain down into the neighbourhood. They stampeded by my house as I was sitting idly on the front steps and I watched five or six patrol cars rounding them up. A Wild West Show on Canning Street. Unbelievable, the whole area was hanging off their galleries to watch the show. All those bad dudes got time for that stunt and since one of them was the President the rest of the gang soon dispersed. I was too young to join as a member, but they considered me an honorary mascot; my only duty was to report on the movements of the Eagles. Yeah, the streets were really tough in those days.

February 26, 1970   Thursday

     Someday I hope to be able to sit in a train station and not feel blue, and be able to say to myself, David Fennario,

15

you've accomplished something in your life. It's a date I
have with the C.N. Station which has played quite a part in
my life. The night of March 13, 1966, Jay and I went to
Toronto. Kay, Elaine, Robin and Carol were there to see
me off. "C'mon we'll be late," said Jay as I kissed them
all good-bye and rushed down the stairs to the train in my
long brown trench coat. I remember the late summer afternoon I met Karen in the station after not seeing her for
nearly six months; how surprised I was that she was
actually glad to see me even tho the Don Jail screws had
cut my hair and I was thin, yellow and ragged. The hours I
spent in the C.N. when I didn't have anywhere to stay and
it was bitter cold outside. The many fags that tried to
pick me up. The station closes at twelve and opens at six
in the morning. When I was sixteen and a runaway, I
came into the station one morning before and soon fell
asleep sitting on a bench only to be awakened by a business man fag offering me a cigarette while placing his hand
on my thigh. "Fuck off," I said. "You guys are like vul-
tures." I acted tough but actually I was very upset and
close to crying out of sheer anguish. To the man's credit
he left a dollar bill beside me on the bench as he got up to
leave. I remember once after refusing another fag's pro-
position I asked him for some loose change. "Ah no,"
he said, "you've got to work for your money. When you're
hungry enough, you'll come across." During the next
couple of weeks I often ran into the same guy in the uptown Ville Marie area and he always threw me an oily
smile as if to say, "I'm waiting kid." Well I never got hungry enough but a lot of other poor boys did.

March 2, 1970   **Monday**

    The magic electricity of the West End. Drunken
hours in the Fulford Street bar downing ten-cent draughts
with James Patrick Bryan O'Neill. Background sound
effects. Derelict orators without audiences philosophizing
to themselves at the back tables. "I've got nobody," one
guy kept yelling every minute until the waiter threw him
out.

16

In the old days the West End used to be called the
Swamp because of the tremendous concentration of people
living in those blocks. Yeah, it felt like a swamp today!
I went up to St. Lawrence Main this afternoon and for
fifty cents watched three movies. An old derelict broke
down crying during a love scene and two ushers came over
and threw him out. The man was young once and had
hopes. Walking off the Main down through Place Ville
Marie I was struck by the contrast of life styles. The
office worker rushing confidently to the train that is always on time, to the meal he is always sure of having.
While just a few streets away men who were once at least
as well off as most office workers are living from hand to
mouth, day by day, obliterating their minds with alcohol
and crying to themselves in cheap movie theatres.

Pat and I tripped over to the Dominion Bar for a few
quarts of beer yesterday night. Dubois the Bouncer had a
lot of trouble tossing out a very skinny, nervous, black, old
junky who wrapped his arms and legs around a post like
an octopus when Dubois tried to grab him. He clung so
tightly that it took Dubois and two waiters to peel him
off. They threw him out for doing a hilarious strip tease
dance on top of a table. According to Pat the guy they
threw out was a real mean dude in his youth. "He's a famous man. He shot a cop on Mountain Street back in the
forties and got life for it. Cop insulted him. A real bad
actor, yeah."
A street song we used to sing as kids is going through
my head - "When I'm dead, bury me deep down along St.
Antoine Street. Place a brick upon my head and tell all
the pretty girls I'm dead."

March 18, 1970   Wednesday

I dreamt last night that I was working for two dollars an hour chopping ice off a lofty church roof, a dome
like that of St. Joseph's Oratory. It was bitter cold up
there and very slippery. I also dreamt I was on a bus going to work and when it came my stop the bus driver
wouldn't let me off. Neither would he let anyone else off
at their stops. I walked up to him and demanded to
know why he wouldn't open the doors. "I'm fucked up,"
he said, "and I just don't want to let anybody off. I'm
sick of being a bus driver, but I have no choice but to
work at this job. "That's all very well," I replied. "I
understand your position, but understand ours. We want
to get off the bus and you have no right, even if you are
disturbed, to keep us on it. Besides your actions will not
ease your problems; matter of fact, you're only intensi-
fying them because these people are bound to get violent
with you if you persist in what you're doing." I can't
recall whether my reasoning influenced him but I hope
so because I hate to think of riding that bus again this
evening.

March 21, 1970   Saturday

Something magic about walking up St. Antoine Street
in the early morning with Jacky Robinson. It's a memory
I know I'll retain because I sense that the time is fast
approaching when our paths will divide permanently, his
into a world of prisons and mine into a work-a-day life.
Some cops in a passing patrol car nearly stopped to hassle
us when Jacky spat at the sight of them. My stomach
cringed but Jacky just laughed and said, "Man yesterday
I globbed through the open window of a parked patrol
car I was passing by and watched the cop later get into
the car and wipe it off the seat with his handkerchief."

March 23, 1970   Monday

I'm writing the following paragraphs under a strain.
What I mean to say is that Jacky just dropped in, hysterically upset by his impossible life, raging on about his partner Billy White fucking him up left and right. Actually all
the troubles Jacky's got he brought on himself. The poor
guy. If there was any decent way of avoiding him I would
do so because I've seen him on these bad trips before and
this one has all the signs of terminating violently. Cruel
as it may sound, jail would be the best place for him right
now. Security, a place for him to lick his wounds. I'm
too disturbed by his visit to write down what I had
planned. The dancing boy is losing his grace, stiffening
rapidly under the blows. Half-mad roaming through the
black alley ways of Montreal, breaking into garages,
stealing car radios to buy furniture for a flat he can't
afford. I've been on the defensive during our recent
rendez-vous prepared to withstand a possible attack; tense,
watching, calculating and frightened.

March 27, 1970   Friday

Another quiet day, at least so far. It's ten-thirty as I
stand writing this note hiding behind some shoe boxes
on the stockroom table. Gord King, one of the salesmen,
told me today that he has been working in Simpson's for
five years, first in Fairview and then here in the main
store. His three kids force him to swallow whatever shit
Oswald the Head Manager throws his way. "Yeah," I said,
"I understand your responsibilities and why you have to
swallow your anger. But as for me I don't have a family
yet so I can still afford to tell sons of bitches like Oswald
to go fuck themselves." He grinned and looked at me as
if to say, "You're O.K. in my books, David Fennario."
Ah fuck, the agonies of working on a Friday pay-day. It
hurts. I feel like destroying every watch and clock in the
joint and walking out.

March 30, 1970   Monday

A young black whore in an expensive mod fur coat
crying to herself, slowly walking along St. Antoine Street,
an avenue unmoved by tears, callous from uncountable
scenes of brutality it has witnessed.

The West End today, in the cold neon light of a
March day looked like a drunken, scabby, old witch festering in an unmade bed. Gangs of wolf-children roaming
the back alleys in packs. I keep a wary eye open on such
nights and never allow anyone to approach me from behind without my noticing. Open man holes, fires, and
wolf-children. The whole area stinks of gasoline fumes,
charred wood and cat piss. Not a winter passes without
some family from the area being burnt out of house and
home by hot oil stoves bursting into flames.

March 31, 1970   Tuesday

The music of the Japanese Koto. A young tree growing. A child laughing. Every time a woman smiles, a death
is forgiven. She kisses her children's hands and the wars
are forgotten. Dried brittle flowers-memories of the
seasons. Spent, burnt out cigarette butt emotions. The
lost melodies of a child's hot green day's growing.

Met Cliff, "the last of the hippies," passing along
Dorchester Boulevard on my way home from work. He
was dressed in a shabby old blue suit, two sizes too big
for him, carrying a wrinkled patched up overcoat over his
shoulder. His hair, his shoulder-length long black hair that
he wore so proudly the last seven years, is cropped short
in the approved wage-slave style. He looked like a wet
sparrow, beaten, down on his knees waiting for someone
to buy him. Ah Cliff, it's all over now, baby blue.

Weird dreams last night of looking for old boyhood friends in High School libraries and people getting killed in music stores. Speaking about boyhood friends I really freaked out Larry Omer the last time I saw him with the acute, almost total recollection I had of his mother's flat down on Canning Street which I haven't visited since I was seven years old. The tiny porch floor of his family's house was laid with coloured tiles depicting a black Scotch Terrier which had a chunk missing from its nose. On the hall wall, the right hand side, a few steps from the porch door hung a portrait of Winston Churchill with a bulldog and a union jack.

Thinking about Cliff again today, thinking about the summer Cliff was managing the Image Coffeehouse and the day Joe McBride walked into the back with a .32 pistol, waved it apologetically in Cliff's face and emptied the till. Cliff's wife Joany ran after Joe as he was walking out and pleaded with him to give the money back but he only nodded his head sadly and said, "I'm sorry, Joany, but I'm desperate. Please leave me alone." Joe was a tall, lanky, very good looking dude from a southern Ontario tobacco town. He first came to Montreal in the winter of '66 after being dismissed from the army on charges of "bootlegging on a massive scale," to quote his own words. He began striking with the Devil's Choice and hanging around the downtown bars pushing dope and hassling the flower children. Joe was a very aware person in a negative sense, similar to many guys I grew up with, and I spent many an hour drinking with him in the downtown bars back then. The last time I saw him, about two years ago, he was drinking with Steve and Snoopy in the Prince Arthur tavern just up street from Cyrano's, a café catering to the bikers. The man looked in a bad way, thin and haggard about the face and really heavy on speed. At the time he told me he was considering having himself admitted to the Douglas Hospital because he had nearly killed a man that week-end.

21

Remembering a conversation I had with Jacky walking uptown together a few weeks back. "Yeah," I said to him, "You guys really made a killing about Christmas time. According to the Montreal Star, there were more breaking and enterings pulled off during the holiday season in this city than anywhere else in the world." "Yeah, well you know," said Jacky smiling, "Christmas was coming, the goose was getting fat, and nobody was putting pennies in the old man's hat."

April 6, 1970   Monday

While I was walking along St. Antoine this morning by St. Anthony's Church, a black hearse pulled up to the curb and a cheap metal coffin like the one my Uncle Art had, was carried up the church steps. One sad woman with a handkerchief up to her eyes was walking beside it. It must have been a very poor man who died, to be hurried to his grave so early in the morning.

April 8, 1970   Wednesday

Had a long drive out to the C.C.M. warehouse on the South Shore this afternoon in order to pick up a bicycle for a customer. The cab driver was a tough old veteran of the Montreal streets, having pushed a downtown hack for over twenty years, and he whizzed by other vehicles and pedestrians with inches to spare, never batting an eyelash. We had difficulty locating the place and spent over an hour meandering through a semi-urbanized country area that had a fascinating ugliness about it. Graveyards, gas stations, taverns, wooden shacks, barns, duplexes, high schools, churches all mixed together like a minestrone soup. If cities have afterbirths, the South Shore is Montreal's. Total anarchy. Picture a long row of duplexes terminating in a dumpyard connected to a cemetary that has gasoline stations blossoming on all sides of it

like poison mushrooms. Add a few bachelor-apartment
houses peppered with the old broken-down farmhouse
heavily sprinkled with a strong dose of drive-in hamburger
stands and presto, the South Shore. A post-industrial
garden of Eden à la mode 1970.

April 13, 1970   Monday

Simpson's department store early in the morning,
with long, dull hours of toil ahead. The salesmen begin
taking the white dust covers off the merchandise as everyone scurries to their departments. Doors opening and
slamming, the banging of the freight elevators stopping
at the floors, unloading trucks full of goods. The buzz
of voices dominated by the crisp dictatorial bass of the
manager. The stuffy air like layers of transparent cello-
phane. The air conditioners are turned on. The day has
begun and I already have those low-down Monday morning stockman blues.

April 14, 1970   Tuesday

There're two jokes doing the rounds here in
Simpson's, being told by the staff all over the store. One
I made up myself. I first told it to Yvon a couple of
weeks ago, and this is the way Gordie King told it to me.
"There's a bum walking up Ste. Catherine panhandling
and he says to me 'Hey, Mister, got any change?' 'No,
sorry. I work for Simpson's'. 'Ah, yes' the bum says to
me, 'I understand.' " The other joke is, if a young whore
uses vaseline, what does an old whore use? Answer -
polygrip.
Sat on the concrete slab opposite the McGill Library
during my lunch hour eating sandwiches in the sunshine.
Watched a black student with a crippled leg trying to
make it with a cute snow white Westmount chick who
was constantly flashing a liberal I-like-black-militants
smile. At least five Bob Dylans, four Trotskys, and sixteen Che Guevaras walked by me in the space of an hour.

23

One sad lonely looking character had the potential written on his face of becoming another Texas sniper shooting down people from a watch tower like they were clay pigeons in a carnival side show. My egg sandwich did a double flip in my esophagus when I saw his grim face looking my way. He was the image Incarnate of the Merciless Avenger Destroying For Peace. The insane Messiah tormented beyond human endurance, storing up tremendous hatred within himself. I know the type. I've seen some explode. McGill doesn't know it, but if my guess is correct they have a Texas Sniper in their class-rooms.

Shortly afterwards I looked up and to my pleasant surprise I saw Elaine Rivers hurrying by on her way to the library. "Elaine!" I yelled, waving my hand. The familiar surprised look passed over her face, the one that makes her resemble a ten-year-old expecting something unpleasant to happen. Then she smiled, came over, sat down and gave me a big kiss. Elaine grew up a stone's throw from the C.P. tracks in lowest Westmount, the daughter of a heavy-drinking Indian father and a French Canadian Mother. She laughs easily and walks like an uptight ballerina. She's beautiful, of the French-Iroquois variety with slightly narrowed coal black eyes, high cheek bones and straight dark hair. Four years ago when I was going out with her I used to parade her down Ste. Catherine Street like a prize. "Eat your heart out boys," I'd say to myself.

"You know, Elaine," I said, while studying the tiny scar she carries over her top lip as a momento of her tom-girl days, "very few girls from your background ever make it to university." "Yes, I know," she said quietly, "I'm surprised myself." Then we spoke about the speed epi-demic occurring amongst people of our age and how sad we thought it was. "Well, you know Elaine," I said, "there are tremendous pressures upon us all, and not all of us can shoulder them especially people who have no hope for the future." We made our departures shortly after I said this because I had to get back to Simpson's. And I left her, feeling guilty as if there were something I should have given her but didn't.

April 15, 1970   Wednesday

Liz had the hiccups when I came home this evening.
She sounded like a mouse with indigestion. "Hello-hic-
sweetmeats," she said as I stumbled through the front door
and down the hall to the bathroom to wash Simpson's off
my hands and face.
Wanna know what is the fastest thing on two legs?
A stockman leaving Simpson's 5:30 on a Friday pay day.
Gangway! Torpedoing for the nearest exit, knocking over
customers like bowling pins. Irate old ladies swiping at
me with their canes, snarling as I bang past them. "Sorry!
Sorry! Outtaway!" Exploding unto Ste. Catherine Street
like a shotgun blast. Kapow. The week is over. Two days
of freedom away from the coal mines.

April 19, 1970   Saturday

Rapping with Shannon and Art Frig this afternoon
for a couple of hours at Jacky's place. Art's just a couple
of days out of OKALA after doing twenty months for
pushing grass. Both Shannon and Art are from the Goose
Village, a neighbourhood famous for its story tellers and
they had some very amusing anecdotes to tell us of the
winter they spent together in Yorkville, 1966. They
crashed out for over a month with twenty other guys and
dolls in a laundry room of a big apartment house on
Avenue Road until it was busted up by a raid. "Yeah,
yeah, we hit the front page of the T.O. Star," said Shannon,
"Hippies found living secretly in laundromat of Ritzy
Avenue Rd. Apartment house." "How the fuck did you
ever manage to get in past the door man?" I asked. "Ah,
easy," said Shannon, "No sweat. The doorman was from
the Goose Village and I used to turn him on."
Yeah, Yorkville, the winter of 1966, the year of the
Hippie. Kids sleeping in abandoned cars, vacant lots,
porches, broom closets, under staircases, nestling like wild
animals in any hole that offered a little security. Homeless
kids, disturbed runaways, misfits, rebels, castaways from
the back streets.

Wolf children with long hair and sharp thin faces hustling
the night streets for food and shelter. All this happening
in the heat of down town Toronto. (Note: Gooseville
was the nickname given to a tiny slum community that
the city of Montreal tore down to build the Autostade
about six years ago.)

April 23, 1970   **Thursday**

Found myself thinking about my grandfather's house
out in Ville Emard with its proud little garden in the back
where my grandad spent most of his leisure time. When
he first moved out there to be close to the factory where
he worked as a stoker shovelling coal in the furnaces, the
area was dotted with single-story tar paper wooden houses
that stood out like gigantic mushrooms in the meadows
surrounding the heavy industrial plants. Today the fields
my father used to play in have all been built upon. My
grandfather's house is now surrounded on all sides by
three story tenement houses that fill the whole neighbourhood, street after street where once only the dandelions
grew.
I was kidding the shipper in the toy department next
to ours saying, "Hey, I heard the Hula Hoop is coming back."
"Fuck! I hope not," he said throwing his arms up in a
gesture of anguish. And I was thinking about my poor
sister Peggy Anne the night ten years ago she got drunk
for the first and only time in her life. While working in
the mail room of the Traveller's Insurance Co., she had
fallen in love with a young man whose job was to bring
the department mail daily to her so she could stamp the
letters and send them out. In the course of many months
Peggy Anne became more charmed by this young man
and it became her fondest dream, her only dream, that
he would ask her to the Christmas Office Party. The day
before the party arrived and he didn't ask her but she
rationalized his cold behavior by assuming that perhaps
he was too shy to ask. I can remember her telling us this
at the supper table. After eating she dressed herself up
and went uptown alone to the hall where the party was to

be held. Not a single man asked her for a dance, as for Prince Charming he didn't even speak to her. The telephone rang at our house about nine o'clock and my mother answered it. After hanging up she came over to me and said, "David, that was Peggy Anne on the phone. She is drunk and very upset and wants you to help her home." I took two buses up to the building on Sherbrooke and found her standing outside alone on the street corner crying. She was more upset than drunk, close to nervous prostration, completely shattered by the cruel treatment she had received that evening. I walked along beside her helping her through the snow and she was half sobbing, talking to herself. "How could they act like that? So cruel, they all acted as if they didn't know me." My poor sister, so simple and child-like in her manners could not understand that the office staff were simply not interested in establishing personal intimacies with a lowly file clerk.

April 25, 1970   **Saturday**

Feeling especially mellow I walked into the Second Avenue candy store just off Wellington Street and was served by the same old guy I knew as a kid, seven years older and more grey. He failed to recognize me. A weird old guy. When I was talking to his wife one afternoon years ago she told me that Burt, her old man, had worked in carnivals nearly all his life and found it hard to break some of the old bad habits, like short-changing. "He does it automatically without thinking," his wife said, "so if you find yourself walking home with the wrong change just come on back and I'll give you what's owing." The boardwalk, the stairs, the children - Verdun.

The Parti Quebeçois was down on Wellington Street yesterday in full force, bearded intellectuals handing out leaflets with a smile, a social worker's smile, the lips turned up benevolently in the corners, the eyes beaming promises of better welfare. Oh yeah!

Back home at ten o'clock and went with Pat for a few beers at the Dominion Bar. "We're all people," said the go-go waitress smiling at us as she handed us some free matches. A black mother, Silky Johnson, well known in the neighbourhood, tough, sharp tongued and very human was sitting with us at our table. She told us a social worker had once asked her "How long have you been in the West End?" "How long have I been in the West End?" she replied, "I never been out!"

April 29, 1970   Wednesday

Delinquent Dave's curly-headed devil of a brother got himself four years in Shawbridge for resisting arrest and other sundries. Whacking a cop with a hockey stick and running down the street. Dave's fourteen-year-old brother is a mean one, disturbed and capable of almost anything. It was a relief to hear that the neighbourhood mail boxes will remain intact for the next couple of years. There're bound to be a lot less fires too. The poor kid's already a hardened criminal, destined for murder. Their mother both sickens and angers me. Mother Rat can be found any night of the week drunk in the Dominion Bar surveying the possibilities with her cold reptile eyes. What happened to her to make her that way? What monstrous experiences has she undergone to make her so corrupt as a woman and a mother?

May 2, 1970   Saturday

We passed the Dominion Bar, one o'clock in the morning and I say to Jay, "Let's go in and check to see if Pat's there." Then turning to Bryan, the kid, I said, "Look, this is the toughest bar off the Main and I wouldn't feel right bringing you in there, O.K.?" "O.K.," he said and he split. "In no way, Jay," I said as I pushed open the Bar door, "did I feel like bringing that dumb kid in here." "Gonna buy me a beer, Dave?" "Yeah, sure," I said, digging up my last dollar as confidently as if I had a hundred

more of them. We were sitting at a table when I noticed
a young hustler, obviously attracted to us, had parked
herself close by our chairs. And I began teasing Jay, "Go
on, Jay," I said, "ask her to dance man. Don't be ignorant, she's in love with you." "Naw, naw," he said, "Never
can tell who she's with. Might be trouble." We had two
rounds and were about to have another but the last call
sounded so we got up to leave. "C'mon, Jay," I said,
"I wanna show you that Castoria sign down on St. James
Street." "Yeah," said Jay, "I'd like to see it. There's
one down in the Point too. Hacher's Castoria Cough
Syrup. Children cry for it. I could never understand as
a kid," said Jay, "what that meant, 'children cry for it';
but now that you've told me that the stuff used to be
loaded with codeine, I understand." "Yeah," I said,
"Fathers, mothers, brothers, everyone cried for it. Fifty
years ago, man, before the Pure Drug Act was passed,
half the West End was addicted to that shit. Sinister, isn't
it." "Yeah," said Jay as we hopped along St. James
Street three o'clock in the morning jumping up and banging with our hands all the no parking signs we passed by
in a boyish contest to see who was the best at it. "The
honour of the West End is at stake, man," I said to Jay,
"but hell all you guys living south of the canal are fuck-
ups anyhow." "Oh, yeah! " says Jay putting on the Pt.
St. Charles tough punk act complete with accent and
phraseology. "Yeah," I said jokingly, "Listen dummy I
grew up on discount Kraft Dinners and stale baloney,
don't you mess with me." And we laughed as we jumped
over all the fire hydrants between the tracks and Notre
Dame Street on Seigneur. "Let's go jump some freights
for old time's sake, Dave. C'mon, huh?" "Naw man."
I said, "If I had another beer in me I probably would but
wow, don't those trains sound good?" "Uh huh," said
Jay, and we stood and listened to the cars shuttling back
and forth, the engineer's bell ringing, the brakemen on
the side ladders swinging their lanterns as the train pulled
out of the yard. Checking through the factory window
of the Continental Can down the street, we spotted Nicky,
Walli's brother working night shift on the rolling machines.

"Hey, Nicky! " we yelled rattling the steel screen on the window to gain his attention, but he was too occupied working on a rolling machine that had broken down to hear us. "Hey," Jay said, "There's an air vent on the side, yell in that and I'll stay at the window." Nicky heard my voice and walked over to the dirt stained window with a puzzled look. "Who is it?" he asked. "Jay and Dave," we laughed. We rapped for a while until the foreman came into the shop; then he split back to his machine. A little time later sitting on the concrete side of the canal bridge smoking cigarettes and admiring the industrial scenery. "Man listen to the noise of all machines, Jay." "Yeah," he said laughing, "Overtime and night shifts were invented along with electricity." A small Rambler with two pretty girls in it passed over the bridge and slowed down to take a closer look at us. We waved. "Bet you they come back again," said Jay, and sure enough a few minutes later the same car came by and this time we blew kisses. "Why do you have to be married, Dave, man," said Jay punching me in the shoulder in disgust.

May 3, 1970   **Sunday**

Delicious memories of mornings without worries and care. Young girls, essence of May and April so green in lilac. Windy street morning sunshine on the warm wooden steps of Mackay Street. Skipping ropes tied to no parking signs. One-a-leery, two-a-leery sing song thin little girl voices. Shadows, whispers, unremembered dreams, forgotten conversations, the golden princesses I never loved. Sidewalks, roof tops, the pallid ghost alleyways, the crooked weather-warped stairs, the hard cruel neon lit hallways, the angry janitors, the broken doors and empty wine bottles. The unmade beds, the hasty breakfasts, the honky tonk evenings, the quiet tables, the musical chairs, the first bold caress of love, the tender yielding, shy but giving. Sparrows and dandelions, rock 'n roll, Salvation Army sofas, harmonica, soul music, sleeping

bags used as blankets, sheets and pillows. The unexpected
visitors, the initiations, the natural comradeship of refuges.
No questions and very little judgement given.

May 4, 1970   Monday

Gravity has us all knotted up in molecules. The
forest is growing, the leaves are young on the trees.

May 7, 1970   Thursday

Thinking of Bruce McDowell. I can remember him
as a little boy with golden straw hair walking shyly through
the back door of my family's kitchen and my mother
saying, "Bruce, do you want any breakfast?" The whole
neighbourhood knew the sad broken life of the McDowells
and their wandering childrens' pitiful existence. They
were welcome in the kitchens of a dozen homes. The
silent boy grew up into a critically disturbed adult. Not
until he reached adolescence did the symptoms of mental
illness become apparent in him, up to that time he was a
very easy-going, quiet boy who generally played alone. I
was his special and only companion and we used to play
together all the time. "What do you think of this? Of
that?" One windy autumn night we were playing in the
backyard, both about eight years old and I remember saying to him as we lay on our backs in a great pile of leaves,
"Bruce, I think the sky is gonna fall today. The wind is
so strong it's gonna blow everything inside out." Mysteries,
puzzles no one would explain to me. The stars, the moon,
the wind, the smell of the earth. Bruce remained silent.
I was his friend. He was safe.

After the films Liz and I went for a walk in the Marguerite Bourgeois Park nearby Wellington Street beside
the Dominion Glass factory. "Last time I was in this
park, Liz, I was fourteen-years-old," and I told her about
how I ran away ten years ago with Bruce McDowell. I
was in my bedroom at 260 Second Avenue reading a huge
anthology of American poetry when my mother came
to the door and told me Bruce was downstairs to see me.
Leaving the book lying open on the bed I rushed downstairs and invited Bruce up to my room. I hadn't seen
him for months. During the conversation I had learned
that he had run away from Shawbridge the day before
and he intended that evening to start hitchhiking out to
Vancouver. "Why don't you go down to the States," I
said, "It's closer and I'll go with you." O.K. with him so
off we went down the street, sixty cents between us and
bound for Florida. It was October and a mild evening
with a scented autumn breeze blowing, whispering of the
changes. We attempted to walk over the Champlain
Bridge to the South Shore but the men at the toll booths
stopped us. We retraced the distance we had walked and
cut along the railway tracks planning to sleep that evening in one of the old cabooses the CN had parked in the
yard. But the railroad bulls spotted us trying to break
into one of the cars and the chase was on. We took off
for the fence like frightened antelopes. I ripped the sleeve
of my windbreaker scrambling over the barbed wire,
nearly landing on Bruce as I fell, and rolled down one
of Park Marguerite Bourgeois' grassy slopes. The thick
carpet of leaves smothered our footsteps as we ran into
the shadows of the trees. Glancing back we could see
long straight fingers of electric light beaming from the
cop's lanterns wildly probing the shaded area for us.
We ran a couple of blocks along Wellington Street to en-
sure a safe getaway and then we slowed down to a brisk
trot in the direction of the Jacques Cartier Bridge. Looking back from the other side of the river for the first time
in my life on the brilliant panorama of Montreal all lit

up in the night, I had to catch my breath. It was the first
objective outside view I had ever had of my mother-city
and she looked like a great whore covered with stolen
diamonds. We walked south along the expressway about
eleven miles until we came to the Notre Dame de Sacre
Coeur exit. Bruce said he knew a camping site in the vicinity so we headed into the bush. We bumped around in
the brush for quite some time before Bruce happened upon a pathway and within a few minutes we were sitting
on a damp old mattress in the middle of a field warming
ourselves before a tiny fire. With leaves serving the pur-
pose of both blankets and pillows we settled down for
our rest. It was to be my first night sleeping out under
the stars and I was surprised at how deep and big the sky
was. We were sleeping about an hour when I noticed
what seemed to me to be bits of dew falling. "Dew don't
fall like that," said Bruce. "That's rain." And in a few
minutes I had to agree with him when the rain began falling harder. Much to my reluctance and at Bruce's insistence we left the camp site and walked into the village in
hopes of finding some old shack we could crash in for the
night. We emptied the change out of a couple of milk
bottles standing on the village's front porches in anticipation of breakfast. Halfway through the village we
came upon a half-constructed house that we decided
would be the most likely lodging place for the remainder
of the evening. By this time we were thoroughly chilled
by the damp cold night air. We wrapped ourselves up in
some cardboard we found on the floor of the house as
best as we could, but all to no avail. The cold wind blowing through the open frame of the unfinished house cut
into us like an icicle dagger. In desperation we retreated
to the basement where we risked chances of discovery by
making a bonfire with the cardboard. Fortunately it
was just about dawn when our fuel supply ran out. "I've
had enough, Dave," said Bruce, "I'm heading back to
Montreal to my aunt's." "Stick it out, Bruce," I said,
"It'll get warmer the further south we travel and once
we hit Florida, man, hah, we'll be living then! FLORIDA.
That's where I'm going." "Not for me, Dave, I'm sorry,"
said Bruce. "I don't think you'll be able to get over the
border." He gave me what change he had on him, then I

watched him for a while ploughing through the mud in a northernly direction towards Montreal. The village was full of kids now on their way to school. I ducked into a church and with the aid of a pen knife I dug a holy candle out of the altar prayer stand figuring it would come in handy later on. Then after spending the fifty cents I had on chocolate bars, I got onto the highway and stuck out my thumb. A half-hour or so later a French Canadian farmer in a beat-up old Chevrolet truck stinking of cow shit drove me within twenty miles of the border. The second and final lift I received was from a suspicious priest who asked me about my destination amongst other things. I told him I was from the farming community of Tadoussac, a name that happened to pop up to my head. He told me that the only Tadoussac he had ever heard of was east of Quebec City. Being a smart kid I dodged the remainder of his accusing questions by firing barrels of them at him. Totally confused, he dropped me off a dozen yards north of the line, apologizing as he opened the door for not being able to take me over into the U.S., and off he went. I walked up to the line fascinated by the idea that with one step I would be in the United States of America, the land of Lincoln, Benjamin Franklin and Davy Crockett. When a long diesel truck pulled into the inspector's driveway blocking off the custom's officer's view, I took my chance and walked across the border. Strolling nonchalantly alongside the highway congratulating myself on how easy it had all been, I spotted a service station on the other side of the road and decided it would be a smart idea to pick up a road map. Humble Gas Station - what a funny name for a garage I thought to myself as I scrambled over the high wire fence separating the North and South highways. Walking into the garage office I had my first opportunity to talk to Americans on their native soil and to my surprise they had the same accents as my cousins from Ontario. They were very obliging and at my request they handed me a road map of New York State. I wondered about the strange grins they had on their faces until I turned around and found myself looking straight into the cold official eyes of a heavy khaki-uniformed patrol man, a badge pinned on his shirt just like a western sheriff and his hand resting lightly near his holstered gun.

34

"Well," I thought to myself as he led me into the
back seat of the patrol car," It looks like Bruce is going
to have company in Shawbridge," Anyhow Wyatt Earp
and his deputy brought me back to their office where they
questioned me for over an hour; and after checking out
my record over radio with the Montreal Police, they
released me to the R.C.M.P. just up the road. There I
sat for an indeterminable amount of time carving my
name on the wooden bench with a pin I had found on
the floor. The sun was almost down before the provincial cops had everything straightened out then they
drove me into Montreal, a very tired and sleepy fourteen-
year-old. In the basement of Station Number One I fell
asleep sitting up on one of the benches. In between
dozing off I witnessed quite a few guys being dragged in
by the cops, some passive, some handcuffed and belliger-
ent, one with his leg bleeding from a bullet wound. One
of the cops standing nearby who had been pointing me
out to his fellow constables as if to say, "What did this
dangerous looking criminal do? Start a riot in kindergarten? " came over and asked me what I was in for. "Crossing the border illegally," I said in as rough a voice as a
fourteen-year-old with his voice changing could muster
up. "How far did you get?" asked the cop. "About
fifty yards," I replied and all the cops broke out in a
chorus of thunderous laughter. "Fuck'em," I thought to
myself." One day I'll be just like Jesse James." After a
while a plainclothes man approached the bench and said
I was to follow him upstairs. I did so and he led me to
an office door. "Go inside," he said as he went away. I
walked in and found myself facing my mother and a social
worker sitting at a desk. My mother rushed over and
hugged me sobbing. "How could you do this, David,"
and I said, "It's O.K. Ma, I didn't mean to hurt you. Just
felt like moving that's all." Well I talked to the man and
listened to his dire warnings about keeping bad company
like Bruce McDowell. I objected to his advice and voiced
my own immature criticism of the social system that had

warped Bruce's humanity. The man seemed to be both
impressed and saddened by my fire. Once I began talking,
he never said another word, just sat there with a deep
sorrowful look on his face. Thinking back I realize what
an exceptional person he was. He walked us to the elevator and said as the door was about to close, "David,
take care of your mother." And that was that. I was
released without charges, went home with my mother, ate
a tremendous supper then fell asleep for eighteen hours.

<u>May 14, 1970</u>   Thursday

Liz defined my uniqueness as a writer perfectly a
few weeks ago when she said, "You know, David, what
makes your writing original is that people like you usually
don't write." Yeah, I've got more balls than brains.

<u>May 19, 1970</u>   <u>Tuesday</u>

Sandwiched in our mother's supple womb lies the
future fat and kicking.
Sitting in Denise's living room with Jacky and Jay,
all of us drunk on wine, harmonizing on guitar, harmonica,
and spoons. "Listen," says Jacky after downing the last
drop of wine, "There's a guy working in a tavern on St.
Lawrence who owes me three bucks. Let's go over there
and pick up some booze." Which is what we did, returning with four quarts of Labatt's fifty.
Jacky was lonely, consequently it was difficult for
us to make our departure. Since we were catching the
nine o'clock train to T.O. the next morning we were
hoping to get home by midnight. But in no way was
Jacky in any hurry to see us go, he was stoned and wanted
company. "Stay here overnight," he said. "But you got
no clock!" I replied. That stumped him. Anyhow we
got home just after three o'clock and I woke up with the
alarm, seven-thirty in the morning, sore eyes, a pounding

brain, shooting pains in my right ear and a toothache. In
short I was in a bad way. Down to the station in a cab
cursing Jacky, bemoaning our lack of sleep. Waiting in
line in front of gate 8 for the T.O. train we encountered
the Mosses who did a double take at the awesome sight
of me hung over in the early morning looking like a condemned man. Liz had never been on a train before and
accordingly she was very excited at the prospect of going
on one. It's a shame my general misery dampened her
enthusiasm somewhat but still she was continually hugging and kissing me, smiling, much to the amusement of
the strangers standing nearby. The gate was opened and
we flooded down the staircase along side the train to the
car we were to occupy. Liz took the seat next to the
window as I lifted our suitcase up onto the rack. Trains
are very social, total strangers talking to one another.
Three new romances were evolving a couple of seats away
from us even before the train started to move. A sudden
jerk and the show was on the road. The Quebec country-
side was in the midst of spring ploughing. I tried to
imagine the slow and methodical lives of the farmers.
Saw a couple of farm kids out in the fields with rifles pop-
shooting at crows. Two other kids raced the train for
awhile riding bareback on some heavy workhorses. As
we were rolling through this pastoral scenery I suddenly
turned to Liz, who was in absolute rapture at the sight
of cows and pigs and said to her, in all seriousness, "Do
you realize that there are 1,200 miles of sewer pipes underneath Montreal and that 40 per cent of them were built
over a hundred years ago?" Liz laughed and said, "What
a dumb thing for you to come up with at a time like this."
I had to laugh myself.

A neighbourhood mob scene is occurring as I sit here
writing. The lonely neurotic old woman who lives down
the street is having one of her monthly drunks. A few
minutes ago she began yelling through her window at some
kids who were checking through the gardens with flashlights for worms. "What are those little fuckers looking
for? Yaller gold yaller gold yaller gold," and on and on
like a broken record. People began coming out on their
galleries. "Shut your fuckin' mouth, you old drunken

bitch," they yelled. "Sleep it off. Go to bed." The old
doll got all huffed up over the insults and came out of
her house and went over to the police telephone on the
corner of Dominion just outside my house. Sitting on the
window ledge I heard her say, "There's people here
frightening me - come here right away." Lonely drunken
old woman. When the cops came she ran into her house.
After the police left she went on with her noise and right
now a small mob of people have been attracted to the
scene, standing in the middle of Coursol Street trading
insults with the old doll. "Ah. You go to bed with all
the drunks in the taverns." "Sing a happy birthday to
the Queen," she replied in a raucous voice that could be
heard for blocks. Was she ever a beautiful young woman
full of dreams and hopes. Did the young men watch her
as she walked along the street?

<u>May 21, 1970</u>   <u>Thursday</u>

        Early this morning I trudged my weary way up the
hill to the Montreal General Hospital to get my bad tooth
yanked out. Of course I was expecting the worst. I took
a note-pad and a pen with me in order to take on the spot
notes, but I was too disturbed to put down more than
the following lines: "Sitting on the bench in front of the
dentist's office waiting nervously to be called. Babies
crying, high heels click-clacking down the halls. The
solemn faces of the patients are in sharp contrast with the
smiling, fresh-faced nurses gaily chatting with the young
doctors. Am I to be plagued with such depressions all
my life? How I dread these vivid confrontations with
the harsh realities of my existence. The tooth has got to
go. The tooth." The dentist was nothing like I had anti-
cipated; he turned out to be a friendly back street mari-
timer with practical advice. "Your teeth are worth saving.
Brush them. Listen," he says, "I was in dentist school
for eight years so I should know something about teeth.
That's why I'm telling you this. I'm sure you could tell
me about things I don't know about." "Yeah, that's right,"
I said, surprised and pleased by his human attitude. With-

38

in a matter of minutes passed pleasantly in conversation, the tooth was out and I was on my way home, stepping lightly.

May 23, 1970   Saturday

Great big Babbette from the Gaspé—tabernack, had some wonderful stories to tell of some of her very full experiences. She told us of an incident which happened to her a few years ago when she was working as a waitress in an expensive "haute culture" restaurant regularly pat- ronized by lawyers and judges from the nearby criminal court. Waiting on a table one afternoon she overheard a couple of hot shot big wheel lawyers laughing about a case in which one of them, the bigger lawyer in the city, had managed to get some poor bastard three years in the Pen for stealing a quart of milk. "You think that's funny, eh?" said Babbette in her usual candid manner. "You're very pleased with yourself eh - getting that poor man three years in the fuckin' jail for such a little thing - eh? You're very clever, eh?" "Babbette!" said one of the lawyers, "Do you know who you are talking to?" "Yes," snapped Babbette as she turned away, "A fuckin' dog!" The lawyers were annoyed at Babbette's refusal to serve them so they called over the manager. "I'm sorry, messieurs," he said apologetically, "but what can I do? If Babbette doesn't want to serve you, I can't maker her do it and I can't fire her, she is too good of a waitress." A human defiance, Gaspé guts, so typical of Babbette.

June 3, 1970   Wednesday

Desolation streets full of children running, bumping, yelling, singing, skipping, bouncing balls and chasing one another around the parked cars. Old men on their door steps. Young wives pushing their baby carriages to the laundromat. Slender young backstreet chicks cutting by saucily in bell-bottom jeans bold as love. Young men out of work tinkering around with their old cars. Middle-aged mothers domestically gossiping with one another on their galleries in the afternoon heat, relaxing before the kids come home from school. The shuttered windows that never open, the cloistered silence of condemned houses. The doors, splintered and cracked, tell the whole story.

June 7, 1970   Sunday

Well I went and sat in the Bistro Friday night and downed myself a couple of pints of beer while observing in envy the well-heeled intelligentsia relaxing culturally over a glass of wine. Their well-groomed looks, the sophisticated tilt to their faces, the cold, cynical glitter of their eyes. I rolled my cigarettes in embarrassment under the table. The fellow next to me was fingering a map of the world which he had placed over the marble table. He began asking me questions and I asked him if he spoke English. "Oh!" he says, "Are you from Montreal?" "Yeah," I answered. "And you don't speak French?" he said with a sly grin. "Lots of people don't," I answered. "Are you a student," he asked. "Nope." He didn't understand and repeated himself. "No, I'm not a student." "Hah!" he said, "you are an artist." "Nope," I said, "I work on trucks." Once he found out I was a loser he soon returned his attention back to his friends, which is what I wanted him to do anyway.

June 25, 1970   Thursday

This afternoon I ran into Vince the "old Fox" still dealing dope, an old veteran. He was stoned and in a deeply philosophical mood. I managed to squeeze a tight but hearty laugh out of him when I recalled the day I saw him running up and down Park Avenue in front of the Image. I remembered how intrigued I was at the time by the spectacle of Old Vince actually running because exercise is just not one of Vince's things. I allowed

him to pass by me a couple of times, then I yelled out at
him as he wobbled by, "Vince! What the fuck are you
doing?" "I'm working up my Speed," he gasped.

June 29, 1970   Monday

Slept in this morning. Didn't hear the alarm. Fuckin'
drag. What to do what to say. How would you like to
live on a tight rope? Or as Mr. Jimmy says - Forget it,
I got it.
    At Robin's yesterday afternoon playing on the kit-
chen floor with the children of Dale Eden. Dale was my
secret love back in grade five. I used to follow her home
from school in a discreet manner. Gail Moore was the big
thing in my life in grade seven. I planned one night to
sneak up to her house on Lansdowne Ave. in East Verdun
and place a pile of change I had saved from delivering
papers on her front gallery, but I never worked up enough
nerve to pull it off. Yes, the stolen kisses I had with Diane
McKay behind the kitchen door when her mother wasn't
looking. I was ten and she was eight. What a flirt she was.
I met Mr. Jimmy uptown on the way home and invited
him down to our place for supper. He sang for his meal
by narrating a few interesting stories of his "brothers and
sisters of the Spoon." Twenty-year-old speed addicts
burning up their brains in dark basement apartments.
Fantasies, dope-concocted dreams so easily collapsed by
the slightest whiff of reality. A many-sided mirror, illusionary character is Mr. Jimmy with a chameleon's ability
of fading into whatever background he happens to walk
into, and right now he is the Junky. Jimmy told me that
Jagger had been in town a couple of months ago. Just
blew in from Vancouver in the usual condition - broke
and homeless, missing his front teeth, down and out.
Wouldn't steal or do anything just sat around in Jimmy's
apartment all day writing poetry and shooting up speed.
He left one night without warning and beat Jimmy for a
jacket and a pair of pants. "Well," says Jimmy, "I guess
there's still hope for him; at least he's still alive enough
to beat somebody."

Yeah, busted disgusted and can't be trusted as the old
cons say. Read in bed until two o'clock last night then
tossed and turned on our hard and bumpy old box spring
bed until four. Up at six feeling bad and mean. Splashed
some water on my face, put on my clothes and went
back to bed after setting the alarm ahead twenty minutes. And, like my sister Peggy Anne used to tell me as
a kid, if you want time to slow down it goes faster. I
never experienced a quicker twenty minutes in my life.
Ram rap ram rap rap rap rap rap. Oh, sweet Jesus, shut
up! Liz got up with me to be in at work by eight and
the two of us stumbled about the house each in our own
individual coma. My head was still none too steady when
I kissed her good-bye, for I pecked her on the nose instead of the mouth. Walking round-shouldered in a stupor
to Notre Dame Street my cap pulled low over my fore-
head so as not to frighten the people with my early morning face. Unskilled labourers, factory hands, packers,
assistant shippers, dish-washers, waitresses, seamstresses
crowd the crack of dawn buses. Slum people, squat,
gnarled with the dull suffering of long hours and small
pay. Skinny, shabby St. Henri factory girls with their
rat-like faces and unkempt hair. Italian seamstresses in
black dresses conditioned by their peasant background to
accept docilely unrewarding toil sat stoically in their
seats staring straight ahead. How long - how long?

July 2, 1970   Thursday

Saw a Chinaman flag down a taxi cab today for the
first time in my life. Somehow it seemed to be very un-
characteristic of those tight-fisted closed-mouthed orien-
tals with their urban-peasant mentality. It must have been
an emergency, I can't explain it otherwise, unless he was
some kind of renegade. There was another unusual Chinaman I heard about who used to frequent the Only Café,
a bar patronized very heavily, I should say almost totally,

by fags, butches and hustlers. Pickles told me about him
one night when I was sitting with her and saw him trip
in. "Wow," I said, "never saw a Chinaman in a bar before."
"Yeah, that's old Tom Ling," she said, "he's been around
for years and he knows the gay scene inside out. He
doesn't hustle and he doesn't drink. The old man just
enjoys the company and sits and raps. We're like a family.
Funny guy, never asks for nothing."

July 5, 1970   Sunday

That early morning number one cigarette blues has
got me. Elevator going down, dull skies leaking, slow
rain falling. The squalor of an unmade mind.

Liz came home yesterday with thirteen dollars in
tips gained by serving huge parties of black Americans
with furious appetites in the Laurentien Motel. Deep
Southern voices requesting grits and ordering extra everything on the breakfast menu. "Good tippers," sighed Liz
as she collapsed on the sofa and nodded off to sleep.
During the time she was sleeping I was up in Pat's kitchen
rapping about his latest conquest - Irish, alias Blue Eyes,
the Virgin German ballerina. "Gonna have to push her
under a truck if she keeps pestering me," said Pat, full
of romantic sentiment as usual. Yeah, he's still searching
for his ideal girl - a blind, deaf and dumb nymphomaniac
who owns a liquor store. It could take some time.

One point of information the narrator of the Dow
Planetarium brought up struck me as being strange. The
Earl of Ross, an extremely rich Irish nobleman, had a
life-long ambition to own the world's largest telescope
and finally managed to have one with a 73" lens constructed at tremendous cost. In 1844 as he was scanning the night sky he discovered a new galaxy. 1844 was
also the year of the Potato Famine which killed nearly
3,000,000 Irishmen of starvation. He didn't need a
telescope to see that.

Again no luck this morning. "A Lundi matin," said
the boss man. The peasants were empty-handed and
grumbling. Deep voices rattling up from their bellies.
But not a stone was thrown. A forty-five minute walk at
fast pace from the truck yard to my house down dingy
Notre Dame Street. I always say hello to Benjamin Franklin as I pass the Chateau de Ramsey where he once resided.
"You were right old man." And Irish ballads always hum
in my brain as I salute Duke and Nazareth Streets in
Griffentown, the mother of us all. Her dark damp tenement lined streets mothered thousands, nursed them with
her bitter hard tits. Her ravaged face, half insane with
cheap booze and bad food, smothered and sweltered in
rat-infested basements surrounded by her red-eyed ragged
brood of wolverine children. So quick to cut, so prone
to kill and many of them never grew old and died in the
explosions of their young wild blood or else survived to
rot in garbage gutters, jails and strait jackets leaving no
families, no names, just bones in pauper's fields. But our
grandfathers flourished on the thin, sparse milk that had
killed so many of their brothers. They came home at
nights, hid their crimes, drank down their hatred, laughed
at their bare-ribbed hungry houses and listened to their
mothers in the kitchen when the old man came home
cut-up and stupid. "Don't be like him, son, pray and work."
And they did and they prayed in the factories, in the
ditches, in the brick yards, in the railway cars and in the
logging camps. And in their faith they had families
and with the muscles of their arms and backs they built
in slavery a foundation for their children's freedom.

Beat up intestines, nicotine-coated tongue, jittery
throat tied up with a cough at the bottom. Sick in
Babylon.

July 11, 1970   Saturday

My pen is no longer a pen but a tool. I pick it up now like a mechanic picking up a monkey wrench.

July 12, 1970   Sunday

Walking back home from the movies on the Main, a head full of memories of past ambitions, hopes and schemes; of the Place Ville Marie world I failed to adjust to; of Beverly Wood, of Karen Chevarie; the young clerk and his lonely evenings. They'll be tearing down the old C.P. Station in a couple of years. The marble steps worn thin by generations of passing immigrants including my own mother who walked down those steps at the age of five, a little Scottish girl with her braided hair covered with a Tam o'Shanter. My grandfather took the family on their second day in Canada for a once-in-a-lifetime meal at Mother Martin's, a very exclusive restaurant in those days and today. And my grandmother Kerr in her broad Scot's broque said as they entered the door, "Ah, Willy do they let working people like ourselves in here?" "All people are equal over here in Canada," answered my grandad in a proud voice. A good sweet man loved by all who knew him.

July 14, 1970   Tuesday

"Coming home on a wing and a prayer! " yelled Sandy from the back of the old derelict truck our drunken driver was zooming us home in down St. Denis Street, "Look out people! " It seems our driver had been dropping in at the taverns all day long; in between loading us up with circulars he had been getting loaded himself. The boys describing the state of the nation during our lunch break. "One thing for sure," said Rival, "a big change is coming. I don't know what it is but it's coming." "Yeah,

yeah," murmured the other guys. And, like I told the Indian, these guys make more sense sometimes than any twenty so-called radical leaders put together. They see things in their total social context. "The boses tell you what they want but you can't tell them what you want. Remember that people!" said Honky in a Moses on the Mountain type voice. Kaliph the Inspector always stays out of these discussions, he's a good nigger. And three out of the ten truck crews are too far gone on the booze to worry about anything except the next bottle of wine.

The suburban fields are splashed with blue corn-flowers. It's the time of year for them. I know because they greeted me on July 21, 1966, when I walked out of the Don Jail, a free man after thirty-one days behind bars; and since that day blue cornflowers have always symbolized freedom for me. Oh freedom when I crossed over the Humber River Bridge in T.O. on foot going up-town for my first decent meal in a month smiling at everyone passing by giving a fond hello to one and all in-cluding a traffic cop in the middle of the street. People laughing to see anyone as hysterically happy as I was walking down Queen Street with every button in my shirt and jacket holding a blue cornflower.

July 16, 1970   Thursday

The workhorses are taking off their blinders.

July 17, 1970   Friday

Dreamt last night that Liz and I were walking along Wellington Street close to sunset looking for a theatre with a good film showing. I was wrapped up deep and tight in my anxiety bag and had to see a film. The theatres we passed by had nothing interesting showing and we walked on and on through crowds at a quick nervous pace, the people like vague shadows. Liz grew fatigued, mildly complaining. "If you want to go home, go home!" I said angrily. "Here's a bus ticket!" She

gave me a hurt look, snapped the ticket out of my hand
and rushed across the street to the bus stop. I walked
on until I came to the last theatre at the end of the
street. The sun was almost down, it was now or never.
The advertisement on the luridly painted billboard showed three old men in hermit robes with long flowing
white hair and beards standing desolately in a snow
blizzard. Stormy Weather was the name of the film.
I walked into the lobby but didn't like the sinister
appearance of the theatre or the ghoulish looks of the
ticket taker, so I split. It so happened that the bus I
got on was the one Liz was taking back home. She
was sitting in the back rapping with an old boyfriend
of hers from years ago and completely ignored me when
I sat down close by her.

July 20, 1970   Monday

     The truck crew sitting in a Notre Dame Street
greasy spoon having early morning toast and coffee before starting work. "It's good to eat, eh, mon vieux?"
said Mario to me as we got off the counter stools to
leave. A short day doing Ville D'Anjou duplexes and
apartment houses knocking off work at two o'clock.
Coming home in a fit of energy I cleaned out the backyard filling up six jumbo garbage bags with trash. Then
I sat on the front stairs reading a newspaper until Liz
came home with a big smile on her face when she saw
me. Pat was over about five o'clock with the news that
he had finally received his first unemployment insurance
cheque, inviting me over to the Fulford Street Bar to
celebrate its opportune arrival - like a ten month baby
long in coming bug good anyway when it happens.
Talking in the bar about farms, motorcycles, girls and
art. "Yeah," said Pat, "I'd like to take up farming, you
know, the simple life. The bare essentials. A couple of
cows, chickens, twenty-three dancing girls." "Ah, ya
better behave yourself, Pat," I said. "I've heard rumours
that Women's Liberation plans to assassinate you if you

continually persist in your idle ways. They will not tolerate your wholesale corruption of Montreal's young womanhood much longer."

Sunday night around five o'clock I cut over to Charly's to find him buried in a thick book on Genetics studying for his American Acceptance Exam. We went over to the Annex where Charly had a beer and myself a coffee. (Visions of my Uncle Art.) Rapping about Socialism, discussing my difficulties in conversing with college intellectuals. The topic of I.Q.'s was brought up. "My teachers never told me I could do better," I said. "They were satisfied that the little I produced was the best I had to offer." Walking back to Charly's we ran into some old friends of mine walking up Maisonneuve Boulevard. Kay, Elaine's cousin, with her angel sister Isabel, two girlfriends, Big Linda and Early, and Mike Smyth. Charly split and the rest of us went over to Mike's apartment on Lincoln Avenue to exchange all the latest news and happenings. Kay is still working as a live-in babysitter with a Dollard Des Ormeaux family as she has been for the last four years. The kids she minds relate much more to her than to their absentee mother. The family took a summer vacation this year without Kay, and the kids cried for her every night. Kay's a tough but tender-hearted girl sad and burdened down with the res-ponsibilities left on her shoulders by a neurotic mother and drunken runaway father. She has stories to tell of the years she spent in a girl's home on Crescent Street. Of her greasy boyfriend, Louie, who grooved on Cadilacs. He'd climb up on the roof of every one he'd find parked on the street and jump up and down on the roof of it with his motorcycle boots. "And, if he was in the mood," said Kay, "he'd also kick in the headlights just for laughs but only Cadillacs." And stories about Elaine's old man, a heavy-drinking full-blooded Cree Indian. "That's why Elaine is so strong," said Kay after I told her that that little girl had once beat me in arm wrestling. "She was always having to go and pick her father up off the side-walk when he came crawling home drunk. Her mother and father have been fighting like cats and dogs for the last twenty-five years."

48

"One Christmas Eve he came stumbling home crazy
drunk, blind as a bat, rolling into the living room while
all of us were sitting in the kitchen. 'Cawlis, Ma,' he said,
talking to the Christmas tree, 'you look beautiful tonight
my lovely wife, cawlis. Let's make love. And boom we
hear a sudden smash and crash, and rushing into the living
room we found him lying on the floor with the tree on
top of him, covered with broken glass, tinsel and cotton
snow." Elaine dragged him out from under the mess and
carried him to bed.

Another time during an evening's drinking bout it
seems that the old man laid a beating on Kay and Elaine
for some small insignificant reason, and they, determined
to revenge themselves, left the house to get out and get
the cops. "We planned it," said Kay, "so that when we
came back with the cops I was to bug the old man into
swinging a punch at me. Then I'd duck and he'd hit the
cop standing behind me. Well, we got the cops up there;
Elaine unlocked the door, and what a sight to see! The
old man sitting down drinking with a friend both in their
underwear and the wife under the table barking like a
dog. I didn't even have to bug the old man because when
he saw me standing in the doorway in front of two big
Westmount cops he came up roaring and threw a punch
that hit the cop just as we had planned. But he wasn't
arrested. He began throwing beer bottles at the cops
and chased them down the stairs out into the street. "You'd
like to get me on the sidewalk, eh?" yelled the old man
as he stood on his doorstep cursing them, "but I know
my rights, est ti. You can't arrest me in my own house."

<u>July 22, 1970</u>   <u>Wednesday</u>

Spent over an hour working on a letter for Eddy
last night and was too drained of ideas by the effort to
be able to write more in my journal. Had a dream of my
father sitting in the kitchen in a dirty undershirt crying.
Liz woke up from a nightmare early in the morning and
I put my arm around her until she fell asleep again. We

knocked off work at three-thirty yesterday and Kaliph told us there'd be no work until Monday. Looks like the boys are gonna have to panhandle their week-end booze money. "Every dollar I spend," said Sandy, "is a dollar stolen from my landlord." The Montreal Messenger has a lot of alcoholics under its steady employment. They work on the trucks year after year, summer and winter, supporting themselves by delivering circulars, living in dingy furnished rooms down around Notre Dame Street, getting drunk as often as possible on "Bingo" wine. They are the aristocrats of the lower St. Lawrence Main Taverns, the working bums good for a free round of beer on pay days, as all the old mission bums know. A working bum dreads having his legs go bad on him more than death itself for lameness would force him down into the ranks of the mission bums, the Untouchables, the lowest rock-bottom status in society. The drifting, homeless mission alcoholic, subsisting totally upon charity, hoping only to live long enough to be able to collect his old age pension at 65. Most bums are old Vets, a phenomenal number of whom were either Black Watch or sailors and they wear their insignia proudly upon the lapels of their shabby jackets, especially when panhandling. "Give an old Vet a dime, buddy" is one of the classic standard lines they use. Their termite world of sleazy taverns and cruddy greasy spoon restaurants lies rotting under the edifice of our tumbling social system.

July 23, 1970   Thursday

I love my mother's laugh. The Celts are not a people much for smiling; the brooding solemn faces of a people weaned upon a harsh and barren land. A long inheritance of bitter disappointments, a wiry acceptance of death as an occasion to celebrate. Loyal, puritanically honest, habitually hard-working and gifted with an innate sense of justice. No Welsh, Irish or Scotsman feels himself to be less than any other man on this earth, or so it seems to me judging from my own family. The Jews have a wise-crack type of humour, the English have a punctuated

laugh, the French are smilers, the Germans heavily jovial
and the same with the Scandinavians; but the Welsh, Irish,
Scots and Bretons laugh like the sea, like a sudden wind,
a ringing explosive burst vibrating, I have seen my mother
laughing when a few minutes before she was in bitter tears.
Of all the European races the Celts seem to have most
retained the human sense of laughter. The Indians, the
Blacks both African and American, yes they have the secret
too. A lingering rapport with the earth that bore them,
a grandfather's wisdom of birth, of wombs and graves and
the interconnections so tightly wired between them both.

July 24, 1970   **Friday**

        A belly full of smoke and a mind full of disconnected
long distance telephone calls.

July 25, 1970   **Saturday**

        And then boom down to the movies. Marlon Brando
in a western doing his thing, the bad-guy hero who just
wants to be left alone. Out of the theatre about two
o'clock and with time to kill began strolling slowly up
Ste. Catherine Street in the bright sunlight smoking Camel
cigarettes and grooving on the crowds. All those young
girls so good to look at. Met Issy on the corner of St.
Mark Street and stopped and rapped with him on the
sidewalk as the shoppers walked by. He's a dedicated
girl-watcher like myself and a connoisseur. "Yeah, Liz
tells me she's gonna get me some blinders," I said. "I
keep coming home in the summertime with acute eye
strain." Dropped in to see the boys at Ribkoff's dress
factory. It was visiting a jail I had once done time in.
Close-caged atmosphere, humid sweat-stained walls,
creaking floor boards. Mike, Butch and Rolly scurrying
about like white-faced termites in a subterranean cavern.
Talking about overtime, motorcycles, Jimi Hendrix's
latest album and girls.

Later at home waiting for Liz on the front steps watching kids play baseball on Dominion Street. Black and white tough little mothers dividing themselves up into teams. "We'll be the New York Whiteys and you guys will be the Boston Blackeys."

July 26, 1970   Sunday

Met Nathan coming down Atwater Hill on a motorbike and I asked him for a lift over to St. Mark Street. "Sure, get on," he said. Slipping and sliding up to Charly's who had just got home from the hospital, and Nathan and I spent an hour in his living room rapping about the bad old days of 63 Craig Street. Nathan's 1956 Hearse, half-a-block long, air-conditioned, with a Rolls Royce engine. We rode it slowly along Ste. Catherine Street one tropic evening back in 1967. Twenty to thirty street people, long hair streaming down their psychedelic shoulders hanging out the coffin windows yelling peace slogans at the crowds on the sidewalks. A whole mob of French sailors in their white ducks and red pompom hats came running up to us on the street when we stopped for a green light. Four of them managed to squeeze in through the hearse windows waving their berets at the rest of the navy left behind when the light changed back to red. What a cruise that was, and the hearse only cost Nathan four hundred dollars.

July 27, 1970   Monday

Dave Ronn has stood still on the same ground I last saw him on six months ago. Thin, sickly, depressed and oppressing in his manner; still hasn't forgiven me for the bitter note I left in his mail box two summers ago. He just barely condescended to pay attention to whatever I said, nor did he make any comment upon anything I uttered. In boyish pride I informed them of the one hundred and fifty thousand words I have written since

December. If total lack of response is the new "in" way of congratulating a person's achievements, then I was highly complimented that evening. But as it is, I am not a cool person, and I felt quite hurt by their behaviour. "Well," I said, puncturing the dead silence, "It's really not as impressive as it sounds. You see I write one word over six thousand times each week so actually I've only written thirty six words and after I've written about sixty times six thousand words I'm gonna toss them all up in the air like pieces of a Scrabble game then type them out in book form just as they landed." Down to the Ben Asch Restaurant on the corner of St. Lawrence and Ste. Catherine for a smoked meat with sad mad Albert Collignon who gave me an outline biography of his pathetic life as we sat at the counter poking the ice cubes in our cokes with a straw.

Born on a farm in Manitoba thirty-one years ago his family moved into Winnipeg when he was ten years of age. Ran away when he was fifteen and stayed on the road two years. Returned and finished high school. Entered university, met Leonard Cohen who encouraged him in his poetry, had a nervous breakdown and left school without completing the year. Came into Montreal the fall of 1965 and met Jean Yves and myself at the Prag that winter. Albert introduced me to Cohen one evening at a table in the back of a coffee-house. Sad, faggish-looking guy in an expensive mod suit. "David I would like you to meet a friend of mine, Leonard Cohen." I nodded, sat down and began talking with Albert. I had hardly ever heard of Leonard Cohen before and I kept confusing him with Irving Layton, Montreal's other Poet Royal. Matter of fact I kept calling him Irving and he corrected me a few times before giving up in disgust. Maybe he thought I was some kind of professional mind-blower trying to fuck up his head. I'm not sure, but we certainly didn't hit it off. He didn't even turn his head when I said goodbye. Well, that's show biz.

Albert went back up to Dave Ronn's after we finished our smoked meats and I continued on my way downtown, walked into the Prag and found Jean Yves sitting at a back table smiling to himself over a cup of coffee. He looked up when I sat down in front of him and grinned mischievously. "Aha," he drawled, "another ghost. Look at all the ghosts," he said, dramatically spreading out his left arm in a graceful swoop, brilliant and charming as only Jean Yves can be when he is creating an atmosphere. We walked slowly up Mountain Street arms behind our backs, heads bent together like wise old men. Jean Yves had a dramatic story to tell about his family and it may or may not be true. Not that Jean Yves is a liar but the nervous breakdown he suffered recently is still visibly affecting his behaviour. Walking and talking we found ourselves meandering along Argyle Street where it all happened back in 1966. Alley cats and hollyhocks, wooden steps puckered with age, patched up hobo houses all with rooms to let signs tacked on the doors. The sidewalk folds and arches like a swelling concrete ocean wave. "Let's go on the tracks, Dave," said Jean Yves, walking in the direction of the railway fence. "Yeah, O.K.," I said apprehensively looking up the street for passing patrol cars as we vaulted the wire. We felt like young runaway boys going into the night for the first time alone. "Let's go to Toronto, Dave," said Jean Yves casually as we walked along the rails. "I can't, Jean Yves." "Why not?" "I got Liz. She'll worry." "Oh, yeah," he said softly. "I forgot." We climbed down the foundation of the Seigneour Street bridge and headed along Fulford Street. Laura yelled to me suddenly from a top window, "Ah you're gonna get it when you get home. Liz told me she's gonna lock you out." It was two o'clock in the morning and I waved hello to Mr. O'Neil who was sitting with one of his daughters on his gallery stairs. A couple of houses down we stopped to talk with Bryan and Stan who were stoned on grass lying on the sidewalk using a telephone pole for a pillow. "Did you hear, Dave," said Stan, "that Dirty Doris stabbed some guy with a fork down on Atwater Street tonight? Done him in 'cause he wouldn't give her a quarter when she asked him on the street." "Yeah? No kidding?" I said. "Well old Doris always was a bit touched." "Yeah," continued Stan, "and some drunks from the tavern busted up the Maoists' bookstore and beat the shit out of everybody in the place. One of the Communist girls was going around today with a black eye giving out leaflets."

Dougie called on us yesterday to tell us that Dawn
was in the hospital having her tonsils out. We walked
back with him up to the General Hospital where on the
ninth floor Peggy Anne was sitting with her daughter in
the children's room. Dawn's eyes nearly fell out of her
head when she saw me walk in, her long-haired comical
uncle that's so loving with her. Down to the Plaza to
buy cigarettes, donuts, soft drinks for everyone and a
mammoth ice cream cone for the little chipmunk.

And Walter O'Neil, Pat's uncle, turns out to be my
mother's first lover. "I almost married him," my mother
said, "but he started running around with some girl from
Ottawa about the same time I met your father. Walter
began coming around while I was dating your father and
asked me to marry him but I liked your old man better.
A month after we were married Walter phoned me up
and asked me how I was doing and said that if he ever
heard of your father laying a hand on me in anger he'd
kill him." She showed me a photograph of O'Neil, a
picture I can remember seeing as a child of a handsome
tough-looking guy with a broken thumb all wrapped up
in a cast. "He told me he got his hand caught in a car
door, but I figure he must have broken his thumb over
somebody's head in a bar. He was that kind of man,"
said my mother musing over the photo.

I painted all the rest of the floors yesterday and
could not find the time for studying. Got a sore neck
and a touch of the flu, not to mention that early morning blues that's got me. Reading the births, deaths and
memorials in the <u>Montreal Star</u> and an article on Intelli-
gence Quotient tests, which are something I never personally excelled in. We had a test in grade 6 in Bannantyne School and I can remember a week or so later Mrs.
Denneberg calling out the names of a half-dozen students

asking them to stay after school. Since the people she named were amongst the best scholars of our grade I knew they weren't staying in after school for bad behaviour but for an interview and pep talk concerning their élite brain power. Wayne Young and Jack Reilly were amongst the six, and I can remember the elevated gleam that came into their eyes when Denneberg singled them out from the others. "Well, maybe I'm a loser," I thought at the time, "but they ain't got the magic I've got. I can see things they're blind to." Wayne is now a French professor, Jack is working on an M.A. in Science, and David Fennario is still working on his magic.

Yes, I would have dreams that I'd tell in the form of stories to my friends including them in the dreams to let them know we were all together. Or should be so. This is the way it should be. I could not accept the prison I was born in because I knew I was innocent of the charges I had been sentenced for, and I knew all of us were innocent and none of us guilty of the judgements passed upon us. The jail we were suffering in was of our own making and the day was coming when we'd free ourselves. Danny Malone, Larry Omer, Robert Taylor and myself playing in the backyards, sheds and dark night alleyways of East Verdun. "Wouldn't it be nice if we were brothers and lived and played together all the time?" and even when I said this, I knew we would grow up strangers in the world just like our parents and lock the doors.

August 6, 1970   Thursday

Even forgot what day it was today that's how hectic a night I had babysitting Jacky Robinson through one of his berserk drunks; putting his fists through windows walking up the middle of the street like Godzilla the monster dinosaur roaring out challenges to innocent passers-by. "Fuck you!" he yelled at a kid no higher than his knee. "Fuck you too," squeaked the little boy as he ran away. "I didn't hit the little kid did I, Dave?" asked Jacky the morning after sitting at the kitchen table while Liz patched up his cuts and bruises. "No, man," I said, "you didn't hit anybody but you make one hell of a fuckin' racket. I was expecting shot gun blasts when you started hitting those high c's." He laughed; then I continued, "Bingo wine does it to you every time, Jacky. From now one, Man, the only thing I'm ever gonna drink with you is carrot juice - rabbit booze, man."

Proverbially it was all Pat's fault. Jacky calls on me about three-thirty in the afternoon and he grabs my guitar as usual and begins strumming out some beautiful R & B numbers. "I'm going down to the bar, Dave," he says. "Come and join me." Agreed we'll go uptown for a short beer but first we'll call on Pat and ask him to join us. And that dumb Mick comes out with this line, "Hey, Jacky, let's go get some bingo. We haven't got drunk together on a jug of wine for years." I throw Pat one of my are-you-out-of-your-fuckin'-skull type looks but he doesn't catch it. Well, from the very commencement of the festivities I'm feeling nervous, just sipping the juice remembering the last time Jacky got drunk on wine and I ended up pulling him out of a snow drift he was swimming in with his shirt and shoes off, all the while yelling blue murder much to the annoyance of the local population. Feeding Jacky wine is like throwing lit matches on a dynamite keg. It generally explodes, and so does he. Last night's explosion was a classic. Jacky, Mary and myself sitting in Pat's living room, and Pat was over at the studio (my basement) trying to make some chick while I remained as a spectator of Jacky's sodden slurpy attack upon a reluctant Mary. I got up to leave when Jacky turned off the light but Mary grabbed the back of my sweater as I was walking out of the room. "You don't want to make out, do you?" I said as I turned and looked at her. No, she nodded with a pleading look in her eyes. "O.K.," I said as I walked over turned on the light and took Jacky by the arm saying, "Hey Jacky come here a sec." We moved over to a corner. "Look man she doesn't want to make out." "So what am I?" he answered. "Some kind of animal?" I shrugged my shoulders, picked up my guitar and left hoping for the best. Looking up from my steps towards Pat's house I saw Mary looking out the window and I signalled to her to let her know that

I was going to get Pat. And Pat after a lot of violent waving of the arms and swearing went up and did the reluctant
hero bit. Ten minutes later as I lay in bed with Liz talking,
Jacky came stumbling through our front door singing and
yelling at the top of his powerful lungs. He did the swan
dive bit on the rug throwing up as he fell and I ran into
the kitchen to get the mop. Coming back I found him
sobbing incoherently and wiping his mouth on my Indian
Print Sofa cover. "Get off the floor, Jacky," I said, "so
I can wipe up the mess." He bounced to his feet pushing
me out of the way, headed out onto the back gallery
and jumped down into the street. Looking out of the
front window with Liz, I watched him roaring up Dominion Street as I described earlier. He made a turn onto
St. Antoine Street and I figured, out of sight he's going
back uptown, but no such luck. He staggered back into
view and I went back into the bedroom grabbed Liz's
arm and said, "Let's go. I don't wanna be here if he
comes back." Boom over the back fence and up the
street; turning on St. James we heard the sound of breaking glass and looking back I saw Jacky putting his fists
through Pat's downstairs door windows. We stayed twenty-
five minutes at the Athens Restaurant over a coffee and
then began cautiously making our way back home along
the shadowed side of Dominion Street not knowing what
to expect. Everything was quiet, a single red light was
burning in Pat's window. I moved softly onto our front
gallery and looking through the open window I saw
Jacky lying unconscious on our living room floor. Stepping over his body making as little noise as possible tip-
toeing around the house. The walls and floors were
splashed with blood. "He's cut himself," I whispered
and I went over and checked him out, but it was nothing
but a couple of deep scratches on his hands and arms
that were no longer bleeding.

All of us got up with Liz next morning who had to
be at work by eight o'clock; at Jacky's insistence I accompanied him up to the John Howard where he hoped to
get some money to pay for Pat's window. As all old
rounders know, the J.H. doesn't open until the stroke of
nine, so to while away the hour's wait we had facing us
we took a trip up to the Atwater Bus Terminal. There I

sat laughing on the steps of John Cabot's statue watching
Jacky on his hands and knees like a dog barking at the
pigeons hopping about the park. "Watch out he's insane,"
I yelled to the mob of work-a-day people filing through
the square on the way to their jobs. They were laughing
just as hard as I was at Jacky's antics like lifting up his
leg like a dog pretending to piss on a tree, and then bouncing over the grass after the birds. After awhile I started
to get a little paranoid. "Come on doggy," I said, "we'd
better split from here before the cops pick you up for not
having a licence." Down we went into the Nihon Plaza
where it took Jacky only five minutes to aggravate two
hefty security guards into ushering us out of the place
with dire warnings never to return. "But, officer, I never
touched her," Jacky said talking about the woman he
chased up the escalator, "I was only being friendly."
"Yeah, well do it somewhere else," said the man pushing
us from behind. The whole scene could have been cut
out of Midnight Cowboy, Ratso and Buck getting the bums
rush again. Calculating that the J.H. would be the safest
place to spend the next hour with Jacky, I talked him into
heading in that direction. "Look," I said, "You're sleepy,
you could sleep on the lawn there and the cops won't
hassle you." Two guys were stretched out on the lawn
when we got there and Jacky knew one of them. Some
half-witted French Indian wearing shabby wino pants,
gum boots and a green boy scout shirt complete with gold
tassles and covered with merit badges. Just the kind of
nut Jacky would know, a derelict boy scout. "Wearing
this," said the guy pointing to his shirt, "I can get into
all the camps. I got all my first class badges too." "I
bet you help old ladies across the street and mug 'em,"
said Jacky laughing. The other guy in his mid-twenties
with a booze-red face framed with a full beard that made
him look like a derelict college prof said nothing beyond
bumming a cigarette. He was the insane Boy Scout's
silent partner and they specialized in hitting churches for
grub and money. "Guess the priests must find it hard to
resist a boy scout," I said listening to the man brag of his
exploits.

The clean brisk social workers, young, fashionably
dressed with styled modish hair cuts complete with sideburns and moustaches nodded good morning to us ack-
nowledging the Boy Scout's greeting as they walked up
the gravel pathway to the entrance past where we lay
sprawled out on the grass. "I guess there was a time,"
I thought to myself, "when these young college guys
found us amusing but they know by now that we're all
just a bunch of winos full of con lines and desperate for
a drink." "Yes, here we are," I thought bitterly, "all
of the same age group and generation, the social workers
and the bums, loving the same music, admiring the same
people and seemingly more together than any other past
generation yet still treading the same old evil roads that
our fathers did even though we wear our hair long, smoke
pot and read radical literature." It was my first sickening
view of the fate in store for the Jacky Robinsons of this
world. Jacky, the wild and charming boy, magically
plastic, his flowing body slowly hardening into that of
a stiff and clumsy scabby old stumble bum, the kind that
wander aimlessly through the crowds on Main Street
talking to themselves fishing newspapers out of public
waste-paper baskets.

Jacky went in as soon as the doors opened and came
out fifteen minutes later with three bucks in his pockets.
"What did ya say to the guy?" I asked as we walked away
from the building. "Well, the guy had long hair and I
figure he's cool so I tell him the truth. 'Look man,' I
says, 'I broke some windows and I need some money to
get them fixed before the people 'phone the cops.'
And I show him the cuts on my hands, and the guy says
to me, 'And where do you think you're going to get the
money?' And I says, 'why from the good old John Howard
of course.' 'Oh no you're not,' the guys says but I talked
him out of three bucks anyhow, one for every window."

Stopping at Baldy's on Atwater to have breakfast
we bumped into an old acquaintance of ours from the
Lagauchetiere Street era, tall and handsome Don, the man
the girls were all in love with. Shy, quiet, speaks with
a noticable stutter, a very gentle person. "Come over
with us and see the house me and Liz got, Don," I said

as we got up from the lunch counter. Walking up Coursol Street together Jacky says, "Fuck man, I hate walking back through the neighbourhood after all the shit I caused last night." "Well tell the people you're sorry," I said. He took my suggestion literally and got into the middle of the street down on one knee and yelled, "I'm sorry, I APOLOGIZE!"

While Jacky was taking a bath that left a ring in the tub about a foot wide and an inch thick I sat in the living room drinking coffee listening to Don's stories about the six months he spent working in the Thompson Mines out west. I finished up our conversation with a well-rehearsed lecture on socialism handing him some literature as he left with Jacky to go uptown. After spending an hour and a half writing down the events of the past evening I took a break and cut over to Pat's to see what was happening. Pat was sitting in the living room his fists all wrapped up in gauze and bandaids talking to Mary. "What happened, Pat," I said gazing at his bruised knuckle, "get into a beef?" "Yeah." "With who?" "Ah with some guy last night who was carrying one of your bedsheets and following Jacky down the street." "Yeah? I was wondering where that bedsheet disappeared to. Did the guy say anything?" "Naw, I jumped him real quick-like and hammered him down, teeth all over the place. I haven't been in a mood like that for a long time." "What did the guy look like?" "A white guy a little shorter than me and heavier." "It might have been a cop, Pat." "Yeah, that's why I'm playing it cool. Don't spread the story around, O.K.?" "O.K. Man what an evening." "Yeah, pretty good for the middle of the week."

August 7, 1970   Friday

Jacky was over at the house about ten o'clock this morning waking me up. Picked up my guitar and started playing an old blues number, "I found a new love". "Guess you didn't make it with Mary last night, eh, Jacky?" I said teasing him. He answered me with a sad smile and continued singing. "And if you ever leave me baby, I

think that I would die". After he had finished singing
all those bad feelings out of him I began questioning him
about his activities yesterday evening. "We went uptown,
Mary John and myself to score a dime of hash. Well we
got some and I went into the back of the Prag to find
some tin foil to put it in; and, fuck, I found a quarter
ounce of hash somebody else had stashed back there in
the alley." And thanks to Jacky's luck everybody got
stoned over at Pat's last night.

August 9, 1970   Sunday

        I spent the afternoon over at Pat's father's place on
Fulford Street listening to his stories about the West End.
Death Valley Jack, Eddy Jackson, Jimmy Fay, Bill Flowers,
Carfare, Johnny Muldoon, Emmett Rooney, Roy Colly,
all real bad actors from the neighbourhood, the Tony
Frank gang and the infamous Hochelaga Bank hold up.
The gang had their headquarters right here on the corner
of Dominion and Coursol back in the twenties. All of
them caught and hanged for killing three motorcycle
cops and a guard. Blind Pigs, Honky Tonks, gambling,
prostitution, the West End was the Red Light district of
Montreal back in the bootlegging days and Ragtime Jimmy
O'Neil was playing piano in some of the toughest joints
while still in his teens. "It was clean fun," says Mr. O'Neil,
now the father of six children and not wishing to impress
young people in the wrong way by his stories of the hard
people he knew. Stabbings, gun battles, guys with their
eyes and tongues cut out, whores beaten to death with
baseball bats by jealous pimps. And a story about a hop-
ped-up drummer who used foul language in front of
ladies at a club one night and got pumped full of lead for
his bad manners by an ex-body guard of Al Capone and
card-playing friend of Jimmy O'Neil. Good clean fun.

August 10, 1970   Monday

Yeah, it was a hot day for working - 95 degrees in the shade with the sweat running down our faces like rain. Bouchard's unemployment cheque is two months late and he was describing the noise he caused down at their office on Friday about not receiving the money due to him. "If you people don't want a Revolution," he said, "you sure are asking for one and I'm gonna be one of the first to pick up a brick."

I found a dollar bill on a gallery and treated myself and the Indian kid to two big family-size Cokes sitting on the steps of an Italian grocery store way up in the North End of Montreal. "Glurp glurp glurp-gasp ah that was good-um-had to get some liquid down that old tube of mine before I faded away, Collin." "Um, yes, I understand," he said burping up the gas.

And on the way home waiting for the Notre Dame Street bus I watched a trailer truck carrying a load of pigs pull up for the green light. The animals were poking their ugly snoots through the vents in the trailer sides, sniffing at me and I guess after all that dirty sweaty work I had done I must have smelt just a few degrees less pungent than they did. And yes they do have eyes like Chicago cops. Pusillanimous beady little glittering eye balls staring from a flesh-heavy obscene face.

August 11, 1970   Tuesday

Suffering again today in 92 degrees of heat and to top it off, the _pièce de résistance,_ you might say, the mosquitoes were out in regiments, big mothers with half-inch stingers out there in suburbia. Bouchard didn't show up today. The general consensus of the boys in the crew is that he's received his cheque and is out on a glorious drunk celebrating. "He's probably sitting in an air-conditioned tavern right now downing cold beer thinking of us poor bastards sweating it out on the streets," said Tobin dreamily. Tobin's a sandy-haired man, thin with a nervous rounder's face, about fifty years old he has worked ten years on the M.M. trucks. He has a flat around St.

63

Louis Square and lives alone with his cats.

The French kid got bit by a dog, it took a chunk right out of his arm. The dog's owner donated a sympathetic band aid.

August 14, 1970   Friday

Up to Charly's and he was talking about another baby he found with no brains. Sometimes Charly reminds me of the Embalmer, a character who drinks in the Pocket Rocket Tavern across the street from the Armstrong Funeral Parlour where he works. All the rounders in the area patronize the Armstrong since the Embalmer is an old rounder like themselves. He sits in the bar for hours every day telling stories about the interesting bodies he has embalmed. Charly and he should get together someday and exchange stories of the horrors they have encountered professionally.

August 18, 1970   Tuesday

I saw the river again today and the sight of it brought tears to my eyes. It's like magic for me.

We were working away out near the western tip of Montreal Island in Ste. Anne de Bellevue. Huge old country houses with long wide verandas that wind all around the house with vegetable gardens in the back just like my Grandpa's old house out in Ile Perrotte back in the early fifties. Little children sold me a cup of Kool-Aid on the street for a penny and I gave them two. "Not bad stuff," I said after downing the cup, "It's worth two cents."

We passed by Verdun High School on the way back uptown and I waved to my old ghost staring out of the window of Mr. Cord's classroom. How I used to dream but never in my wildest imaginings did I ever think that one day I'd be delivering circulars and pass by the school in the Company truck. Mr. Steele our guidance teacher never spoke to us of these things. They weren't on his charts depicting what salaries we would make in the future depending on how far we went in school. Of course since I was in Science III and one of the back-seat boys, the subject of university was never approached. That was left to the élite Latin class, but at least we were led to believe that with grade ten or eleven we would be able to make a comfortable living.

Mr. Steele's world of commodity values has never appealed to me, I've hated it all my life, but in high school I didn't know there could be anything different from what he described. I had vague hopes that the beatniks might have something different. In my early teens I once saw a young couple walking down Ste. Catherine Street in their bare feet carrying their sandals. I was fascinated by their appearance by the cool beatified air about them, and I followed them for blocks walking five yards behind them hoping to work up enough courage to speak to them but the courage never came. I feared their rejection.

I used to look with envy upon the young university couples walking arm in arm through McGill Campus wrapped up in intellectual discussion. So young to have the world at their feet, born into a lifestyle that I would never know except from the outside with my nose pressed against the windows. And I dreamed that I could somehow transcend a world I wanted no part of. I would become a famous and brilliant author constructing word bricks I could toss through all those fuckin' windows separating me from the good life. I'd B & E that world crashing through on my own terms. Yeah, mothers, here I am regardless of all Mr. Steel's charts.

The feelings, an understanding of laughter and sorrow. A sympathy not only with pain which is natural, but also with joy and pleasure.

August 20, 1970   Thursday

The old woman down the street went on a drunken berserk again last night "My brother's dead! " she was yelling. "Everybody should be dead, might as well be dead. I live alone. I live alone." "Ah sleep it off! " the neighbours yelled back. "Dry up! " I was sitting on the edge of the window s'll taking all this in when one of those militant French Separatists came up my stairs and dropped a newspaper in my porch. "Pouvoir Ouvrier," "Quebec Libre." "Quebec aux travailleurs." I watched him passing others at the houses down the street. Very stiff face, wire-rimmed glasses perched upon a thin social worker type nose that had a CBC cultured moustache underneath it. More than likely a lawyer's son majoring in political science. In my head silently I was saying go back to where you came from friend, you're not needed. We all live alone down here and can take care of ourselves.

August 21, 1970   Friday

Denise didn't show up by three o'clock so I taped a note on the front door telling her to go through the window and that I'd be home in an hour. Went up Atwater hill and parked myself by a tree outside the Reddy Memorial Hospital to wait for Elaine. Three Camel cigarettes and twenty-five minutes later out she came accompanied by a teen-age boy who obviously had a hopeless crush on her. Elaine, electrically happy and activated, so glad to have finally finished working at a job she hated, bouncing along the sidewalk beside me attracting the attention of everyone on the street by her candid manner. A big compulsive hug given to me unexpectedly while crossing Ste. Catherine Street left me gasping for a few seconds. Behind Elaine's small fragile appearance lies the strength of a full grown man. "I used to play a lot of baseball when I was a kid," she said in explanation. Years ago when I was going out with her she challenged me to an arm and hand wrestling match. I smiled condescendingly as I placed my elbow on the table and extended my hand expecting a very easy, almost effortless contest but to my shame and utter astonishment it took me about five minutes of blood, sweat and tears to get her little hand down on the table. As it is I have the sneaking suspicion that she allowed me to win knowing how sensitive males are about being beaten by a woman in a strength contest.

66

A long day on the trucks, arriving home at a quarter
after nine. The summer boys were complaining of sore
feet but not the old winter veterans like Bouchard, Collin
and myself. Yeah, we've seen the elephant.

August 25, 1970   Tuesday

Now about the Massiwippi trip. Around 7:30 that
night we packed up to leave - Liz and myself - to meet
Neil at the Metro and then up to the Provincial Bus Ter-
minus getting on a Grayhound bus to Magog. A long hot
bus ride sandwiched in the back seat with three young
giggling French girls who were passing around a bottle of
codeine cough medicine. And I was strung out, strung
up tight, three quarters drunk and in a fine state of confusion. Depressed and sickened, unsatisfied with myself,
tormented by the deep set irrationalities of my nature.
Worrying about worrying like my mother says.

The Allens were there to greet us with their stationwagon and the kids when the bus rolled into Magog. Rattling down the long dark country roads Betty Ann talking
about C.C. the 93-year-old farmer who was born and
brought up in the area. "We brought Bungy the Siamese
cat down with us once when we visited him and old C.C.
said, "By gar that's a strangely marked kitten you've got
there folks." Their country house has the same odour
about it as my grandfather's old place in Ile Perrotte.
Strawberries and cabbage - home made blackberry wine
fermenting in the shed. I downed two nervous beers while
sitting talking to Ray and Betty Ann in the kitchen table
making foolish unnecessary attempts to ingratiate myself.
"Fuck it," I thought after awhile, "I'll sleep on it." and I
excused myself and headed for the bedroom. Yeah,
Massiwippi, good night.

I was the first one up the next morning sucking in all
that oxygen-saturated air outside on the porch feeling
vaguely like a marooned sailor. All of the familiar land-

marks were missing - the Stelco chimney, Northern Electric, Redpath Sugar, Five Roses Flour signs that I grew up with. The country's great, I guess, everybody says so but I've yet to see anything as beautiful in the sticks as the sun rising over Coursol Street or dipping below the tenement buildings on St. Antoine Street. I don't know, you see one tree you've seen 'em all and the same goes for cows, pigs and barns. "Give me sidewalks anyday," I said to myself looking through the screen windows at all that monotonous green stuff. Yeah, bright lights, big city. Nine o'clock in the morning and the C.N. brakemen are sitting in the Fulford Street Tavern having a cold beer before going into the yard.

Yuppie came into the kitchen first in his pyjamas rubbing the sleep out of his eyes. "C'mon, Yup," I said tousling his hair, "let's play a game of cards." Janey, Gavin and Liz joined us later sitting at the table in the sunshine living room. Betty Ann in the kitchen mixing up a batch of blueberry pancakes for breakfast.

Afterwards I went for a walk about the property with the boys checking out a tent they had put up in a field. A two-man tent that five of us squeezed into. "Hey this is fantastic," I said in a Brooklyn accent as we sat all squashed together a mass of arms, elbows, legs like a broken jig saw puzzle. "We really made it. This is gotta be a world record, Neil! " And somewhere from the bottom of the pile came a muffled voice. "Get your elbow out of my ear, Yuppie."

A few hours later we were banging down the country road in the battered old Grapes of Wrath stationwagon loaded down and spilling over with kids, food, towels, beer and other beach apparatus to the lake. Neil and I took two rubber rafts way out on the water bouncing around like dolphins and I swallowed enough water to start my own goldfish colony. Other highlights in the afternoon were a rock skimming contest and Yuppie's premature buriel under a great mound of sand complete with a driftwood tombstone.

Betty Ann had been invited by a neighbouring family, the Browns for supper; so after changing and drying out we piled back in the car for the trip out to their farmhouse. Norman Brown is a professor of anthropology and

a Quaker by religion. Ray and he spent hours discussing
the ins and outs of establishing a commune. A very heavy
intellectual evening, not my style at all, and I spent most
of my time messing around with the kids. I had a Thal-
idomide Baby's Boxing Champion fight going on in the living room for a while. The kids playfighting each other, their
arms locked inside their sweaters with only their fists and
a small part of their forearms showing outside the sleeves.
Old man Brown, curious about the noise and laughter
glanced in through the patio door and freaked right out.
You know, Quakers and shit like that. So the game was
busted up. The strange thing is that the Brown's son
was much more aggressive than any of the other kids. I
had to rap him on the head more than once before I finally discouraged the boy from trying to rupture me during the game.

   We quit the Browns around twelve o'clock with
nothing decided or agreed on after four hours of conversation. And that's a lot of talking just to say nothing. The
experiences of that evening emphasized for me the actual
break in communication between the intellectual and
manual sections of the working class. The different roots.

August 29, 1970   Saturday

   After we got back to Montreal I went down to the
Pt. St. Charles Health clinic for a check up. Like with
my imagination, I figured they'd take one good long look
at me and ring up the City Morgue for a hearse. Nothing
more frightening than having a physical - I'd rather face
three psychopathic killers in a blind alley than have one.
"Well," says the doctor after an hour of thumping, pumping and bumping, "I can't find anything wrong." I nearly
fainted with joy. As I was sitting up on the edge of the
examining table putting my jeans back on he says to me,
"About your chest rib deformity - has it affected you in
any way?" "Well," I said, deliberating a few seconds,
"it's made me a poet."

September 1, 1970   Tuesday

    A nice thing did happen Sunday now that I think of
it. Some kids came over to tell Liz that they had a kitten
for her if she wanted it. A lady across the street had one
to offer us. All the kids trooped back with us to our
house. Standing at the front door - "Can we come in, can
we come in?" O.K. and boom five of them in my house -
black and white - Linda, Polly, Johnny, Jacky and Jerome
tearing about the living room after sitting shyly like a row
of sparrows on the sofa for five quiet minutes. Liz was
more sensitive to the noise than I was, I'm more used to
it, having grown up in a huge noisy family. Polly's a
little darling, curly hair, big brown eyes with a smile that's
gonna knock the men right over in the streets ten years
from now. I put an R & B album on the machine and we
all did the "Funky Chicken" just as natural as walking
down the street.

September 2, 1970   Wednesday

    We did N.D.G. today, No Damn Good as the resi-
dents like to put it. Walkly Street freaked me right out.
Here in the middle of a semi-exclusive suburb lies an
oasis of cheap cold-water apartment houses inhabited by
typical backstreet people. I knew that a lot of old West
End families and moved up into N.D.G. but now I know
where. Yeah Walkly Street - it was like someone took a
chunk out of St. Antoine Street with a carving knife and
tossed it up on the mountain. Freckle-faced snot-nosed,
red-haired little Irish brats bashing about the streets with
their black buddies just like down home.
    An air of exploding vitality, totally foreign to the
rest of the community hovers over this one long, heavily-
populated street. I saw more kids on Walkly Street than
in all the rest of N.D.G. It was like magic to turn a street
corner and enter a totally different world, a familiar world
of heavy men with tattooed arms leaning out their car

windows rapping with their drinking buddies on the sidewalk, of heavy set mothers with great flat feet and voices
like diesel whistles yelling for Johnny to stop hitting his
brother with a hockey stick. Ah yes I almost cried, it
was too real to be true. So warm, so human and good after
witnessing the sterility of N.D.G.'s other disturbingly
clean streets, so calm, so green, so pretty, so unbelievably
dead. And the dogs don't bark at you on Walkley Street.

September 3, 1970   Thursday

And Pat and I sitting in the bar rapping about the
bad old days in Ribkoff's dress factory and Rolland Denny
the head shipper. "He's been working there too long,
Pat," I said, "his whole life consists of Ribkoff's and getting stoned. He doesn't talk much to me 'cause we don't
have anything to say. I mean we respect each other but
we've got nothing to say - just a big chunk of silence sandwiched between hello and good-bye."

September 6, 1970   Sunday

And Friday evening was a very low evening for me
and Pat sitting in the Fulford Street Bar downing ten-
cent draught trying to find words for the blues we had.
Pat came closest. "It's like trying to get a hard-on and
you can't," he said. "Or worse," I replied, "It's like getting a hard-on and not having anything to fuck." Deep
drinking and thinking rolling home later singing "Gil-
garra Mountain."

Down with Liz to my old man's birthday party
Saturday night. All the Hannahs, McCluskeys and Rob-
ertsons were there, Jessie, Betty, Jean, Margeret and
old Aunt Maggie occupying the matriarch's chair. "Do
you remember me, David?" asked my Aunt Margeret.
"Sure I do," I said, "you taught me how to wink when I
was six-years-old."

The Amyots were down also. Old man Amyot fool-
ing Elizabeth into believing that the rabbits out in Chateau-
guay no longer have long ears or white fur because they're
been mating with the cats. My Aunt Maggie, 70 odd years
old was asked by the family to sing some old Scotch
songs and she sang in her full throated deep wild and
ringing voice, "Don't Go Down in the Mines" and "The
Poor Little Blind Boy". Not a dry eye in the house when
she finished. Yeah my mother's side of the family are
all singing birds with rhythmic flowing voices that sing
words even in ordinary conversation. My Aunt Jessie especially has a sweet voice. I could sit back for hours and
listen to the music of her sentences.

The party went on until four in the morning. My
mother attempted to do the sword dance but she's getting a little too old and heavy for the foot work. My
Aunt Margeret and Jessie asked for two kisses when I got
up to leave. "He's as cute as a button," they said to my
mother.

Sunday night standing on the street corner with Liz
wondering where to go. "Let's go over to Zotolie's for
a hamburger and say hello to that good old man behind
the counter, the one that looks like Maurice Chevalier."
And he was there drinking his glass of beer and mixing
up tomorrow's soupe de jour in a huge pot on the stove.
We sat on the stools for a half-hour under the neon lights
feeling like ghosts, my whole mind aching with sorrow
and like a fool I was shaking my head as if I could throw
off the weight loading me down. Maurice Chevalier probably never saw a sadder looking man than me in his whole
life behind a short order counter. The rainy Sunday night
nowhere to go Fennario blues.

Jacky was over at our place the same night, borrowed sixty cents from me and said he was going to Expo. "What do you think I should do, Dave?" "What do you mean?" "Do you think I should go back to stealing?" I looked at the floor and said, "Why don't you stick to pushing, it's easier." "Yeah," he replied, "but you need dependency." "Your hair's looking good," I said in order to change the unanswerable subject.

September 8, 1970   Tuesday

Jacky called on us around twelve thirty last night as we lay in bed. "Can I crash for the night?" Silence. "Just for one night, no more." Silence. A groan from me. "Ah Jacky isn't there any place else you can stay?" "Nope." Squirming silence. "Ah O.K. Jacky." Crash on the couch and boom he's right to sleep and snoring before I even had time to turn another page of my book. I lay awake a long time thinking and consequently slept in the next morning. Too late to go into work so I walked over with Jacky to Baldy's Restaurant for breakfast. And he's sitting beside me at the counter wearing the Davy Crockett fringe suede jacket he stole at Expo making faces in the mirror, freaking out the waitress. "John William Robinson, alias John Sebastien, alias John Beauchamp," I said looking at his reflected image, "You're looking good this morning with your eyelids glued together and your tongue hanging out." "Yeah," he replied. "I started out on burgundy but soon hit the harder stuff."
And we went up together to the John Howard where I asked a counsellor about some legal matters. He typed out the address and phone number of Legal Aid for me and suggested that I call them. I phoned the place three times and each time the operator said, "One moment please" and left me hanging on the open line until I hung up. I really don't think the place exists at all, they just give a telephone number to some desperate poor slob like myself in order to fob him off upon some non-existent community service.

And down to the Prince Edward Chest Hospital next
for a T.B. x-ray. Jacky found himself a sunny spot on the
lawn outside the clinic saying to me as he lay down, "Don't
be gone for hours eh, Dave?" Inside I encountered the
usual bureaucratic system. Pick a number, sit down and
wait. Starched angels of mercy with emotions well buried.
"So here's your card Mrs. Roberts and call us, phone us
in February, six months from now." I did the thing, was
x-rayed and an hour later walked back out on the street.
Jacky sprawled out on the grass like a hobo using his jacket for a pillow. "Wake up Jacky," I said lightly kicking
his thigh, feeling like an officer of the law. I lit up a cigarette and watched the nurses go by as he struggled back
to consciousness. "Sure is nice here in the sun - there
was a beautiful girl in the clinic that you missed Jacky."
"Ahuh." "I gotta go down to Dawson." Silence. A
flick of cigarette ash. "C'mon Jacky wake up." "Yeah,
yeah," he groaned rolling over rubbing his face. "So I
gotta split," I said getting up. "Yeah, O.K. Dave. I'm
going down to Welfare. Take care." "Yeah, take care."

September 9, 1970   Wednesday

I sat on the front gallery with Jay until three in the
morning rapping about Jacky and speed. A cold rain was
falling, dripping from the tree. Deep shadows lined Jay's
face as he was talking. It was like we were both wearing
masks and apologizing for not taking them off. Both of
us looking for the key that would open the door locking
us each to ourselves.

September 10, 1970   Thursday

Lying in the bathtub this morning reading Cohen's
Beautiful Losers a book that has been recommended to
me many times in the past. It's impossible for me to
read Cohen without thinking of Moe Nichols, a fanantical
fan of Leonard's from Strathroy, Ontario, a dull little
town situated somewhat south of London. To Moe Mon-

treal is a holy city, a Mecca, because Cohen grew up here. The dirty old System Theatre is a shrine to Moe because Leonard Cohen wrote a poem mentioning the place, and, come to think of it, the little French guy behind the candy counter does wear a cowboy string tie.

I don't know, I admire Cohen's style but the guy really has fuck all to say to me. Like Rimbaud or Hart Crane brilliant but freakish, the loneliest guy on the block writing poems to himself.

September 13, 1970   Sunday

Saturday afternoon and boom it was decided that all of us, Vivian, Charly, Pat, Mary and ourselves would drive up to my camping spot near St. Marguerite. By seven o'clock, sun going down, we were sitting by a camp fire drinking beer, rapping (just like in old contree eh?) singing. Pat playing guitar, me on the harmonica harmonizing on the kind of song the old Harps sing in the Arrowona down in the Point when they're crying in their beer, "They Built a Sewer Where My Mother's Grave Used to Be." Nearby campers voiced their criticism of our taste in music by howling like timber wolves. "Ah go fuck yerselves! " we yelled back, "this is government property."

Vivian and Charly wandered off by themselves for awhile down by the river just like young lovers do. Pat and I, old married men long impervious to moonlight, not an ounce of romance left in us, decided to get right down with it and began chasing Liz and Moe through the fields crashing through the bushes yowling and grunting like movie monsters. Boris Karloff would have admired my style.

Eleven o'clock on the way back to the village up and down rocks, boulders, gullys the sky as black as ink. "Avalanche! " One casualty - Pat with a cut hand and a bruised knee.

The Existentialists stand bankrupt and stranded in their own personal despair. Since they have no hopes for the future they either attempt to transcend the world as it is today or else train themselves to accept their lot stoically. The intellectuals, the clowns and philosophical jesters of the ruling class are rapidly losing their old position as the privileged major domos of the Capitalist class; these insolent creatures who for generations felt only contempt for the great "unwashed", who dealt with the working class only as a means to their ends are being shown the door now that their masters have automated machines to do their thinking. It's hard to resist saying to the intellectuals as they sit entangled in the chaos of their ruined Ivory Towers - so how does it feel?
Revolution is our birthright.

September 16, 1970   Wednesday

I was wandering around uptown this afternoon checking out the Prag scene and rapped for awhile with Murray Smith, a politically aware unemployed philosophy graduate and mutual friend of Jean Yves. It hurts to write his name. Jean Yves. The pen moves in sadness as if I were drawing tears on a dead friend's photograph. As for Murray, he's older now, less nervous, more tight together and I like him better.

I rapped with Murray until ten o'clock and then went home down lonely dark Seigneur Street. Something always tears in me whenever I cross the tracks down into the West End. I am crossing a boundry line. It hurts, a wrenching, a blow, the opening and closing of a stiff-jointed tight spring door. Pat doesn't feel that way, for him the West End is home. For me it is the dark side of my brain.

I'm not trying to be a saint, I just wanna be an honest man.

Wednesday morning, nine o'clock, Jacky's at my door and I'm to go with him to court. He has his long hair tied back with a rubber band to look clean cut for the judge. I give him a shirt. "Button it right up, man, judges got this thing about unbuttoned shirts." "We're there by nine-thirty checking out the trial lists posted on the main lobby - John Boudain, Court Number 21. We rush up there hoping we're not late but end up sitting in the nicotine yellowed marble hallways of justice for two hours. Lawyers, black-robed, like great ravens flitting up and down the halls. Well-dressed, overfed sly-faced corporation lawyers grouped together in knots about their upper class clients flashing their hearty high school guidance teachers' smiles. Backstreet, rat-faced spindle-legged whores in short skirts barely touching their crotches, priming themselves, rehearsing their excuses. Vicious young hoods in shabby suits strutting around, petty thieves. Finally our turn came and we were informed that because Jacky didn't have any defence the trial would be postponed until the second week of December.

September 19, 1970   Saturday

Uptown about two o'clock ringing Billy Shaw's door bell on Clark Street. A stranger answering the door, "Is Billy there?" "Yep c'mon up he's asleep in the front room." And there he was lying asleep using his knapsack as a pillow. "Billy fuck it's good to see you," I said waking him up with a hug. "I didn't think I'd miss you this much but I did." Just as I figured, he had spent the summer travelling through the States. "Lots of heavy things happening to me, David." He's flunked out of McGill and left his poor little rich girl Michele, the Queen Bee.

When I first met Billy back in early '66 he was making it as a folksinger under the alias of Billy Shaw. I crashed at his place for awhile back in those days in an apartment up on Park Avenue near Villeneuve. The first night of our acquaintance we sat up until dawn smoking butts, drinking endless cups of sugared tea. I remember Billy asking me what my life's ambition was and me answering dead seriously, "Well I'd like to have an all-dressed pizza every day of my life, I guess." Billy, a heavy user of hallucinatory drugs in the past is at present deep into the Yippy thing. He comes on very intellectually now but emotionally he still retains a backstreet flavour. The Duke of Earl thing - don't touch me or else. Yeah Pretty Boy Shaw from the Junction. His sister Ruthy is back with him, taking care of him now that Michele is gone. Kidding Ruthy about the short romance she had with Polish Jay from the Point, I said, "You know Ruthy you've broken Polish Jay's heart. He's been carrying it around in a sling ever since you left."

Well after a lot of heavy rapping Billy decided to go out visiting friends living nearby and I went with them. Vegetable type people whose whole philosophies orientate themselves around dope, the axle that their life-functions unconsciously revolve around. No man dies comfortably: that is not the way of life and filling your brain full of smoke will not help you on your death bed. Death has no bondsman, you cannot pay him off. Anyhow, later for that type of shit.

September 20, 1970   Sunday

Pat, Mary and ourselves spent the afternoon shopping for vegetables at Atwater Market enjoying the open air spectacle very much. Suntanned country boys in faded overalls to remind us that this was Quebec and that Montreal was not Quebec. Pink-skinned plump heavy-breasted farmer's wives like Mother Earth.

September 21, 1970   Monday

Saturday night at Pat's house cutting out pieces of coloured bristol board for the war game. Rulers, crayons, scissors lying all over the living room floor. People dropping in seeing us down on our hands and knees like little kids. "What are you doing?" "It's a rehabilitation programme a social worker recommended to us," I replied

78

winking at Pat. "I'm designing a picture," said Pat too embarrassed to explain the situation. "Yeah," I said, "it's called A Dull Saturday Night."

Sorrowful Glenn was over with his kid. "Why does he always drag that poor kid around with him?" whispered Pat. We gave Glenn the nick name Sorrowful because of his pathetic attempts to impress everyone he meets. Unbelievable as it may sound Sorrowful's 180 pound wife is a professional go-go dancer. She does the Northern mining pulp and paper town circuit, I guess the guys up there in isolation are not too fussy about how a go-go dancer looks just as long as she can shake that money maker around the stage.

Glenn's twenty-eight, one of those real old hippies who can remember when there were dinosaurs in Yorkville. When you could light up a joint on Main Street and nobody would know the difference. Ah yes, Glenn those halycon days of yore glimmering in the golden filtered light of nostalgia. I remember the bad old days too Glenn, 'course not as far back as you can. I was still getting drunk in the back of my high school locker room and trying to make it with sweet little miss sixteens when you were my age but still I can remember with fondness the vintage year of 1965 when there were only about a dozen guys in the city with hair over their ears. Mobs used to follow me around the streets, there were only three restaurants I could eat in and I needed a bodyguard to get in and out of a tavern alive. But the girls loved us.

September 23, 1970   Wednesday

Hung over and sick in Babylon. Yesterday stands unrecorded. The Day of Registration. Location - The Royal Montreal Armoury in Westmount. The scene - chaotic. The actors - young. The rules - very old. Hundreds of boys and girls confronting the bureaucratic machinery they may, one day, have the privilege of joining. After fifteen confusing minutes this poor boy wanted to rush right out of the place and go find a job in a warehouse somewhere. And if a kind-hearted sweet tempered girl hadn't taken me under her wing to baby-sit me through the whole process I probably never would have got through it.

Yes, the whole scene shakes me, rocks me, has me wondering about myself. So foreign to me, drawing me away from everything I've ever known. I'm frightened by this new environment I'm entering, afraid that it might estrange me from Elizabeth, from my roots, from my home, afraid that it might kill me, knock me over.

So I'm actually in college taking international political science, History of the Western World, 20th Century Literature and Humanism and an Introduction to Social Sciences. Yeah, I really make it.

Phoned my mother to let her know about the news and she says, "Yes David your grade three teacher told me she'd never forget you walking in class carrying a huge encyclopedia under your arm." Yeah Miss Bateman was rather freaked out by this backstreet boy carrying books around like other guys carried sling shots. "And even Mr. Patry said you should be brilliant after all the reading you were doing in high school," continued my mother. "Yeah, well Ma," I replied, "I don't know where I put it all."

After registration I walked in the rain past the Pom Bakery I painted with Sonny and Ray on pump scaffolds two summers ago. College was the furthest thing from my mind in those days dangling fifty feet in the air slapping paint on the walls while listening to old Ray's stories about the whores in Singapore. "I sailed for twenty-five years," he told me, "I've been everywhere almost, seen everything almost and here I am fifty-five years old slapping paint on a fuckin' bakery. It's hard. You don't know what I mean kid you're young but wait 'til you get my age and nobody wants to hire you."

There are secrets sleeping in my brain that are sometimes whispered about in my nightmares. Fear, mostly it's fear. Anger in my voice, I don't want to be afraid.

I met Bob Paully yesterday on the street recognizing
him from twenty-five yards with his back turned to me.
A familiar hunch about the shoulders, a tenseness in the
legs, head held up proudly in the West End style - yeah
it was Bob and I went up and gave him a great hug. "Ah,
prick!" he says, "You didn't write because you didn't
think you'd see me again eh? - Well game's over now!"
"Listen," I said dodging the playful punch he threw at
me, "I just live across the street, c'mon over and see Liz."
"Well, just for a few minutes, I'm working," he said.
"Oh?" I replied, "You're with that Warner Bros. film
that's going on down here?" Yeah I'm working as an
assistant camera man" "You still on that farm in Ontario?" "Ahuh, same place." Liz came out on the back
gallery to shake a rug while we were standing on the
curb of Dominion Street. "Hey Liz look who it is!"
"Oh Bob!" she says her face beaming, smiling, "how's
your family? I heard Barbara had another baby boy."
"Yeah, Donovan," he replied, "Sure it's a good Irish name.
So listen Dave give me your phone number and I'll
give you a ring before I leave town." Hope he keeps his
word cause it's been good two years since I had a good
long talk with Bob.

This afternoon I treated myself to a couple of movies
on the Main, afterwards taking a slow walk along Ste.
Catherine Street looking at the people, feeling unappre-
ciated and deep in self pity. Not really self pity - just
on a kind of childish ego trip. There I was, the unknown
hero and nobody recognized me. Movies do it to me
everytime.

I sat for twenty minutes drinking a cup of coffee in
the Sir George cafeteria. The inevitable first year student
folk singer was wailing out the inevitable Codeine Blues.
"And it's Reel-al yes it's real, one more time." Everyone
looking solemnly wise especially the long hair existentialists. We know the games everyone is playing, don't
we? Ha ha ha. And that's where I came in, the unknown
bad looking but good guy, sensitive withdrawn tormented
and shy hero. The kind of guy who flunked out of his

courses years ago but keeps haunting the campus because there he can be someone. A sad-eyed philosopher,
radical derelict making the rounds of the Youth Culture
trying to make a connection and getting older by the
minute. Tick tock stop the clock, tick tock make it halt.
Just lonely that's all. Just wanna be somebody anybody
that's all. Make a movie out of my life so someone will
know. Write a book so someone will know. Stand on my
head and spit quarters on the corner of Peel and Ste.
Catherine, each one personally autographed. Somebody
please I'm lonely. But who has the time, everyone is tired
of the same old songs, I'm lonely, I'm misunderstood,
I'm in torment. It's like going around complaining about
the measles when everyone else is suffering from the same
disease. It's a drag but I got it too and a lot of my own
troubles besides. Yeah trouble, T-rouble, bad news everyday travelling fast and furious. Wake up in the morning
and wonder if today's the day it happens. People whispering, something's brewing, the shit is gonna hit the fan
any minute now. Hang on to your safety belts the
ground is coming up fast. Don't you want to dance in
these streets, don't you want to release that unbearable
tightness wedging your mind?

September 25, 1970   Friday

Having trouble regulating my time, I've been sleeping in too late in the morning then frantically diving into
my studies to get them over with before Liz comes home.
And Kenny Weaver that wild Maritime boy writes
to tell us, or rather Liz whom he has a crush on, that he's
getting out of the Kingston Pen on parole in about a
month. Look out Montreal! Eddy also writes to tell
me he expects to be out sometime next fall. It's hard
to pinpoint just exactly where Eddy's mind's at, he's
such a deep and hidden person in great contrast with
ol' Kenny who's about as subtle as a nuclear explosion.

Friday night we helped Pat and Mary knock off a
25 ounce bottle of Vodka in their living room. Then we
grabbed a hack up to the System Theatre and took in
two movies. Pat left before the second feature was over
because Moe was falling asleep. "We'll meet you later
at the Bistro O.K.?"

The films were full of unreal violence, it was a relief
to walk out into the night air, into the reality of common-
place people crowding the sidewalks looking at one another. "Everybody's talking about the same things, Liz.
Listen to them, they're all talking about Revolution. It
makes this bad old Socialist heart of mine feel good."

And it's true the people passing, young couples, old
couples, some well-dressed, some not, with long hair and
short hair all were rapping away on political subjects.

The Bistro was packed that evening with its usual
clichés. "We're all graduates here," I overheard one guy
say at a table as we entered the door. Yeah they really
make it.

Pat and Mary were sitting with us, Moe's eyes rov-
ing all around looking for the ideal stranger to talk with.
We have little in common with her (the daughter of an
Indian colonel) and she finds us to be dull company
most of the time. She drifted away from the table just
as Pat got into an argument with a very drunk derelict-
philosopher who stank of piss. I know, I was sitting beside him having my usual paranoic fears of a vicious
fight breaking loose at the drop of a hard word. But of
course nothing happened, Pat is an old hand at bystepping
obvious insults while all the time egging the guy on into
deeper anger and confusion. I was not around to witness
the termination of their gigantic mental contest because
I joined Mike Smyth at a small side table where we sat
drinking beer, rapping until the last call was sounded.
The waiters began putting the chairs up on the tables
and I said, "Well Mike we went and closed the bar again,
just like in the old days eh? Remember when we used to
close down the Empire Tavern nearly every Friday night
and Claude the waiter used to help us down the last

83

couple of beers on the table so he could go home?" Ah yes
the golden mellow glow of a tavern table brimming over
with ten cent draught beers and a half-a-dozen good old
thirsty friends to help you drink them down. Love, it,
love it.

The walk home, the short-cut across the C.P. tracks,
Liz afraid of breaking the heels on her new shoes and me
with a close eye on the passersby 'cause two o'clock is
mugging time down in the West End. (Kind of sounds
like a song doesn't it?)

Saturday afternoon we placed a long distance phone
call to Kenny Weaver in Toronto as he had requested in
his letter. The prison authorities granted him a three-day
pass to visit his family so yesterday we heard his voice
again for the first time since February 1968.

"Yeah," he says, "Billy my brother got me fixed
up with a date, some real ugly broad with a nose like
Cyrano de Bergerac. But after three years and no tail I
ain't gonna be fussy - hey I'm getting out on Hallowe'en!
Isn't that a trip?"

"Yeah, yeah," I said, " and how's your brother Billy
doing? Is he still putting his hands into mail boxes?"

"Oh yeah, off and on."

"Have you heard any news from old Paul Trottier?"

"Who? Old Paul? Oh yeah - ha ha - Billy saw him
about a month ago drunk out of his skull on Yonge Street
walking along with some ninety-year-old hag holding
hands, arms around each other like teenyboppers for
Christ sake. Yeah crazy old Paul. So he hasn't seen me
or Billy for two years and you know what the first thing
he says to Billy?"

"What?"

" 'Billy Billy,' he says,'I know where there's this
crackerbox safe'; and fuck they're standing on Yonge
Street, millions of people all aroung right in the middle
of the afternoon. Yeah crazy old Paul."

Hey Dave, how about Andrea that long tall Chinese
chick, is she still around?"

"Robin tells me she went to Japan and now she's
in Tibet."

"Tibet? What part of Montreal is that?"

"It ain't a suburb Kenny, it's a weird country in Asia."

"Asia wow, hell I'm going to miss her."

Signing off he said he was gonna come and see us as soon as he could. "O.K. Kenny," I said, "We'll warn Montreal that you're coming back."

Bob Paully came down the same afternoon around four o'clock. With the exception of a story Bob told of a beef he had in a Greek restaurant last week in which he knocked out some ignorant dude with a sugar bowl the general conversation was about Bob's life on the farm. His three-quarter-acre vegetable garden, his pigs, chickens, pheasants, rabbits and tractor. The long lonely blizzard-filled winters without electricity, without music.

"That's the one thing we missed a hell of a lot," said Bob, "We were starved for music after a couple of months. I'm putting in electricity this fall, I mean why should Barbara wash clothes by hand when we have a washing machine. Not only that I've got an eight hundred dollar hi-fi and a collection of over two thousand records I haven't heard for years. Like once I lived for a month in the bush with only a pen knife but why not have luxuries if you got them."

"Right," I said, "it's a fuckin' crime to have your wife going through unnecessary drudgery when the appliances are available."

"Well," he said, "you learn by your mistakes and I found out that it sounds romantic you know to live the farming life as it was a hundred years ago reading books by kerosene lanterns. But fuck man a couple of months of reading under that kind of light you feel like you're going blind. The words jumping up and down on the page like flying birds."

Up to Tyndale's Saturday night for a poetry reading bringing Pat along with me - "You're my ice breaker Pat."

Good people with us that evening. Louie, a young backstreet poet from the Maritimes whose hang-ups I readily identified with and long tall Mark a 6'6" giant who grew up on Shannon Street in Griffentown. We were rapping about family background Mark informing us that his grandfather was from the bush. "Mark," I said, "I think your grandfather must have been a tree."

After an hour of us backstreet boys bragging about the hard streets we grew up on I said to Mark's girl Kerry, a little shy thing from the Town of Mount Royal - "Hey Kerry aren't you afraid of being the only girl surrounded by such a heavy crew of desperate characters?"

September 29, 1970   Tuesday

Still have the feeling while sitting in classes that I shouldn't be there at all. An Industrial Arts student placed in a Latin class by mistake. I wasn't trained to be where I am now, sitting in the midst of the élite, the brains. I never rated as a brain nor did any of my former professors (excluding Dugan) ever attempt to cultivate what potentialities I had.

October 1, 1970   Thursday

Sitting in the kitchen with the oven on and it's the only comfortable room in the house because Credit Foncier hasn't turned the furnace back on yet. Warmth. It's important. A red hot stove ought to be on the coat of arms of Montreal's native capitalist class. Imagine back in the 1890's, January 1896. A scene from one of Norman's photographs of that era. Little bourgeois children all bundled up in warm winter clothing are playing on the huge snowbanks lining the sidewalks in front of their parents' limestone mansions on Sherbrooke Street. Sleigh bells ringing as the Drummonds, the Redpaths and the Molsons pass by all wrapped up in expensive furs on their way to pay social calls. The coal furnaces of Westmount are going full blast, God is in heaven and all's right with the world.

In Griffentown they are praying for April. They're wearing their overcoats to bed. Drunks are falling asleep in snowdrifts and freezing to death. Down the hill the hollow-cheeked ragged little children are shivering. They will remember their father sitting by the unlit stove. They will remember.

October 3, 1970   Saturday

Done it again. Sick as a beaten dog from that Old Niagara wine, does it every time. The school day was hectic, I mean it was hard to take on a Friday. Class after class the teachers droning on and on, me fidgiting in the seat trying to concentrate on subjects I have no interest in at all in learning. But I must get that diploma, gotta get trained for the machinery and be a good boy. Yeah the nigger as a student. I really make it.

Drinking in Pat's living room last night, Charly and a new girlfriend of his, Mary, a Woman's Liberator. Pat really laid on his male chauvinist act thick once he discovered what her political views were. He was hilarious and almost got a good stiff kick in the balls from No nonsense Mary. "Ah he's only putting you on, doll," I said. "Don't call me DOLL," she replied balling up her first, causing me to jump behind Liz in self-defense.

And Moe dressed up Liz in a green sari. "It's like wearing nothing at all," she said, "I feel naked."

I went down to my place and got my collection of early Rock'n Roll songs. It was a real treat for everyone to hear Jerry Lee Lewis pounding out raunchy down home funky tunes on the piano like "Great Balls of Fire" and "Whole Lotta Shaking going on." And believe me watching a girl rock'n rolling in a sari is something else.

October 4, 1970   Sunday

Back at the desk again and writing without really having anything to say this quiet afternoon.

Liz has been off the pill for a month now by doctors orders. Her period was due on Friday and it didn't come. I don't even like to think about pregnancy. Liz

87

is going for a check up on Thursday and is understandably upset by the whole thing. Like I said I don't even like to think about it.

I have nothing to say. It's all the same to me, that's how I'm feeling now. Can I do it? Can I do it? A thought ringing constantly in the back of my ears. One part of my brain keeps saying, don't try it you'll only fail. You'll only discover that you're as stupid as you think you are. Keep dreaming, dreams can't hurt you.

But here it is. The work of my lifetime, a six hundred and forty page journal upon which my own personal esteem rests today. I have done something. There is a definite level to my apathy now, I can only fall so deep whereas before there was no bottom.

October 5, 1970   Monday

Last night I spent two and a half agonizing hours writing a criticism on Cleaver's <u>Soul on Ice</u> and went to **bed** very worried in mind about it. This morning I arose - hallelujah - at eight o'clock from a warm seductive bed, splashed some cold water on this sad face of mine and went into Dawson's for my French class.

Returned back home and got into my criticism again almost totally revising it. I should have cut out the little biographical note on myself at the beginning. I'm blushing now for that little piece of egotism taped unto my objective essay on the "racial" question.

October 7, 1970   Wednesday

Tuesday night walking back home from the Westmount Library with Liz. An old freaked out hobo with about a hundred withered dandelions pinned to his shabby jacket warned us as we passed by him to watch out for the Hallowe'en Wagons (a local term used by Westmounters to describe their municipality's black and orange patrol cars). "Thank you," we said to make him feel appreciated.

This morning I jumped out of bed feeling like an ex-junky refusing a fix he really wants to take, wrestling with a deep sense of apathy, fumbling through my guitar, typing, writing exercises in very poor spirits, then sitting down for a lunch of peanuts and raisins. In vain I tried to prepare myself psychologically for my afternoon in school. It had all been so clear the night before but my self-confidence dissolved into panic before the final class was finished.

While sitting in one classroom a vision came to my mind of some poor wretch going berserk right before our eyes attacking the person closest to him with a carving knife. I imagined the ensuing panic after the attack. The screams, the stampede for the door, the victim's cries growing more and more feeble with every thrust of the black boards. The maniac butcher heaving with insane strength his eyes crackling with electricity squilling like a tormented demon pumping the knife with short quick blows into his prey.

October 8, 1970   Thursday

At this moment there is a Rolls Royce parked across the street from my house. It's being used in the movie being shot down the street, the Warner Bros. production about some Indian kids blowing up the bridge going over to Caughanawaga.

Well I'll tell ya, Dominion Street hasn't seen too many Rolls Royces in its time.

October 9, 1970   Friday

Pat went over with me to Dawson this afternoon at my request. I wanted to expose him to the torments I've been undergoing the last two weeks. We sat in on a conversation the kids were having about why people sit in the back seats of class rooms. Really constructive.

It's terrible how some people abuse their minds dwelling upon useless metaphysical problems, problems with no solutions because they aren't really problems. Clutching for non-existent parachutes as they fall through the air when all the time they know how to fly. Better learn to spread your wings quick baby 'cause the ground is coming up fast and hard.

"I can't understand these kids Pat. When I was sixteen, man my blood was so roaring hot that all I wanted to do was ball. Use what was between my legs whenever I could, dance and get drunk when I couldn't. And travel if nothing else worked."

<u>October 11, 1970</u>   <u>Sunday</u>

That little group of people at Charly's tonight sitting around in the living room, all medical students discussing community projects. And I walked in with my sad face, my desperate uptight mind, smiled and sat down.

Charly was very pleased to see me, something clicked between us Friday night, opening up a new compartment in his heart. I felt the rise in temperature.

Well I'm sitting with Charly's student friends this evening feeling envious of their balanced lives, of their confidence. What would happen if I jumped up and kicked one of them right between the eyes, I wondered. Could they understand how upset I am, how tormented I feel by the social problems they can discuss so flippantly. I was the only one in the room without a parachute.

There was an evil air about the streets tonight. I hurried along quickly not looking anyone in the face. What is wrong with me? I am so afraid that I will never learn how to speak, that I will never learn how to untie my tongue, that I will die as uselessly as Andrew Boyle, my grandmother's first husband, dead in the battle of the Somme, 1916. His body was never found. How did he die? He was married only three months and hardly knew one end of a rifle from another. What were his dreams, his ambitions, what was he thinking of a minute before he died? I would like to know. I imagine him

90

to be about 5'7", thin with sandy-coloured hair and a
slow sad smile. A dreamer, a gentle person bewildered
by the kaleidoscopic events that had placed him in the
trenches. He was killed in his innocence, butchered,
slaughtered, sucked up by the mud in no-man's-land
and never found. More than likely a Krupp shell blew
him into smithereens as he moved with his squadron towards the German lines, his head bowed down like he
was facing a driving rain. Missing. No longer here. No
more dreams, no more Andrew Boyle; and Jenny Boyle
waited two sad long years then married William Kerr a
coal miner, my grandfather.

October 12, 1970   Monday

I had a dream last night that I was a McGill University student with long hair in 1953. It was a groove sitting there in class checking out what it was like to be a
student back then. Yeah how times have changed with
nearly everyone now wearing their hair long and fewer
and fewer people getting hysterical over Grey Cup games.
I learnt something tonight, I learnt what gentleness
is in depth by practising it myself in a conversation with
my old man after a Thanksgiving dinner. The subject
was about campus uprest and my old man in his bitter-
ness was lashing out against the students in that cruel
thin voice of his I've hated all my life. "The trouble is,"
he said, "that we were due for a war ten years ago and
didn't have one. They should get rid of all those misfits
on the campus." The context of what he said is unim-
portant, it's the manner in which it was spoken. The
pessimism of a man who has undermined all the natural
joys and happiness I have ever known. I have never in
my life openly confronted my father but tonight as I
sat beside him, my head bowed, flashes of white anger
surging through me, I knew who it was I hated. But
instead of striking out against him I felt the cold white
ball of anger in my gut uncoiling as rapidly as it had
tightened and in a very tense voice I said, "Misfits are
made, not born." There was a noticeable pause then

my father continued with his diatribe even more bitterly than before but by then I had gained control of myself and, in the course of events, had him condemning the socio-economic system rather than the people trying to function under it. What a triumph for me to hear the tension melt away from his voice and know that I was responsible for the good feelings that had been generated. To know that, at times I'm capable of such understanding is very encouraging. The depth of a man is gauged by his gentleness.

October 13, 1970   Tuesday

Man the dreams I've been having lately are really out of it. Last night I dreamt I was working on a very mysterious case with Sherlock Holmes as an adviser. I found him to be quite dense actually.

Liz didn't go into work this morning because we sat up late last night discussing what was to be done if her pregnancy test proves positive this Thursday. Her fears were somewhat calmed by my own matter-of-fact approach towards the subject. "It's only a hassle, Liz, if you're pregnant. It won't destroy anything, it's only a hassle." I pretended to believe that her chances of being pregnant were slim but actually since she hasn't had her period for two weeks I think the chances are that she is. Still, somehow I feel that luck is with us; that old Celtic intuition that everything is bound to turn out all right. If it doesn't kill you, you learn something.

Yeah the theories cracked right down the middle this afternoon when exposed to real life. Sunny-side up, tight-assed little chicks with liberated breasts bouncing beneath T-shirts, tempting the eye, tightening the stomach. It's sheer fuckin' hell for a married man with a promiscuous gut but an unwilling mind believe me. Gonna hafta get some blinders.

<u>October 14, 1970</u>   <u>Wednesday</u>

Pat is having a lot of trouble with Mary; tonight she
walked out on him after a big quarrel. The girl is very
unhappy living down here in poverty-stricken low-spirited
reality. She can't cope with the dull desperation of this
life and I can't say I blame her. I get the idea that she
won't be with Pat much longer; either she'll split home
which would be best or else escape back into the Student
Ghetto Never Never Land to play her flute for a few
months in between nervous breakdowns. It really looks
that grim from my perspective but then again I've had
a pretty grim life. Boo hoo. Cry. Cry. Sob. Tears on
the beer glass. But, seriously, I sense how trapped she
feels in her position. It is grim. The maze she is lost in
very few people ever get out of. It's too early yet to
tell whether Moe and Pat are dying or changing.

<u>October 15, 1970</u>   <u>Thursday</u>

This morning I was down at the Pt. St. Charles
Health Clinic with a sample of Elizabeth's urine for
a pregnancy test. Perhaps tomorrow we'll find out the
results but more likely on Monday. Liz is very much on
pins and needles, poor girl. Little Miss Gloominess I
called her tonight as she sat sulking at the kitchen table.
Sally came up with something valid today in class
upon the topic of writing. "To learn to write well,
you must write a lot," she said. I sense that here is a
subject, a craft she is skilled in and knows well enough
for me to learn from her regardless of her confused per-
ception of the social problems evident in today's world.

My sweet mother phones me up this morning to tell
me to take the 3' by 6 foot flags I pinched from Expo off
the walls. "I'm hearing on the radio David that the police
are raiding all over the city and they raided one place on
Prince Arthur Street that had flags on the wall." Thanks
Ma," I said, "but I don't think they'll bust me for having
the Jamaica flag hanging in my bedroom."

Pat got up and went with me into Dawson this afternoon sitting with me in one of Sally Nelson's classes. We
both felt so old, our brains racked with pain listening to
the words. I'm not saying we felt superior, just different
because all our dreams were pounded out of us years
before leaving just one sweet hope behind - Revolution.

The strain of waiting for the results of the pregnancy
test is visibly wearing Liz down. She woke up crying
from a bad dream last night as I lay reading. "Oh David
I dreamt there was big spiders crawling all over me."
"Hush it's O.K.," I whispered, hugging her as she lay
half-awake, tears in my eyes.

Friday night over at Pat's drinking beer in the living
room. Charly with a sudden gesture says, "I'm tired of
just sitting around boozing it up. Let's go up to the
Nihon Plaza and get a game we can play." O.K. agreed
and we ended up at Crazy Eddy's Adult Games on
Sherbrooke Street arguing with one another over which
game to select. And finally compromising on a game
called "Group Therapy" going for $12.95. Not exactly
a bargain.

Pat and Mary have been quarrelling all week. A big
storm was brewing and I felt certain that the combination
of booze and group therapy would bring it down on our
heads. Charly has a fault sometimes of looking so far
into the distance that he can't see what is right in front
of his nose; consequently he ignored me when I suggested
that we should postpone playing the game.

The cards used in this game request an individual to perform certain pertinent acts as honestly as possible. The other players judge whether the actions are honest or not thus deciding whether the player in question moves forward or backward on the board. Liz proved to be the most honest of us all, in my opinion.

Meanwhile Mary was getting very drunk and more hostile towards Pat by the minute. The final explosion occurred when Pat picked up a card asking him to explain to everyone why he was not worthy of them. "I'm a rat" he said for a beginning. "You're goddamn right you're a rat," yelled Moe, "and you're a fuckin' son of a bitch too!" The lightning flashed in Pat's eyes. "Game over girl," I thought to myself as they began shouting and pushing each other around. Yeah Group Therapy was packed up quick. "Let's go," said Charly, and that's just what we did, moving on leaving Pat and Moe roaring at each other in the living room. My parting words to Charly as he scrambled into his Volkswagen were, "See I told ya Charly we should have got a war game. It would have been a lot more peaceful."

October 18, 1970   Sunday

Saturday afternoon Sorrowful Glenn lent us three dollars and accompanied Liz and myself up to the Français Cinema where we took in three films, all of them pretty shitty but entertaining.

It was bitter cold when we walked out of the show and went down on St. Lawrence Main for some all-dressed dogs. Standing up eating under the garish neon lights of that nightmare street. The sidewalks stink of hopelessness, it's in the walls, in the people's faces. The bones of October a skeleton wind rattling.

We couldn't get off the Main quick enough for Liz who hates that street with a fervour. It holds no charm for her, only terrible sad memories of the broken-down brooding days we spent together on Hotel de Ville Street back in '68.

On the way home Sorrowful made a peace sign to
one of the heavily-equipped combat soldiers standing
guard outside the Unemployment Office; the soldier
cradling his submachine gun in one arm flashed the sign
back at Glenn as we passed by. "What regiment do you
belong to?" asked Glenn. "Vingt Deux - I'm not allowed
to talk," said the soldier.

We walked through the Place Ville Marie - Bonaventure complex on the way down to dirty old St. Antoine
Street. "Ah, what a comfortable world they have," I
said watching well-dressed young couples looking idly
into the store windows. "So secure and regular. So
safe just like in the Doris Day movies." Yeah the Chem-
cell world I slammed the door on five years ago.

October 19, 1970   Monday

Our phone is out of order otherwise I'd know by
this time (one p.m.) whether Liz is pregnant or not. I'll
have to use the phone at school.

Rather a memorial day for the fact that I got up
this morning at seven-thirty even though my troubled
mind kept me awake until five shadow-boxing with my
problems.

This afternoon around two o'clock I stood with the
phone to my ear in front of the Registration Office making whispered enquiries about the results of Elizabeth's
pregnancy test to the clinic doctor. "It's negative, the
doctor said. "What does that mean?" I asked. "It
means she's not pregnant." "Well Hallelujah! " I replied
straightening my back as the boulder rolled off.

I waited until four-thirty, the time Liz generally
gets home then I rang her up and listened to her crying
for joy. I wish I could have seen her fact but I didn't
want her to suffer in agonizing suspense any longer than
I could help it. So now the tension of the last three
weeks has melted away and everything's back to normal.
We're both in a party mood tonight feeling like young
healthy people again instead of trapped animals.

October 21, 1970   Tuesday

Yeah I forgot to mention that last Friday night
after the group therapy thing was over I came home with
two pints of beer stuck in my pockets, put a Lightfoot
album on the record machine and sat down at my desk
for two hours writing a love poem called "Questions for
Elizabeth," "What are cities to me if I cannot sing in
them with you, what are railways if they do not lead
me to you and what are beds to me if I cannot lie in
them with you?" The only excuse I can offer for this
poem is that the great qualities of alcohol I drank brought
out the Robert Burns in me. I wanted to sing a few
words about the sweet sonsy lass I love as many a man
has and will continue to do as long as balls and brains
are inseparable. Divorce one from the other and you
have a sick lop-sided man, a Steppenwolf.

October 27, 1970   Tuesday

There is to be an exam on the structure of the U.N.
based on Nicholas's book this Thursday in Political Science
so I've been spending two hours every night since Sunday
reading the required and very dull text book underlining
highlights. It amazes me that a man so obviously intelligent as Nicholas with such a vast range of vocabulary
and knowledge can be so blind to the social implications
behind the structures of the U.N. What makes him so
blind, so limited in his perceptions of the whole scheme?
It's like the old story of the Turkish philosophers com-
missioned by their sultan to study and research the Elephant. They did so, all of them writing specialized re-
ports on the toe nails, the eye lids, the ears, the legs,
the feet, the tail, the skin, the skeletal structure without
describing the whole elephant itself. So the sultan never
did find out what the animal looked like because each of
the philosophers felt that the elephant looked like the
tail, the ears and so on.

There's nothing connecting the work of all these individual researchers delving into explicit studies of certain defined social questions, such as racial prejudice. The solutions they offer as possible answers to these problems are themselves limited by their own specialized insights into the subjects they have researched. You may know the tail of an elephant inside out but it's not the elephant and must not be misconstrued as such; the fact is that the vast majority of the so-called political and social scientists are in the same category as those old Turkish philosophers. The data they have processed are very informative in general. Some of them are of great value when used as factual proof to support the programme and platform of bona fide socialism but in most cases the data is of an irrelevant nature. Their findings, although of irrefutable sicentific relevence in themselves, when measured beside the titanic crises facing mankind daily are puny and insignificant indeed.

October 31, 1970   Saturday

The telephone rang Friday night, Pat on the line asking me if I was ready to help him move that evening. "Sure thing Pat," I said, "but who have you got to move you?" "Leroi." he said, "a black dude from the neighbourhood with a small pick-up truck. He's charging me fifteen bucks." "O.K. Pat I'll be right over."

We waited until eight o'clock in the Dominion Bar for Leroi to show up. "Guess he's out getting drunk somewhere Pat?" "Yeah let's split." I went home with the intention of taking Liz uptown but she said to me, "Dave I think you should invite Pat and Mary over here for a couple of beers. They must be feeling really down. Remember when we were down? Imagine if someone would have called on us and asked us if we would like to have a couple of beers?" "Yeah, you're right Liz," I said giving her a kiss.

They came over but neither of them were in the mood for drinking. Moe, because she had been feeling bad all day and Pat because he didn't want to fuck up his kidneys like he did last weekend. "Well," I said, I wish there was someone who could help me kill off this case of beer." The words were no sooner out of my mouth when the door bell rang and in walked Stan with some hashish. The evening was saved; the three of them smoked up and everyone got pleasantly stoned. "You might say we were saved by the bell," I said watching everyone go into convulsions over my outrageous pun.

Anyhow Pat and Mary only stayed awhile then split to go look for Leroi. Twenty minutes later he phoned back to say that he had contacted Leroi and would come right over with Stan. But Stan had to confess that he was in no shape to move furniture so I went over myself. Leroi was there, a bug husky dude with a white friend both of them sporting prominent beer bellies. Friendly, full of laughter, in a hurry to get back to the girls they had waiting for them in the Dominion Bar. "Shit Pat let's step on it, those girls ain't gonna wait forever." The heavy stuff was moved down first, bureaus, beds, cabinets, book cases, drawers. I supplied the guys with what was left of my case of beer and we did it all, sweating up and down those two flights of narrow stairs, in three strenuous hours.

Predictably Mary was more trouble to us than help. Nothing was packed. She walked in and out of the rooms whining in self pity getting in our way letting the cats run out of the open door then insisting that we go out and find them. Five grown men, two of them over thirty, chasing three dumb cats through back alleys and under cars. That was the first time, the third time they got loose I felt like strangling the girl. But it's not serious. Like Pat said what can you expect from a McGill dropout and the daughter of a university literature professor?

The last drive down to the new house with the second load, mattresses piled up on top of the roof, two bureaus tied down on the back board with me standing beside them making sure they didn't bump off onto the road. The truck drove slowly up deserted St. James Street the wind blowing against my face. I felt as good as I have ever felt in my life standing on the back board of that old truck feeling the wind, looking all around me. The trains, the steel mill, the settlement project, the bridge, the derelict houses. What will I live to see? How many men have asked themselves that question? What will I live to see?

Liz bought a pumpkin at Poncho's yesterday for fifty cents, carved a face on it, put a candle inside and placed it in the front window. Hallowe'en. Within an hour hordes of little kids screaming trick or treat - charity please had cleaned us out of every candy in the house.

A little later we went over with Charly to Pat's with a case of beer. Mary answered the door. "Where's your costumes?" she said. "Ah Charly convinced us," I said, "that it would be a childish thing to do." "That's right Fennario," said Charly, "Put all the blame on me." We sat in the living room waiting for Pat to come downstairs in his costume. Predictably he swooped into the living room in a black cape as Dracula. Eyes blazing, teeth flashing in a dead white face covered with talcum powder. Liz decided that we should get into some costumes so Pat walked me back over to our place to get what we needed. I wanted to dress up as an old hillbilly granny so I tried on some of the old dresses Liz's sister had laid on her but they wouldn't fit. Pat phoned his mother, a big heavy woman, and asked her if she had some old dresses around the house. She did. "Mrs. O'Neil," I said as we were leaving, "you're one of the few women in the neighbourhood that wears my size." She shook a fist at me and Pat nearly fell down laughing.

Liz dressed up as a boy wearing my vest, Pat's navy beany, bellbottom jeans with sideburns and a moustache I charcoalled on her face. She's really an excellent mimic and easily took on the stance and mannerisms of a backstreet juvenile delinquent. We did a spoof in which Liz, alias Franky, tried to pick me up. Me with an old lady's hat on my head, army boots on my feet and my jeans rolled up past my knees displaying a pair of very unfeminine hairy legs.

Sunday night I walked up Clark Street to call on
Billy Shaw only to be told at the door by his roommate
that he had left town two weeks ago for Boston, "So,"
I said, "I guess his plans for a Political Information
Bureau didn't work out?" "Nope." said the guy smiling,
"It didn't even get off the ground." He paused, then
said, "Billy will probably be writing me a letter, does he
have your address?" "Ah, it doesn't matter," I said,
"I'll be seeing him again. He'll be back. Just tell him
Dave Fennario still worries about him, O.K.? " He laughed
and we said good-bye.
      Poor Billy he's been fucking up for the last two
years and now that Michele's out of his life he has no
one to take care of him. Last time I saw him I tried offering advice but he was too uptight, too involved in himself,
to take me seriously. Matter of fact he's never taken me
seriously and thinks of me always as the charming folksy
backstreet hustler-poet I was four years ago. I've grown,
he hasn't. He doesn't recognize my changes, but I realize
his limitations. It saddens me to think of all the people
I've lived with on the streets, so very few surviving. One
little two little three little Indians.
      The urge was strong in me to see Robin, to walk
down with her to the Prag in reminiscence. To talk of
the golden days of '66. The lights were on in the house
but no one was home. I passed by in front of the Prag
myself and watched a young pusher kick the shit out of
some college kid who had burnt him for some grass.
Well that's your rotten life kid, making bad business deals.
It's your tough luck for mixing with people who can be
much more vicious than yourself over a buck.
      I didn't stay 'til the end of the fight. A very large
silent audience gathered on the sidewalk outside the
Prag to watch the massacre. Not a word was uttered.
They stared blankly at the scene as if it were occurring
on a television screen. So much for the Youth Culture,
as for myself I've got enough miseries of my own. Still,
if the guy who had the beating laid on him was a friend
of mine, I wouldn't have stood by idly like his pals did.

I felt guilty about all the Weekly People's piling
up in my closet so I put a hundred of them in a
shopping bag and went uptown yesterday night to dis-
tribute them. Walking through the vacant lot just
north of Campbell's Park I ran into Laura and she
asked me where I was going. "Up to Pat's new place
on Wexhall Street." "Oh great! " she said, "I'll go
with you." Walking along St. Antoine together Laura
telling me that her old man had thrown her out of
the house for fighting with his mistress. "I knocked
out two of her front teeth," she said.

Both Laura Corcoran and Andy Beauchamp are
slowly sinking into insanity. Laura's at the point now
where she can't distinguish her fantasies from the
truth. And Stanley told me a story the other day
about Andy. "Andy was walking down the street,"
he said, "and a girl passed by him on the sidewalk.
You know how crazy he's been getting lately so he
gets behind the girl and puts out his hands as if he's
going to choke her. Some dude sees what Andy's up
to and jumps him, knocks Andy to the sidewalk
and climbs on top of him. 'I surrender,' Andy says
looking up at the guy with a smile on his face. The
dude let him up and walked away laughing. Andy's
a funny guy."

Pat wasn't home. I said good-bye to Laura all
wrapped in dreams of herself as a famous singer.
"Oscar Petersen's gonna pay me four thousand dollars
for a song I wrote as soon as he uses it." "Yeah?!
That's great, Laura, good-bye."

Walking alone along dirty old St. Antoine Street
in the direction of Place Ville Marie doing imitations
of W.C. Fields to chase away the blues. "First Ti-mme
I was ever bit by an Eye-talian-yas-s-s" Then up the
marble stairs of Windsor Station. One paper placed
on a radiator, two in a telephone booth, one on the
sink of a washroom, then down into Place Bonaventure
where I placed papers on the sides of escalators, phone
booths, window ledges, benches. What a way to spread
the news of socialism.

I was taking a break, sitting down on one of the benches when a French kid with a farmer's face crowned with a mop of kinky hair came over towards me, bent down, looked in the shopping bag and asked me the time. "About nine o'clock," I said in a hostile voice. "What is this guy?" I thought to myself. Probably hustling fags. I felt insulted by his attempt to hustle me but he looked so forlorn and lonely that finally I looked his way and said, "Where are you from?" "H-ottawa," he said and then we got into a long story about how hard it is to pick up girls in Montreal. "Did you ever try the Prag?" I asked. "Yes," he said, "but h-all day want h-is money, est-ti." And it seems one weekend last year he went down to the Prag from Ottawa in his friend's car and they messed around all evening vainly trying to pick up some tail. Towards the early morning they were getting desperate and asked some guys hanging around if they knew where they could get some girls. The guys were wearing Devil's Choice's colours. "Yeah, sure," the Choice said, "we know where there's a whorehouse out in Pt. Aux Trembles if you drive us out there." They did and were held up on a country road and relieved of all their money and the car. "We walked back to Montréal," Frenchy said. "Yeah, it's tough picking up girls in Montreal," I said consoling him with a pat on the shoulders thinking to myself, "Man what a born loser." It's a damn shame. Us losers ought to form some kind of mutual protection club.

November 6, 1970   Friday

Yeah it's hard and this poor boy is all wrapped up in the Friday afternoon coal miner blues. Only will-power keeping my head from collapsing into my chest. ("Some blues are just blue, mine are the miner blues.")

November 8, 1970   **Sunday**

Damn near four hours spent this afternoon doing
a report on George Sules' article "Are We Going to
Have a Revolution" for a Wednesday history class
panel discussion. Yes and it had me walking up and
down the living room floor talking to myself. The
budding academic - how sweet it is.

November 9, 1970   **Monday**

Sunday night Liz was up at her Mother's and I
was at home working on my journal. I began thinking of Karen Chevarie, my old girl, my first love, so
beautiful that people used to stop on the streets to
watch her go by. Around eight o'clock I walked up
to MacGregor where she is living. MacGregor Street
has a lot of embassies on it and Sunday night they
all had soldiers standing guard in front of their doors
because of the War Measures Act. I didn't have
Karen's address but I knew her house was located
on the north side of MacGregor just west of Simpson
Street, so I started going in and out of the houses
checking the mail boxes for her name feeling all the
while very paranoid about the soldiers who obviously
found my movements to be very suspicious. Who is
that dude going from door to door kind of thing.
Finally I stepped into a lobby that looked familiar
to me. I knew her apartment was somewhere up
on the top floor and once up there I rapped on a
door that was partially open. A middle-aged very
pleasant European fellow answered my knock. "Yes?"
"Ah hello do you know if Karen Chevarie lives up
here? A very pretty girl with long black hair?"
"Ah yes I think so," he smiled. "She used to live
in apt. 35 with a young man from Ontario who had
a motorbike." "Well I don't know about that," I
said, "I haven't seen her for a year. You said she
used to live here?" "Yes I think so," he replied,

"They moved two months. I helped them with some of their luggage and they told me they were going to Switzerland." "O.K. thank you."

I went over and knocked at the door of apt. 35 and a young girl answered, "Hello," I said, "Does Karen Chevarie live here?" "No," she said smiling, "We just moved in." "Ah do you mind if I look inside your place from the door? I want to see if I can recognize if this is the old apartment." "Sure," she said stepping out of my way. Yes it was the place. I remembered the colour scheme, red and black and the shape of the rooms was familiar. "O.K. thank you," I smiled.

Ah Karen sweetheart so you've found another man. Gone to Switzerland with some dude from Ontario with a motorbike. Does he have my poetry Karen? Can he sing as sweet as me? Do you realize that our love never really had a chance to grow, that I walked down Simpson Street last night wondering where you were and if you ever think of me.

I dropped in on Charly on the way back home. Being in an intolerant mood I argued with Charly over a couple of scotches as to the validity of community organizations. Liz came over from her mother's and cooled me down some what. Charly understood. What are literature, culture, beauty to me but words and often lies? Last night they meant fuck all to me. I was so conscious of my slave status, of my bondage. "I'll talk to you of poetry Charly," I said, "when I'm a free man." And I walked home with Liz down dirty old Seigneur Street with a song in my head that I couldn't sing.

November 10, 1970   Tuesday

Tomorrow is Remembrance Day lest we forget the millions of Andrew Boyles that were slaughtered in the last two great wars. Dead and silent, voicing no criticisms on their gravestones.

There's hardly a family in the Western World that didn't lose someone, an uncle, a grandfather, a brother, a father in the slaughters.

"Years ago," my mother says, "on November 11 at 11 o'clock even the traffic on the street used to stand still for one minute of silence." Such was the reqard the working class gained out of the four years of blood letting 1914 - 1918. One minute of silence in which they did not have to work by law. Such was the reward allotted by the capitalist class to the faithful slaves who survived the holocaust.

I can remember as a little boy hearing the school bells ringing at eleven o'clock on Remembrance Day and the teacher asking us to stand up and say a prayer for the dead who were killed in the wars. I was really confused by the whole ritual and I remember thinking to myself, "Boy these poor dead guys must look forward to this one minute of the year." Visions of them sitting up in their coffins rattling their bones calling to their underground neighbours, "Hey guys it's O.K. they're still thinking of us. We can go back to sleep now."

What would happen if we stopped thinking of them I wondered? I used to shiver with fright thinking of all those millions of musty bone soldiers clawing their way out of their graves to march in regiments on the cities destroying people and little boys like me that didn't think of them. Remembrance Day in my boyish mind was like some kind of a pact the living made with the dead soldiers. "Listen we'll have a minute of silence for you guys if you agree to stay in your graves and not haunt us."

The military graveyards are haunted on Remembrance Day. On November the Eleventh millions of thin voices can be heard vibrating, blowing amongst the poppies. "We were young men once and we did not want to die. We died in vain," they whisper, "We died in vain."

I've got to stop getting so excited in classes when
the subject of Socialism comes up and making a glassy-
eyed fool of myself. Coming home with my stomach
upset, my mind in a whirlpool and wishing I hadn't
said a fuckin' word about Revolution. Shit I feel
lousy about myself when I think back about how I
behaved today yelling down other people, waving my
arms. I guess I can only hope that my classmates are
understanding people. Never again if I can help it.
What I said during the day and what I should have
said kept running through my mind. I couldn't stop
it, couldn't turn it off not even by reading a book.
"I've got to take a walk, Liz," I said, "It's the only
thing that will calm me down. I'm going over to Pat's."
It was raining. I had my cap and leather jacket on.
It was lonely and dark, ten-thirty at night, going to
see people I wasn't sure of as friends anymore.

On Monday Pat and Moe went into Dawson with
me to pick up some application forms for themselves.
Mary's mother told her over the phone that if she
went back to school she would mail her one hundred
dollars a month. They attended one of Black's Political Science classes with me. Mary sat in her desk
like a renegade nun returned to the church glassy-eyed
and in deep penitence. Pat has always been the kind
of guy, like his old man, who is in awe of anyone
with a professional title. Black was back on his old
nationalist's kick and came up with the idea that a
Canadian Car Industry could produce cars much cheaper
and of better quality than those of General Motors.
Well I hammered him on his assumption and more than
a dozen voices in the class agreeing with my words,
"If it ain't profitable it isn't done and it isn't profitable for any capitalist, American or Canadian to make
good cheap cars that last for years." Both Pat and
Moe insisted that I was in the wrong. "David you
didn't get his point." "David don't be so narrow-
minded." Hum I thought to myself things are looking
up again for Pat so good-bye Socialism.

After class Mary went running, literally running, up to Black to ask him if she could get into his January class. I was stunned because I hadn't sensed which way the wind was blowing. Both of them want desperately to get into Dawson and here was I all the time telling them it was shit not realizing how much they, especially Mary, resented my criticism of people they wished to be themselves. You see while Charly over-estimates people thinking everyone is as calculating as himself I under-estimate people thinking they're all as dumb and naive as myself. Little Moe, the wounded butterfly, has never appreciated being talked down to by an ant. Definitely a change in the weather.

So anyhow now I have explained why I felt the way I did walking through the rain yesterday evening to their house. Pat answered the front door and I walked into the living room where he was colouring a cartoon serial he had done on glue-sniffing for the N.F.B. "Where's Moe?" I said wondering where she was but happy she wasn't around. "Ah she's upstairs taking a bath."

I told Pat about how I've been making a fool of myself in school banging my head against a brick wall. "It's no use David," he said, "talking to professors about Marxism. They studied it in college, wrote an exam on it and filed it away in the back of their brains, forgotten and dismissed. They know what Socialism is but none of them think it can ever happen so they're all advocates of reform." "Yeah Pat," I said, "I agree with everything you say except I feel the professors were uninformed by their professors in turn upon what Marxiam Socialism is." I told Pat I wanted to stay off the subject of politics, that I had had it up to my ears with Revolution this week but he insisted on discussing an article he read in the Atlantic Magazine written by a "right wing" sociologist dude, Bancroft. Bancroft maintains that the economic status of a person has very little to do with determining how a man thinks and he divides people up according to his own conceptions of class.

"What do you think of him?" asked Pat. "I find him to be insulting," I answered. "I'm against any theory that divides people any more than they already are. It's bad enough that there're two economic classes of people in society without worrying about the sub-divisions."

108

Mary was by this time sitting on the sofa listening in on the conversation. She sensed that Pat, impressed by my logical analysis of Bancroft's theories was weakening and she broke directly into the discussion swinging her two years of McGill lectures at my head like a club. I rolled with the punches. I had learned my lessons well. I listened. I saw the weak points and threw quick but powerful jabs to her head. Pat came in on her side. I was bombarded. I lay back and took it. Why fight something I couldn't handle. I lay back, reserved my strength and waited for the beating to slow down. It did. Then I threw a punch that knocked Pat out of the fight and stunned Mary into confusion.

I said, "Hold it, hold it! This is not just simply a discussion on theory, this is a personal attack; it's personal and I know why. I've been mouthing off telling you guys these last few weeks how dull and stupid college is, how much I hate it while all the time both of you want desperately to get into that kind of life. My criticisms are a personal insult to yourselves. You attack Marx because of me, because I seem to be saying to you people, slapping your faces and saying you'll never get anywhere, nowhere, without a revolution. Now, neither of you believe in this revolution as I do so. You resent my philosophy. 'We're gonna make it,' you keep yelling at me, Mary. Make it as what? What do you mean? Do you mean I'm saying that you're not gonna make it and that's why I'm being attacked tonight? I want a higher standard of living too Moe just like you guys. I'm on your side, do you understand that? I'm not against you, I'm with you."

"It's not a personal attack," said Mary rallying back from my master blow which had stunned her momentarily into silence, a puzzled look on her face which seemed to say "I didn't know you had it in you."

"Yeah," said Pat, "It's not personal, you're just taking it as personal."

"Well," I replied, "if you're criticizing me for measuring every idea by Marx's theories what can I say? It's a philosophy I accept. I'm incurable and it's my opinion

that Bancroft's ideas are strictly off-the-wall intellectual
ball playing. Clever, but big deal. A show off, don't take
him serious."

We said our good-byes, both of them sincerely trying to bridge the gap they had made between me and themselves. We smiled but inside we knew yeah well it's all
over now.

November 14, 1970   Saturday

Thursday night after the big deal at Pat and Moe's
I came home nervous, upset, with a throat feeling like
it was lined with sand paper from all the mechanical
smoking I've been doing lately. I picked up my tobacco
papers, walked onto the back gallery and threw them
out into the lane. Friday I didn't smoke all day and up
to two o'clock this afternoon I'm still nicotine free. The
urges haven't really been great so far although, I do miss
it.

My inkwell is almost empty, hardly a drop left. One
bottle of ink a year on the average. That's a lot of words.
Speaking of words there's none in my head right now.
Empty, dry, dull.

Liz is at her mother's and I'm at home fucking the
dog. Reading, gorging myself upon peanuts, wondering if
Liz will get some money from her old man so we can go
to the movies tonight.

This college life is killing my spirit, eighty per cent
of the time feeling like a vampire's victim, weak and blood-
less.

Friday night we stayed home, got a little drunk,
read books, babysat Glen's little boy who speaks only
French.

What's the use of writing when I have nothing really
to say except how come I don't have anything to say.
We're all niggers with nothing to do on a broken Saturday
night. Sit around and smell each other's farts. Yeah it's
been a sad day. I wander from chair to chair, stare out
the window for a second. The streets are wet and a cold

110

wind is blowing the leaves off the tree in our yard. A gang of kids are cheering one another, "It's gonna snow tonight for sure," one of them says, "Yah hoo!"

I fear it is to be a sad lonely evening for us all. Six o'clock and Elizabeth hasn't phoned yet. What am I supposed to say? Define how it is to be a young man of twenty-three feeling empty and helpless? Dig up the roots of my despair when I know it'll take a revolution to solve my hang ups. Everyone is sitting around like ice-ridden old beggars displaying their sores to one another. Look, I'm more miserable than you.

November 15, 1970   Sunday

Saturday evening later turned out to be more varied than most of my weekend nights. I waited for Liz's telephone call until six-thirty, then I phoned her only to find out that her father had come home drunk and broke.

"Well good-bye," I said hanging up on her before she finished what she had to say. Woe is me, woe is me - type thing.

I loaded about a hundred Weekly Peoples into a shopping bag then walked uptown through the first snow fall of the year slipping and sliding up the C.P.R. embankment onto the top half of Seigneur Street. Then along the newly-constructed Dorchester Blvd., my head full of memories of people and places I remember like ghosts. Where are they?

Nov. 15, 1969. I quit Ribkoff's dress factory the Monday of that week spending my time looking for another job.

Nov. 15, 1968, a Thursday. I was home in our furnished room on Laval Street having supper after a hard day of slugging up and down snow-covered stairs delivering circulars for the Montreal Messenger. Liz had just started working at Murray's.

Nov. 15, 1967. It was just about this time of the month that the house we were living in on Coloniale Street burnt down to the ground after the oil stove exploded. We lost everything except an empty suitcase which we still have, all charred black on the outside.

Liz was pregnant and I was a hippy with hair past my shoulders waiting for something good to happen.

Nov. 15, 1966. Argyle Street was totally busted up by the final and biggest police raid. Three paddy wagons with a couple of patrol cars to escort us all down to station number one. Eddy Greenfield, me, Spider, Bob Soucy, Jay Dee, Dave McMillan, Boogala, Bob McMasters and many others. After our acquittal (charged with harbouring minors and sleeping in a deserted house) all the guys broke up into couples, partners. I paired off with Dave McMillan, a speed freak hustling Y.M.C.A. queers for a living. We were crashing out at a pad in the infamous Amesbury Apartment house, Cockroach Heaven as it was fondly referred to by the regulars.

I was still going out with Karen Chevarie on the weekends and during the rest of the week meeting Elizabeth at the Prag. My hair, which had been cut that July in the Don Jail, was beginning to grow long again.

Nov. 15, 1965. I just had one of my back teeth pulled out and I was back living at home after a three month's absence from Verdun spent living in New York City and uptown Montreal in a furnished room on sleazy Aqueduct Street.

I had a job as an assistant shipper, working in a dingy shoe factory down on St. Paul Street in Old Montreal. And I mean dingy! Like very very old and dark with stone walls, creaking floorboards and dust-covered windows that hadn't been opened since Armistice Day in 1918. The little elevator was an antique, an oblong box five-by-eight feet that took a half-hour to go up three floors. Rattle bang crank rattle bang. I remember a little song I made up to go with the weird noises it used to make. Carved into one of its painted tin sides were the names K. Ross loves M. Schartz and a date, 1943. My bosses were two fossilized Polish Jew businessmen complete with vests, cuffed pants and double-breasted jackets of a heavy material that must have been the in thing in Warsaw circa 1910.

Nearly every night after supper I would take a Verdun street bus uptown to the Prag hoping to see Christiane D'Orais whose acquaintance I had recently made. We used to neck in the back dark coffee tables until Kurt

112

threw her out one night for licking my ears.

Well, all of these memories were shooting through my mind as I went about discreetly placing Weekly Peoples in various parts of Sir George Williams University and the Place Ville Marie - Bonaventure complex.

In the C.N. Station I watched two railroad cops escort three drunken rowdy crew cut teen-agers out onto jhe street where one of them pulled a gin bottle out from under his overcoat and in defiance of the law drained the last few drops of liquor remaining in it.

And I recalled the fall evening five years ago when Toni, Jay, Mike Smyth and me got ourselves drunk on a case of twenty-four sitting in the little concrete plaza above the P.V.M. Shopping Centre. We drained everyone of the pints in an hour and got super humanly plastered - out of it just like those kids the C.N. cops threw out of the station. I remember Toni was all for tossing the empties through a plate glass window but reason prevailed and instead we piled the bottles up in a pyramid on top of a flight of stairs leading into the Queen Elizabeth Hotel. A little note reading "Fuck yas all" was left sticking out of the top bottle forming the apex of the three foot pyramid. It was to be our motto for many more evenings to come.

On the way back home with thirty papers left in my A & P shopping bag I took a detour up St. Mark Street to call on Charly. As I expected he wasn't home. Passing back down the stairs I almost scared the life out of some young housewife who shot me a frightened look that seemed to say, "Oh no there he is, the Lincoln Street stranger the cops haven't caught yet!" She scrunched up against the wall as I passed by wet from the snow, my cap shading half of my unshaven face, bleary-eyed from nervous tension, sticky damp hair dripping over my ears, cradling a sodden damp tattered shopping bag in my arms. The poor girl's heart was audibly playing the Mexican Hat Dance on her rib cage. She made me feel even creepier than I looked and I found myself slinking the rest of the way home in the shadows like Jack the Ripper.

Charly and I stayed at the Swiss Hut until twelve
o'clock last night talking generally about my relationship
with Pat and Mary.

Don was sitting at our table for awhile, good looking
Don with the Cary Grant face that had all the girls on
Lagauchetiere Street falling in love with him. His mind is
very spaced out. Charly gave me the psychological term
defining his mental behaviour but I've forgotten it. Something to do with a break in his ability to communicate.

"It's not that I'm saying he's stupid," Charly said,
"I know quite a number of people with deep psychological
problems who are very intelligent."

I talked to him about school, about the difficulties
I have maintaining my cool when the subject of revolution
is brought up in class. "I really get uptight and excited
but I don't like to," I said. "I get along with all the kids
but not the professors."

Charly laughed and said, "I'm gonna give you my
wise saying for the month. Stop trying to climb on top
of church steeples." Charly was referring to the dream I
had months ago which he analysed as me trying to impress
my father.

Sunday was such a quiet day that I can't remember
any of the events that occurred. Oh yes I moved all my
books and my writing desk upstairs into the small front
room of Jones' old flat (not rented yet) and made a study
out of it. It's a cosy seven-by-eight foot cubicle with a
little attic window over looking Coursol Street and the
C.P. tracks. A make-shift book case constructed out of
old bureau drawers stands against the south wall. My desk
faces the window and I watch the trains go by during my
smoke breaks. I like it up here. Peaceful, quiet, easy to
concentrate, a pilot house.

Friday was a slow day, empty of any events worth
recording. I'm still growing - what else is there to say. I
grow. I'm not brilliant, far from being a genius, with
more balls than brains, but I grow. Slowly, in pain.

Twelve o'clock walking home with Liz from a club,
arm in arm feeling no pain singing songs along Dorchester
Boulevard. "Sing loud! " Liz said, "Don't be afraid."
"I'm not afraid," I said, "but I don't think you realize
how loud I can sing." And I demonstrated by booming
out the song, "If Tomorrow Never Comes", my voice
vibrating, echoing off buildings blocks away. Some old
dude walking a dog nearly fainted on the spot. "O.K.",
Liz said smiling, "Quiet down."

Saturday morning Liz went in early to work. I got
up around ten and finished my studies more or less by
three o'clock. Jay came over to rap with me for awhile
in my pilot study. We talked about the 23rd Club, the
Independent Order of Anonymous Misfits, in a mock-
serious manner.

"You know Jay," I said, "sometimes I have grandiose
dreams, judging from the way we've grown in numbers
the last five years, that one day we'll be rivals of the
Shriners and the Elks. You know we'll have huge con-
ventions, big parades and shit like that."

But seriously we're expecting about twenty-five
guys to come down this year and if the Club, if I may
be so bold as to call such an informal meeting a club,
grows any larger within the next few years we may have
to abandon the Empire Tavern and resort to renting a hall.
1970 marks the fifty year of our existence making us
some kind of an institution. Its structure is a farce based
very loosely on Robert's Rules of Order as perceived by
twenty drunken young men. Politically we lean towards
the absurd and morally we are all in favour of warm
beds, wine and good loving girls.

Saturday night a long anxious stroll through the student ghetto, along Sherbrooke Street past the limonsines
parked outside the Ritz-Carlton over to Charly's. ("I may
go crazy before that mansion on the hill.") Some kind
of merry-go-round going on in the back of my brain. I
couldn't settle down and speak on any particular subject.

"Well," says Charly, "guess we still have time to go
out for a beer," "Yeah," I replied, "let's go down and
hear that country 'n western band playing at the Kat's
Den."

Ronny was sitting at a table all decked out in his
only good suit, waving to us as we walked into the Bar.
The last of the small time spenders with a bar bill of
$29.00. Very proud of the fact that he is bankrupt for
$6000. That's big time in the small time, man, to be
in the hole for that many grand. Typically the only customers in the joint were all friends of Ronny's most of
whom were broke, sitting in front of beers that had been
opened two horus before. Still some of them were better
off than Ronny who even had to bum a dime from me
for a telephone call. There were about twenty people
in the club. "Hey yeah it's packed tonight eh Dave?"
said Ronny. (His uncle owns the place.)

God knows what they're paying the band, union
wages, I presume. Western bands are really out of it as
far as the club business goes in Montreal. The small town
touring circuit is about the only thing left for them. It's
a shame because Paul, the leader of this three-man group
is a fine fiddle player of the bluegrass variety good enough
to have played several times on the old Carl Smith T.V.
show. He's an old professional working in the show biz
since 1949.

The youngest guy, Wayne, the Jimmy Rodgers fan
(the original Jimmy Rodgers, the brakeman who died
of T.B. back in the thirties) has an excellent country
blues voice. He can really put heart into a song he likes
to sing.

Terry on the bass guitar, the M.C., has an easy going
sense of humour couples with a smooth tenor voice good
for old standards and harmonizing.

Kind of a shame that they can't make a decent living in their chosen field. Anyhow ol' Paul had the fiddle going Saturday night and Ronny was there on the dance floor with some country boy from Renfrew, Ontario, doing an Irish jig. Everybody tapping their feet and yelling like cowboys.

"You're great!" Ronny yelled to Paul as he got off the stage. "That's class, that is agriculture!" said Paul smiling, a veteran of a thousand honky-tonk brawls, a philosopher.

"It's all the same to me," he once said, "not too much can happen that I haven't seen before." A stoic smile playing around his mouth. Twenty-one years in the night life. He has met and sat with thousands of Ronny O'Neils, David Fennarios and even the odd Charly Larson or two. People are all just variations of the whole sum Paul has met in his life. A shade more here, a little less there, taller, shorter, more sober, more drunk, loud, quiet. Faces. He smiles. It's his job and his life making music.

December 1, 1970   Tuesday

Saturday - weak as a sick sparrow. Dragging my ass around all day. Feeling ashamed of myself, worrying about how blue I've been feeling. Really down, under water and short of breath. Didn't-do-my-studies-and-I-am-suffering-the-consequences. Suffered them to come unto me. Smothered myself under a cloud of nicotine all afternoon and then went out to the movies with Liz, Pat and Moe. While it lasted, it was good, but afterwards I only came down all the harder. Splashed deep down in the blues when I returned home. What is happening to me?

I suppose I'm beginning to sound like a broken
record. Why bother repeating again today that I feel
the same way as I did yesterday and the day before?
No changes yet in the atmosphere, still dim and gloomy.
Mind wrapped up in ego pains. Looking at my face in the
mirror to see if I look as sad as I feel. Yep. Very impressive, Fennario, a stranger would almost take you for a
philosopher. Interesting face, like that of a reformed
derelict. An old convict doing his time as easy as possible.
What else is there for me to tell. No stories in my head,
no tales to be told.

Walking down Dominion Street coming home from
school in the slanted December 3 o'clock sunshine. Red
shadows on the sidewalks. Kids playing hockey on streets
not yet covered with snow. I passed by singing blues
songs out loud, trying to find the one that fitted my
mood. "Whether I'm right or wrong I know you're gonna
miss me when I'm gone. You're sure gonna cry when I
tell that I ain't coming home no more." The words are
from an old Jimmy Rodger's ballad that Robin loves to
hear me sing whenever I'm drunk.

Hey I've never told the story about how Eddy Greenfield escaped from Kingston back in 1968 and made the
front page of every major Canadian newspaper. I remember reading the story in the Gazette while at work and
laughing at the idea of a convict escaping from a Christmas
concert making fools out of all the big government officials
who were attending the programme. Weeks later I found
out from Robin that the convict who escaped was Eddy
Greenfield. Here's how Eddy told me the story through
his letters.

Eddy has a very fine baritone voice and consequently
he was made a member of the penitentiary church choir.
The Kingston authorities decided to make a big deal out
of the annual Christmas concert by inviting government
officials and having the whole performance televised. The
choir members were permitted to wear their civies and
allowed to mingle with the dignitaries. R.C.M.P. officers
in formal red jacket uniform stood guard at the doors.

The Governor-General was in attendance; it was really a classy affair. Elderly matrons smothered in furs and diamonds flashed their expensive teeth at the prisoners thanking them royally for their performance. Eddy offered his arm to one old lady who was leaving the scene early and escorted her downstairs past dozens of R.C.M.P. officers who saluted them as they passed by. "I never found out who the old doll was," Eddy says in his letter, "but she must have been something else 'cause all those horsemen were clicking their heels with hands up to their boy scout hats as we passed by."

It was as simple as that. Eddy walked the old doll right outside to her Rolls Royce, handing her over to her chauffeur, then he took off down the street grabbing a hack into Kingston where he got on a bus to Montreal.

The story of how Eddy was picked up by the cops in Montreal was told to me by Eddy's old girlfriend Beverly. It seems the greyhound bus stopped for a coffee break at a restaurant on the South shore and Eddy, perusing the Montreal Matin, found his picture on the front page and decided he'd better take a cab the rest of the way into Montreal. He figured the cops would surely be checking out all the bus stations for him.

He took the cab right down to Contact (an organized haven for street people) on Ste. Famille Street, shocking Dave Robb out of his wits as he came busting through the front door. Robb rushed him immediately upstairs into a backroom giving him a change of clothes, some false I.D. and my address.

Eddy was on his way over to my place on Laval Street hurrying along Prince Arthur when he ran into Christine Wilma. Both of them walked over to my place. I wasn't home. Wilma invited Eddy out to her home in the suburbs. "It's O.K.," she said, "My parents are on vacation in Florida."

From Wilma's house Eddy phoned his girl Beverly talking with her for over an hour on the line. "I'm coming over Eddy," she said. "Be careful," Eddy replied, "Take a cab and make sure the cops aren't watching your house."

They were. She didn't see them. She was in Eddy's arms only a few minutes when the cops came busting into the house through the windows and doors carrying sub-machine guns.

Eddy lost his nine month's good time and all his chances of a parole. He's be out by now if he hadn't tried to see his girlfriend that Christmas.

December 5, 1970   Saturday

The blood of Scottish coal miners runs in my veins. My poetry, my Aunt Maggy singing "The Poor Little Blind Boy" in a high shivering voice that could bring tears to the eyes of a man of stone. The story of my family is the story of the working class; particularly of the Scottish workers with wild tragic ballads in their hearts and voices. Eyes deep with memories.

December 7, 1970   Monday

How long is it going to take me to recuperate from my adolescence? If ever? Can I really change what has been part of my life for so long? The torment of mind I was born with distorting all my thought-processes fucking up my relationships with other peropld. The bruised memories of my sad family life continue to haunt me in my nightmares.

Crazy paranoia dreams lately. Huge automated machines like giant typewriters rolling down city streets systematically killing people. Refugees in the suburban fields of the South Shore across the river. The downtown section of the city is on fire (like in War and Peace). We can hear the machines - a high pitched hum. "Well," I said crouching over in the wind to light my cigarette, "I guess they decided to get rid of us." I wondered how many of us managed to get out of the city. I thought of my friends - how many were alive? How long will I live? There was no question about whether we would get away;

the machines would get us eventually, it was only a question of when and where. No one was panicking. The slaughter had been expected a long time although their tactics rather caught us by surprise. Just another ordinary working day until the gigantic machines suddenly appeared on the noon day streets as if they had been suddenly released from secret subterranean storage chambers underneath the city. Machines big as houses rolling along the main arteries in an impersonal mechanical fashion killing everyone in their path. Enormous typewriter keys raining down on every human within their range squashing them like cockroaches spat against the concrete sidewalk. White guts leaking out of them like ants that have been stepped on.

I was up at Betty Ann's tonight after looking up some material in the Westmount Library on World Poverty. No more invisible dogs biting at my legs in their home.

Betty Ann and Ray left around nine o'clock to attend a meeting at the Free School leaving me behind to tell tales to the kids. "Make sure David has all the beer he wants," Betty Ann said to Neil as she walked out the door.

What kind of a man am I to spend two hours telling dreams to children seven, ten and twelve-year olds rapping with them like I was a classmate of theirs at school. I felt like my Uncle Art. Yuppy sitting cross-legged on top of the table, his eyes big as saucers listening to my monster stories.

December 8, 1970   Tuesday

My mind does not like to think, I would rather dream. A storyteller's mind gifted only to entertain children with dreams and fairy tales. Fennario's nightmare world of lonely people, cigarette butts, bus transfers, empty pop bottles, stale popcorn, steamed hot dogs, greasy french fries, cheap wine, basement apartments, sparrows, dandelions, skipping rope, sidewalks, roof tops, no parking signs, dead-end streets, cockroaches, garbage pails, slush, wet feet, old socks, bad early morning breath, dirty fingernails, stained teeth, blue jeans, patched tattered shirts, country 'n western music, battered suitcases, hunched shoulders, old cars, broken windows, weeds, nervous laughter, young girls fresh as April, empty rooms, unmade beds, kitchen floors, tall grandfathers, low and heavy grandmothers, crowds coming and going, barbed wire highway fences, stop lights, headlights, the velvet warm blackness of a country road, cold left-over pizza the morning after a drunken party, pissing in urinals, dirty dishes piled up in a sink, guitars with broken strings, rusty harmonicas, sunsets in a strange city, battered up cowboy boots, rawhide jackets, pockets with holes in them, girls with warm beds and lonely hearts, coffee-houses, smoke, last call in the tavern, the waiters putting chairs up on the table, rock 'n roll juke boxes, dance halls. Questions, answers, doubts and laughter. Don't worry about nothing 'cause nothing's alright.

December 10, 1970   Thursday

Mother Capitalism is nine month's pregnant and her baby has been doing one hell of a lot of kicking lately.

December 26, 1970   Saturday

Don't look into my eyes, you may guess what I'm thinking. Deep shadows flickering. Flashbacks of memories. I don't want to be like my father, yet I can never fully escape the consequences of being his son. I wish I had the magic words to untie all these tangled sorrows. Yet it isn't all sad. All the males of my family are strange, all of us very deep, moody. Witches in the family. Inherited nightmares. I must know, I must see, I must be ready.

Boxcar words with no verbs to drive them along.

Lady on the mountain, gypsy boy in the kitchen drinking her wine, "It's a new year for all those that are still living but no one can sing songs that sad & live long."

It was a very sad evening.

122

"Here's a story you've never heard, Ma," I said leaning back on the sofa picking up my beer glass. "It's about
the time I got my fat head stuck in-between the bars of
the Willibrord Park fence gate back when I was four-years-
old. You know that was away back in the days, bad old
days of Duplessis when no margarine could be bought in
Quebec and all the playgrounds in Montreal were locked
up until one in the afternoon. God knows for what reason,
but anyhow, anyway one Sunday morning I decided to
go and sneak into the park before the gates were opened.
Two little girls from the neighbourhood came along with
me. The orthodox method of sneaking into the park was
that of vaulting over the barbed wire but these two little
girls somehow managed to squeeze through the chained
bars of the main gate. It looked easy but I got my fat
head stuck trying to go in head first instead of sideways.
You know I was one of those kids who had a head that
looked like a pumpkin stuck on a broomstick. I was
stuck and no matter which way I twisted the old head
just wouldn't budge and the more I twisted the tighter
the pressure got on my skull. Meanwhile Fat Pop, the
park caretaker, the meanest old man in the West End,
the same man who once chased me out of the park for
standing up on a see-saw scaring me so bad that I pissed
myself, was sitting directly across the street from me, sitting on his front stairs twirling the gate key in his hand
with a satisfied smirk on his face. I struggled, twisted,
cried and screamed for about an hour until finally some
of Pop's neighbours came out on the stairs telling Pop
to let me loose. "It's only eleven-thirty," the old bastard
grumbled, "the park doesn't open until one o'clock."
"Well Jesus Christ! " one of the guys in his pajamas said,
"I can't eat my breakfast while that poor kid is screaming
his lungs out." And he went across the street over to me
with a couple of other guys, "Hold still kid," they said
and then boom-boom-boom, kicking with their feet,
they loosened the chain holding the bars together until I
was able to squeeze my head out and run home crying.
Yeah that Pop was a real mean old man I'm telling ya and
on that day he probably had the best laugh of his life
thanks to me."

January 6, 1971   Tuesday

Windy nights always make me restless. Liz asleep
on the couch after a hard day's work and I put on my
long black overcoat, my beige peaked cap, stepping out
lightly into the night. Skeleton winds whipping the last
ragged leaves spinning wildly breaking off from the
branches. Thin shadowed silent memories of the October
winds and the stars they pushed around the sky for me as
a little boy, not long out of the womb but old enough
to question my birth. St. Antoine Street now stripped
of its festive Christmas decorations and back to its standard dingy appearance. Dark rows of scabby-faced houses
swollen and rheumatic with old age.

January 8, 1971   Sunday

I was born at the cross roads of the twentieth century. In 1947 there were men alive not yet in their fifties
who had lived and acted out a part of the drama known
as the Russian Revolution. Children who had seen bar-
ricades in the streets of Paris during the days of the
Commune were old men in their seventies. I envy their
memories.

January 11, 1971   Sunday

Gordy Lightfoot's song "Bobby McGee" always
reminds me of the time little Bobby Archer and I hitched
out to T.O. together back in 1966. We were out on the
401 all day, our last lift dropping us off in a residential
section of Toronto a mile north of the downtown section
around two o'clock in the morning. Nobody on the
streets except us and the cops. A ghost town - Toronto
on a Sunday morning. Everytime a patrol car passed by
we'd duck into the shadows. The cops seemed to be
everywhere as if they knew we had come to town putting
out a dragnet for us. "Look out Bobby," I said, "I think

124

that patrol car spotted us." And we took off around a side street up a dark back alley climbing into a huge refrigerator box someone had thrown into the garbage. From inside our refuge we heard a car shriek to a halt, a door slamming and some heavy footsteps coming up the alley way. A big cop passed right by us waving a flashlight, checking out the roofs and the sheds. He was about thirty feet away from us when Bobby said, "Dave there's rats in this box." "Shut yer mouth dummy!" I hissed punching him in the shoulder. "Pipe down or we'll spend the rest of this summer in the Don Jail." The cop moved further away from us and Bobby says, "So what are we going to do? Stay in this stinking box all night?" "Just be patient alright Bobby?" I whispered. "Be a good boy and wait till the cop gets out of the alley way. This is the last trip I'm ever taking with you anyhow 'cause you've been nothing but trouble for me."

Yes the more I thought about it the more I regretted having taken Bobby along with me on that trip to Yorkville. A fifteen-year-old neurotic middle-class runaway kid with Pot, Grass and Acid written all over his jeans in indelible ink, actually paying me forty dollars to make him a hippy, bribing me to take him to Yorkville, the Mecca of the Canadian street scene.

The cop finally left without finding us, and once the patrol car left the scene we climbed back out of the box. "Well," I said, "we better be careful and stay back here awhile until the cop finishes combing the area for us."

Sitting on the ground, knees up, back against the wall staring blankly ahead into the darkness wondering if we'd ever make it to Yorkville on the other side of town where I had friends with floorspace for us to crash on.

"You know Bobby," I said, "I think maybe we should stay back here until the sun comes up then there'll be less likely to pick us up. And yeah we'll have better chances to panhandle and maybe save ourselves a long walk.

"Speak for yourself," Bobby mumbled, "I'm not staying here, there's rats here."

"Ah, there's no fuckin' rats here ya dummy!" I
said raising my voice. "What's wrong with your head
anyway? When are you going to grow up?"

"I know there's rats in the garbage, I can hear
them," he said pointing at the mound of refuse.

"So what? Big deal so maybe there is," I said,
"they won't hurt us but that cop's liable to lay a beating
on us for making him climb up roofs walking in garbage
looking for us if he grabs us on the street."

Bobby saw my point and about twenty minutes
of total silence passed finally interrupted by the sound
of a patrol car driving by.

' He's still looking for us," I whispered. A few
more minutes of silence.

"Wow," I said, "I wish I had some tobacco left,
man, I'm about to have a nicotine fit."

"Well," Bobby said, "if you hadn't busted up my
harmonica at least we would have had a little music to
listen to."

"I didn't bust up your harp," I grumbled, but I
was lying, the kid was right. Earlier in the day while we
were waiting for a lift on the highway the kid had nearly
driven me out of my skull playing the only three-note
song he knew over and over thousands of times. Finally
he went for a piss in the fields leaving the harp with
me and soon as he was out of view I lay the harp down
on the concrete and dropped a heavy rock on it. I
held what remained of it up to him when he returned
saying, 'Sorry I dropped it on the highway and a car
ran over it."

More time passed. I grew sleepy, but every time
my head nodded down on my knees Bobby would shake
me awake. "Hey Dave; I'm afraid to be alone with the
rats."

"Well Bobby," I finally grumbled, "if you're so goddamn terrified why don't you crawl back into the box
where the rats can't get ya. Here, take my jacket, I'm
not cold, use it as a pillow and you'll go right to sleep."

He did so leaving me to slip peacefully back into
my dreams. A truck backfiring woke me up a few
hours later, broad daylight, seven o'clock in the morning.

126

After straightening the kinks out of my knees I walked over and gave the refrigerator box a few kicks, "Rise 'n shine, breakfast time, Bobby."

A kind-hearted man on his way to work gave us two bus tickets along with fifty cents for coffee 'n donuts. And an hour later found us bedding down on newspaper in the kitchen of an old friend of mine with a flat on Bay Street in Yorkville.

And I never did go back on the road with Bobby Archer who later became a big wheel on the campus dope scene.

January 14, 1971   Thursday

A bitter cold day. I'm sitting upstairs in my study with a blanket wrapped about my shoulders, the house is so chilly. Old houses are hard to heat properly, the wind always finds a way of getting in.

Yesterday evening I was over to my family's to pick up my government loan application which was returned in the mail this week as incomplete. My father had to fill in the back page informing the government of his income level. I sat down with him for an hour at the kitchen table working it out. "Well David," my old man said fingering the paper, "these figures shouldn't stop you from getting your grant." His total income for 1970 was $4,036 dollars. Below the poverty line. It makes me wonder how the hell we lived when the old man had six kids to support yet we never thought of ourselves as being poor.

January 15, 1971   Friday

Eleven-thirty yesterday evening I walked up Atwater hill to the Children's Hospital to call on Robin as I promised I would. In the snow, in the night. Coursol Street deserted except for one frightened little old lady scurrying along with a wary eye open for potential purse snatchers. She practically fell across to the other side of the street after hearing me come up behind her. There was no one at all on Atwater, I had all my memories to myself, memories of the many times I've walked up that hill.

Robin is at present working as a night receptionist in the Emergency Ward. Through the window I could see her sitting at a desk. "She could be a stranger," I thought to myself, "Just a young woman doing her job typing out the information people give her. That's just what she is to the people who come in here. A red-haired girl with a soft voice and sad brown eyes. A stranger until I go in and say "Hello, I know you, we were in love many years ago."

She looked up when I walked in, not recognizing me until I was within three feet of her desk. For nearly two hours I stood talking with her. Babies wailing in the background, orderlies rushing to and fro, security guards huddled in a corner smoking cigarettes to kill time. Neon lights burning, the smell of chloroform. "How do you spell diahreia?" asked Robin. "I don't know." I answered.

Just for the hell of it Robin pulled my family's hospital admittance card out of the file cabinet and I discovered that I had been admitted through emergency at the age of six months. "Probably for convulsions," I said, "I suffered from convulsions when my teeth were coming in."

Robin told me she can tell whether it's going to be a busy night at the Emergency Ward by checking out the pollution count in the newspaper. "If the count is high, I know I'm going to be kept busy by kids with asthma coming in," she said.

Two emergency cases were entered by Robin while I was there; one, a little brown-eyed girl choking with asthma, and the other a boy with possible brain damage from a beating he got for supposedly squealing to the teacher. Eyes and face twitching.

I looked at Robin's face and I knew I would always remember that evening.

January the sixteenth, a Saturday, my kid brother goes into the army and I write a poem about the Golden City.

Down to my mother's by two o'clock, Jimmy sitting on the sofa in the basement with his girlfriend playing records. My mother scurrying back and forth getting all the last things prepared, tears already in her eyes.

The nine of us troop down together to the 58 bus stop, I'm carrying fat little Jean, walking beside Virginia. It's a long bus ride uptown, my parents sitting together up front, little Sarah hopping from seat to seat. The frost is thick on the bus windows. My mother and father sitting silently together. They are getting old; I know they are getting old. The river is frozen over and Sarah's melting the ice on the windows with her warm fingers. I look at Jimmy's hands lightly resting on his thighs, long slender hands like my own, out of the same womb. Virginia gaily speaking to me of her many boyfriends past and present the many hearts she has touched. "It's been a long time since we've been on a bus together." My mother looks back over her shoulder and smiles to see her family.

A short walk down windy Dorchester Boulevard brought us to the C.N. station. Seven old boyfriends of Jimmy's were waiting there for him. "C'mon over here," says one of his friends winking, "I want to speak to you." I see Jimmy's friend pull a small flash of gin out of his overcoat pouring the contents of it into an empty soft drink cup. "That'll warm ya up on the long train ride Jimmy."

Virginia takes a snapshot of me and Jimmy with our arms around each other.

I go to the washroom and on my way back a drunk comes up to me making what I thought at first to be a peace sign but no he just wants two cigarettes which I give him.

"Is it time yet for Jimmy to leave?" Sarah keeps saying. "No, not yet, not yet." And finally she breaks up crying. "Are you crying yet Ma?" says Jimmy smil-

129

ing, my mother with tears in her eyes comforting Sarah.

Jimmy's gang of friends form a circle back to back to allow Jimmy and his girl some privacy to say good-bye to each other. A long-haired guy passing can't resist peeking over the circle of shoulders on tiptoe, "I see you." And everyone cracks up laughing. An announcement comes over the speakers, the train to Val Cartier is delayed fifteen minutes.

"Where's the giant cake and the twenty-three dancing girls you said were going to be here?" says Jimmy laughing.

"Ah so they're a little late," I replied, "That's show biz."

Janice, long and slender, dark-brown, almost black hair past her shoulders. Haunted blue eyes moody. The blood of Lancashire witches runs in her veins.

My father, rather stiff and formal, occasionally laughing at some of my antics; an old soldier.

People say I resemble Janice the most of everyone in my family. Heather commented upon the strong resemblance, Janice saying to me, "You're good looking David." "You're pretty too," I replied.

The final moment arrived, the crowds began filing through the conductor's gate. My sisters and Elizabeth kissed Jimmy good-bye. "Good luck Jimmy," I said shaking his hand. Then my father greeted him and last of all my mother now in tears hugging him, watching him go down the stairs, shaking with grief. All the girls were crying, even my father had tears in his eyes. He cleared his throat and said, "Well Mother you still have David left."

That evening Liz and I did the Mountain Street circuit. The Bistro was loaded with atmosphere that evening. The ghost of Leonard Cohen was afoot, the scent of roasting chestnuts permeated the air. A large gathering of journalists was standing at the bar exchanging witticisms while Liz and I lingered over a couple of relaxing brews. Occasionally our conversation was interrupted by one or more of the assorted intellectuals shouting political slogans at one another. "There's something lacking in these people," I thought, "sometimes their words are good but their ideas fail to touch me." Then a phrase, a verse formed itself in my mind and turning to Liz I said, "Liz, tell me what you think of this verse - 'The scientists and

the philosophers have all forgotten, but the children are
singing in the streets about the Golden City' - does that
sound like poetry?" "It's lovely" Liz said, "Sure it's
poetry. I like it." "You do? It sounds like poetry?"
I said. "Well of course it does," she said, "and I think
it is one of your best." That little verse made the whole
evening seem worthwhile, made me glad to be alive that
bitter cold January night.

January 18, 1971   Monday

    Sunday was a very quiet uneventful day spent
reading and working on my journal. That night I spent
a few hours with Caul Wilson in his living room drinking coffee, rapping about politics. I told him a story.
    "Had a friend of mine, Little Rick McGarnahan
from the West End, living down on Vallée Street back
in 1967. A real sleazy dead end street with crumbling
houses just off Jeanne Mance, running parallel to Ste.
Catherine Street. We used to call it Vallée Alley. Man it
was a mess, I was afraid to walk along the sidewalk in a
high wind in case a house might tumble over on me.
There were a couple of factories, warehouses on the same
street in no better shape than the rooming houses. Well
anyhow Little Rick had a flat down there at the time and
I used to go up and visit him a lot helping him drink down
the gallons of homemade wine he had stashed away. Rick,
Louise, Snoopy, Joe McBride and me were sitting at
Rick's kitchen table one evening, you know drinking
wine getting comfortably stoned, shooting the bull when
all of a sudden cr-unch bang crack - a crow bar comes
smashing through the kitchen wall just above the stove, a
couple of feet away from the table. We're sitting there
wondering what the fuck is happening while the hole gets
bigger and bigger with every smash of the bar. Well when
the hole is about yea big, two-by-two feet, this guy sticks
his head through the wall looking around with a puzzled
look on his face, blushing when he spots us sitting quietly
at the kitchen table with wine glasses in our hands. "Sorry,"
he says, "I thought this was the warehouse we were break-

ing in." "No man," says Joe, "You're working on the wrong wall. The one you want is on the north side." "O.K. Thanks," the guy says smiling sheepishly as he ducked back out of the hole.

"And what did you guys do about the hole in the wall? " Caul asked. "Ah we put a poster of John Lennon over it," I said.

January 22, 1971   Friday

Can I ever forget the afternoon I met Karen Chevarie in the C.N. station and the events leading up to it?

I was released from the Don Jail on July 21st, 1966, and the blue corn flowers were in full blossom as I have described. My former cell mate, Tonto, had promised to meet me outside the Don the day I was to be released, however he was nowhere in sight.

I walked up Queen Street with a young delinquent from Glace Bay, just finishing a thirty day sentence for being caught in a public swimming pool with a wine bottle. With the train fare money my mother had mailed me I treated the boy and myself to a massive bacon, eggs, pancakes and toast breakfast at the Rainbow Grill. We separated on Yonge Street. I went into a cheap three feature movie house and Billy went off with some friends he met on the street.

Later on in the afternoon I checked out Yorkville for Tonto and found him sitting on the rail outside the Grab Bay. He apologized for not meeting me outside the jail that morning. "I slept in Dave," he said, "crashed out in the basement of the Hamburger Joint. The owner's a fag and lets me sleep down there sometimes."

Tonto was a dark-skinned Indian boy, Cree Indian, about twenty-two years old, an incorrigible drifter. We became partners in the Don Jail after the screws laid a beating on us for protesting against getting our hair cut.

Tonto had plans about sitting up all night in a restaurant. "Not me man," I said, "I'm gonna get me a bed down on Shuter Street. Catch ya tomorrow."

The lodging houses on Shuter Street were all filled up, but a kind-hearted fag attendant in a house down on Jarvis Street allowed me some free floor space in the corner of a dormitory filled with dozens of snoring transients. He even went to the trouble of supplying me with a thin army mattress and a blanket. "One of the guys has to go to work at four o'clock so I'll wake you up at that time and you can sleep in his bed." "Thank you," I replied somewhat flustered by his kindness. A saintly fag. "No trouble, no trouble," he smiled.

I was back in the Village by ten o'clock the next day and found Tonto sleeping in the vacant lot behind the Avenue Road Church, the last resort for many homeless street people during the summers of '66 and '67 even though it was raided almost nightly by the cops.

Tonto lay close to the fence in warm company with six other ragged long-haired drifters.

"There were about thirty guys here last night before the cops raided us," said Tonto sitting up yawning, "me and a couple of other dudes climbed up the pear tree but all the others got hauled away in three paddy wagons."

Handing Tonto a cigarette I told him I was planning to hitch-hike back to Montreal that afternoon asking him if he wanted to come along. "Sure, why not?" he said flipping grass and leaves off his pants and jacket. "I've never been to Montreal."

Stocking up on chocolate bars after a couple of hot dogs for breakfast at the Grab Bag we got on a north bound subway taking us out to the 401 highway. Six hours and forty miles later we stood stranded outside of Oshawa, a Toronto suburb, watching countless cars filing by full of paranoiac office-workers on their way home for supper. By this time we knew we weren't gonna get a lift so we began clowning around entertaining the people. An audience of thousands when Tonto grabbed my throat in a simulated fit of rage, eyes flashing, teeth gnashing, tripping me to the ground waving his ten inch hunting knife over my face as if he intended to scalp me. We took turns being the victim. The people driving by really freaked out, little old ladies had their hands to their faces peering through their fingers but still no one stopped. Tonto threatened to pull out his cock and piss on them. "Cool it, Tonto," I said grabbing his arm. "Do that and you're good for three months in the Don for indecent exposure." Reason prevailed. Tails between our legs we crossed over the highway and got a lift back into town.

Tonto and I went our separate ways from then on. After another night at the Jarvis Street lodging house I went back on the 401 by myself in a second attempt to make it home. It was around ten o'clock when I first stuck out my thumb, six o'clock found me in St. Zotique, a small town about forty-five miles west of Montreal Island. One hour, two hours passed by, the street lights went on, the smell of a thousand suppers cooking in the air and no one would pick me up. Stranded again. There was a church directly across the road from me, figuring maybe I could bum some money for bus fare I went over, knocked at the porch door requesting to see the priest. The lady interrupted his supper and brought him out to see me. He didn't speak a word of English. I managed to explain to him in broken French that I needed a one way bus ticket to Montreal. "Non, non! " he said emphatically, a frown passing over his face, "Vat-en! Allez, allez," shooing me away with his hands. "You fuckin' bastard," I mumbled curling my lip at him. "Do you want me to phone the police?" he said suddenly breaking out into perfect English. "I'm going, I'm going," I growled as I turned, walking out the porch door letting it slam behind me. I walked back to the side of the road contemplating homicide and stuck out my thumb for another half-hour. "Goddamn Pepsis! " I yelled every time a farmer bombed by me in a truck kicking up dust in my face.

"Man if I only had a dime I could get myself a chocolate bar," I thought to myself and then the idea struck me, I could sell my rawhide jacket to the guy in the grocery store and get a couple of bucks. That's just what I did catching the ten-thirty bus into Montreal. Hah, it was good to see Place Ville Marie looming into sight. I hurried down to the Prag from the bus station figuring someone I knew was bound to be there and maybe I could find a place to stay.

I walked down the coffee house stairs only to have the waiter tell me that the place was closing. "Strange," I thought to myself, "Generally the place doesn't close until two or three in the morning." I sat down on a nearby flight of steps wondering where the hell I was going to sleep that night. A cop passed by - "Well why not?" I thought, "I'll ask him. Sir, sir," I said skipping up beside him, "I don't have any place to sleep for the night, could you tell me where I can go?"

"Sure," he said smiling, "I'm walking up to Station 10. Come along with me, you can sleep there overnight in one of the cells."

I signed a registration book in the cop shop just like I was entering a hotel, then one of the cops escorted me over to the cell block. "You're lucky," he said, "We have only one empty cell left." No bed, not even a bench, just a concrete floor to sleep on, but the concrete could have been razor blades and I still wouldn't have had any problems dozing off (I was that tired) using my corderoy cap as a pillow.

"O.K." boomed a voice six o'clock the next morning. "Levez-vous, levez-vous, mes vieux - it's time to go - allez."

After a breakfast at Kiery's Restaurant (the old man knows I always pay my debts) I walked over to the At-water Library intending to pass away the morning browsing through the magazines however the old maid librarian caught me sneaking a smoke and threw me out. "Gotta be some place this poor boy can go to," I thought as I walked aimlessly along Tupper Street. "Maybe old Joe Coté's down at the Empire Tavern. Maybe he still has a few dollars left over from his old-age pension cheque to lend me."

But before heading down to the bar, I decided to make a detour up to the Prag just in case someone I knew had come in for an afternoon coffee. Daniel the waiter was sweeping the front steps of the coffee house as I walked up to the entrance. I nodded, we didn't know each other too well, just enough to crack the odd joke together now and then.

"Anybody inside?" I asked.

He answered me with a long slow nod, barely lifting his head. Daniel never was a jovial type person but that morning he looked down right miserable.

"Something bugging you Daniel?" I asked while leaning on the steel railing above the steps he was sweeping. "It can't be all that bad."

"It's that bad," he said in a surly voice suggesting that I should mind my own business."

"Yeah, I guess it is," I said moving away.

"Hey Fennario attendez un instant," he cried suddenly coming up the stairs after me.

"Yeah?" I said turning my face towards him.

Moving over to me he said, "You're a good friend of Jean Yves', eh?"

"Yeah."

"Well Jean Yves was busted in the Prag last night."

"For what?" I said frowning realizing then why the Prag had closed down so early the night before.

"For carrying dope."

"What kind of dope?"

"Junk."

"And where the fuck did that dumb kid get junk?" I said my voice stiff with both tears and anger.

Daniel seemed rather surprised at how moved I was by the bad news he had to tell about Jean Yves, not realizing how fond I was of the boy.

"Ah you know Jean Yves," he said, "always trying to be a bad boy, a tough guy. Well he knows I'm pushing and he kept pestering me for some junk so finally I gave him a little. Last night he was showing the stuff to some friends in the Prag and a plain-clothes Narc busted him."

I stood pondering over the bad news and Daniel continued.

"I've got a couple of thousand dollars worth of dope in my apartment but I'm afraid to go home."

"How come?" I asked.

"The cops are watching me. Jean Yves must have told the cops where he got the junk," he said.

"Naw, not Jean Yves," I said, "He's too smart."

Taking his apartment keys out of his pocket and handing them to me, Daniel said, "I can't go home. If the cops find my stash I'm good for seven years up the river. It's all yours if you want it. Do me this favour and the dope's all yours."

I took the keys. Daniel wrote his address down on a slip of paper, a house on Seymour Street.

"Big favour! " I thought to myself as I walked away. I never pushed dope, let alone junk, but I decided I'd do Daniel this favour in the hopes that Jean Yves wouldn't get any more entangled in the affair than he already was.

The closer I drew towards Seymour Street the more paranoid I got; the streets seemed to be festering with under-cover Narcotics agents disguised as office-workers. People who just a short time before looked like harmless tourists now appeared to be following me fingering their cameras in anticipation.

Daniel's apartment door was ajar as I walked into the foyer; a cleaning woman appeared to be making his bed and dusting the furniture. My legs said go, but my brain said hold it. I'd gone this far, so I'd might as well go a little further. I walked into the apartment after rapping lightly on the door.

"Hello"

"Allo?"

"I'm a friend of Daniel's," I said showing her his keys, "I've come to pick up something for him.

"Oh, c'est bon," she said smiling, "Go ahead."

The first drawer I opened had about one hundred and fifty plastic tabs of speed rolling around in it. I scooped them into my pocket. Two cabinets and one dresser later I walked out of the room with a half a pound of hash, a two by three inch plastic container filled with a white powder (presumably junk) plus the hundred odd tabs of speed. As soon as I stepped out on the gallery I threw the powdery contents of the plastic cup into the garden, dropping the container itself down a sewer; then I slunk along the side street deep in paranoia casting furtive glances up each alley way while heading in the general direction of the Empire Tavern. The idea of going back behind bars had me sweating with fear, quaking in my cowboy boots every time a patrol car passed by.

The tension became unbearable. "Fuck it," I said suddenly out loud as I pulled the dope out of my jeans. I hesitated, deliberated a few seconds while holding the stuff in my hand then with a nervous jerk of my shoulders I tossed the speed and hash as far as I could up the middle of a lane way. "Nothing is worth that much torment," I thought to myself giving way to spasmodic sighs of relief as I walked west along Dorchester Boulevard.

As I think over my past situation today I realize how easily I could have been busted on Seymour Street. Think of it. With a good lawyer I might have got off with five to seven years; that means with good behaviour. I would have been back out on the street sometime in 1970. I would not have met Elizabeth, I wouldn't be a socialist nor would I be going to school with ambitions of becoming a teacher. Just another messed up young ex-con hanging around the John Howard hoping to latch on to a good score.

Old Joe Coté was sitting at his favourite corner table when I walked into the Bar. "Hey Dave," he cried or rather wheezed, "where ya been Dave? -cawlis-I saw Mike the other day and he says you were in Toronto."

"Yeah I was in Toronto alright," I said taking one of the cigarettes he offered, "inside the Don Jail."

Joe paid for the round of beer and told me he could put me up for a couple of days in his furnished room. "The janitor's o.k.," he told me.

"Yeah but Joe," I replied, "you ain't a millionaire, you need your money."

"Ferme ta bouche! " Joe said holding up an admonishing finger, "I have the money."

"From your cheque?" I asked.

"Non, non," I won ten bucks from Porkchops on a bet on the Stanley Cup game and he paid me today."

Joe's one of the oldest and best known rounders on the Montreal scene. 78 years old, a veteran of two world wars and there's hardly been a day in the last fifty years that he couldn't be found sitting in the Empire Tavern having a glass of beer.

As usual people coming into the Bar all came over to say hello to Joe as we sat drinking, talking about the guys we knew in common. One fellow in particular came over and sat down with us after ordering a round of beer for Joe and myself. A middle-aged man, balding, stocky with limpid blue eyes that had a strange, childish quality about them. The eyes of a five-year-old child in the head of a forty-year-old truck driver.

"David," Joe said in introduction, "this here is Alex Macgregor." A slight nod, hello and then into conversation. The name rang a bell in my mind but it wasn't until Alex mentioned that he had grown up away out on the Western tip of Montreal Island that everything fell into place.

"Alex," I said suddenly joining into the two-sided conversation, leaning over towards him as I spoke.

"What! " He replied sounding rather irritated at my behaviour. Obviously he thought of me as just another wild young kid destined to spend the rest of his short life walking in and out of jails.

With a wide grin on my face I said, "What I'm going to say right now is bound to shock you Alex."

"No kidding," he replied with a bored partially hostile look on his face.

"You grew up in Ste. Anne de Bellevue. Right?"
"Yeah."

"You had an older brother, a big man well over six foot, called Gege Macgregor right?"

"Yeah! " he said, a confused look, almost a blush passing over his face.

"And he was killed by a sniper in the Second World War, right?"

"Yeah, that's right," he said squinting his eyes, giving me a puzzled stare, "Who are you?"

"Me? I'm Peggy Kerr's son," I said laughing.

"Peggy Kerr's son! " he said emphatically his baby eyes as big as saucers, "I can't believe it. Peggy Kerr's son!!"He extended his hand to me for the first time. "I grew up with your mother, you know that, eh?"

"Sure," I said, "I've been hearing stories about you and your family all of my life."

"Ah your mother was a beautiful woman when she was young David, and very proud," he said musingly.

We spoke for sometime about my family, Alex telling me he thought I should go back home.

"Well, in time Alex," I answered, "in time. I have no quarrel with my family, only with the world. Do you understand me?"

"Yeah, maybe I do at that," he said giving me a warm smile as he pulled a glass of beer on the table over towards himself.

"Look David," he said after glancing at his watch, "I've got to go meet my girlfriend uptown in a few minutes but I'll be back in a couple of hours to pick you up alright? You can stay at my apartment for the night, that is, if you don't mind sleeping on the kitchen floor since I'll be in the bedroom with my girl."

"O.K." I nodded.

"It's just a little place I have," he continued, "since I've been driving trailer diesels across Canada the last couple of years doing most of my sleeping in the cab itself."

"Sure thing Alex," I said, "see you later."

He was back by eleven o'clock taking me up to where he lived in a taxi, stopping off on the way for an all-dressed pizza.

At his apartment I took the time to give Karen Chevarie a ring; her mother answered to tell me that Karen wasn't home but if I called so-and-so she'd probably be there.

I wasn't even sure if Karen remembered me for it was late July and I hadn't seen her since early March. "Surely," I thought, "such a beautiful girl must have found another man by now but I'll ring her up anyhow."

A strange female voice came over the line, there was a lot of background noise, music, voices, laughter, obviously a big party was happening. "Hello?" I said. "Is Karen there?" "Who?" Karen Chevarie." She laughed and said, "I don't know - there're so many people here. What does she look like?" "A beautiful girl," I replied, "with coal black hair and the eyes of a witch." She giggled and said, "Oh yes . . . I know who you mean . . . one minute please." A minute's silence on the line and then a soft, questioning voice said, "Hello?" "Hi Karen, it's Dave." "Dave Fennario?" "Yeah Karen, it's me, how have you been?" "Oh David," she said, "I've missed you so." Once she spoke to me in loving terms I realized how broken I would have felt if she had proved to be indifferent. I was too full of joy to do anything but stutter a few loving words to her in reply. "I'm going uptown tomorrow," she said, "can I meet you somewhere?" "I'll meet you in the CN Station at any time you want." I said. "Then I'll meet you at one o'clock.

Alex and his woman were still asleep when I got up the next morning, washing myself, looking in the mirror thinking, "Jesus I don't know if Karen will even recognize me, I look so bad." My hair all cropped off, short and bristly, my gums bleeding with pyorrhoea, my skin a dirty yellowish colour thanks to the Don Jail. Yes, I in no way resembled the charming gypsy boy Karen was so much in love with half-a-year ago and naturally I was worried about what reaction she would have to my pitiful appearance.

I arrived at the C.N. Station about ten minutes to one. I scurried through the corridors. "She won't be there," I thought, ' and if she is, she won't want to see me again when she sees how broken up I am." I walked into the station looking this way and that and straight ahead of me was Karen sitting on a bench and obviously very happy to see me, broken or not.

January 28, 1971   Thursday

Well, Sally Nelson has given me the word that she thinks I am a gifted writer. There's a story behind this.

Sally spent her Monday afternoon class more or less informing us that we were all a bunch of lazy clots and that the top mark in the class was a generous B minus. Only three people made it into the eighties and there was a large percentage of incompletes. Of course while she was talking everyone in the class was speculating as to who were the lucky three that rated a B minus. Since I had faithfully attended 95 per cent of Sally's classes and done all the work I figured my chances of an 80 per cent were fairly good.

When the class ended, a mob of people, including myself, moved up to her desk to find out our marks. Three people were ahead of me and then it came to my turn. "What's your name again?" she said. "Fennario," I replied while scanning the class marking sheet she had on her desk, "There it is. Incomplete," Sally said looking up at me. "Incomplete? I don't understand!" I exclaimed, still leaning over the sheet, stabbing it with my finger."

141

"Well," she said with a sigh. "I have one mark for you, a B for an essay you handed in a few months ago. But nothing else." "Yeah but I did all the work and handed it into you," I said tensely, "My journal and an essay on King Lear besides the essay you've already corrected. Something's wrong!" I felt hurt by Sally's coldness towards me. I had expected my journal would make some kind of impression upon her, but no, she couldn't even remember my name. Sally again slowly turned her face towards me and said, "Well, I do have some papers upstairs in my office with no names on them, perhaps some of them are yours." 'There's my journal," I said, "It's my year's project, all neatly printed out by hand and there's my essay on King Lear." My words brought a new light into Sally's eyes, a puzzled frown melted away into a shy smile as she said, "Are you the one who wrote about the West End?" I shrugged my shoulders, "Yeah." She slapped her hands together, "Why, it's fantastic David," she said, "I don't know what to say, it's unbelievable. And all this time the journal's been in my office without my having the slightest clue as to who was the genius who wrote it." Then turning to the people who were standing around, she said, "I wish you could read it." I stood flustered and quaking before this most unexpected storm of praise. "You qualify as a professional writer," continued Sally. "Well," I said, rubbing my nose, "Give me a B minus." I then made an awkward exit while the class was still laughing at what I said.

Coming home I phoned my mother and told her of my triumph, "Just call me Genius, Ma," I said. "Well, if you're so smart," she said, "how come you forgot to put your name on the papers?" I thought that one over a bit and then replied, "Guess I didn't want her to know who I was."

•

January 30, 1971   Saturday

Yes, and I had a good time with the kids on Tuesday afternoon. The five Free School drop-out kids that I've been hired to teach creative writing to, once a week for two hours. I started last week and this week they

142

applauded me as I walked into class. For two hours I sat
on a stool telling the kids stories of my travelling days,
ending with a couple of Don Jail episodes. Suddenly realizing that I hadn't heard a peep out of the kids for a long
time I said, "Um, these stories aren't so funny - maybe
you'd like to hear something else?" "No, No!" they
chorused, "Go on, go on." "I've got a history class at
Dawson at three-thirty, but I'll see you guys next week.
O.K.?" Yeah, I really make it.

<u>January 31, 1971</u>   <u>Sunday</u>

     Friday was very hectic, with nothing done, wander-
ing about Selby Campus with a troubled mind all that
afternoon. That's the way it goes, up and down, brilliant
one day and tongue-tied the next. I've seen it all before,
I've talked about it and I'm getting older. The world is
still outside of me, walls and clocks, stairs and hallways.
No, I've never asked myself why I was alive, or if I did,
it was so long ago that I can't remember now.
     The audience is not yet conscious that they are a
part of the movie they're watching.
     I went uptown after school, walking around for a
couple of hours; and on the way home, stepping out of
the C.P. Station onto St. Antoine Street near the Empire
Tavern, I thought to myself, "Guess I'll go in and check
on old Joe Coté." Bill Howe was standing just in front of
the door when I entered, a blunt, fat and round red-faced
man, drunk on a pay-day evening at the tavern. A fifty
year old adolescent who's been working as a clerk in the
C.P.R. for the last twenty-five years. I first made his
acquaintance eight years ago when I was working in the
Passenger and Freights Department.
     "Say, Bill," I said, "how ya doing? Have you seen
old Joe Coté around?" "Nope. Come and join us," he
said pointing to his table. I double-checked the tavern
for Joe, then I walked back to where Bill was sitting with
the boys, about a half-dozen of them and most of them
the same age as myself. We were introduced, shaking
hands all around. Yeah and it was a refreshing change to

be sitting down rapping with ordinary working stiffs after
five months of Academia. We spoke about girls, hockey,
jobs and pollution. "Well things gotta get better," I
said in conclusion, "because they can't get much worse."
"We'll drink to that," they chorused. And then one of the
guys said, "The company my partner and I work for went
bankrupt today and that's why we're celebrating." "Why,
what's the name of your firm?" I asked. "National Sweat-
shop," they said. "That's what we call it anyhow."

I had three draught beers with them and then I split
home down St. Antoine Street singing to myself. Poor Liz
was at home very sick with the flu and groggy from all
the codeine cough syrup she's been guzzling lately. "Charly
phoned," she wheezed, "and he wants you to phone back."

"Come on over, Charly," I said, "I've got a bottle of
Old Niagra you and Sharon can help us polish off."

February 1, 1971   Monday

Sunday afternoon, down to my mother's. She was
sitting alone by the living room window, sick and depressed. The old man was downstairs in the basement watching
the lunar-flight rocket blast off. "I hope he goes to the
moon with them" my mother said, laughing at her own
words in spite of herself.

The lights were off in the room. I sat on the sofa
opposite my mother, with Sarah curled up in my lap, listening to her troubles with the old man.

"Well, Ma," I said lightly, "maybe you should have
married Walter O'Neil." I half expected she would laugh,
but instead she replied, "Well, I used to have a lot of
fights with Walter, but still, it probably would have been
a happier marriage."

"Was Dad always this way, Ma?" I asked.

"No," she replied, "No, when we were first married
he couldn't do enough for me, but he came back from
the war a different man. Very bitter and cold, fed up
with everything. He was not the same man I loved and
married. That's why I'm afraid about Jimmy going in
the army." She paused and cried a bit, "You're selfish

144

David and don't try to deny it. You'll do anything to get what you want, regardless of people. But Jimmy's more giving, more warm and I'm afraid the army might kill the love in him."

"He'll do alright, Ma," I said. "Don't worry."

"I've been searching for love all my life," concluded my mother. "I never knew my own mother. I was taken out of school in grade two to take care of my step-mother's children. I brought them up and then I brought you kids up and now I'm bringing up Virginia's kid."

The key to most of my nightmares can probably be found in what my mother had to say to me yesterday afternoon.

February 3, 1971   Wednesday

Yes, Mr. Cord my science teacher was right when he told us in his grade nine class that if we could know what we'd be doing ten years from that time we'd all be very surprised. I'm surprised. I bet he is too. "Fennario," he said one time, "You'll never amount to a hill of beans," And that was way back in the early sixties, in the days of John F. Kennedy and the "New Frontier", the apex of American capitalism's Golden Age.

"It's tough out there! " Mr. Cord would say, "It's the Survival of the Fittest. Most of you will fall by the wayside and only a few of you will make It."

All of us were worried about making it, although most of us weren't too sure about what making It meant. All very puzzling indeed and then John F. Kennedy was killed. We were having our November exams and the teacher got up from his desk during the test and wrote on the blackboard, "John F. Kennedy has been murdered." I felt like a sudden strong wind had blown up from nowhere, I felt like I did as a kid when we used to go around the night time alley ways of East Verdun busting windows for the hell of it. The same feeling. Something had been broken and I was scared and glad all at the same time.

The room broke out in loud vibrations - is it going to happen now? "Quiet," the teacher said, "the examination isn't over yet. Get back to your seats." We obeyed and returned to our places, but none of us would ever look at the world the same way again because now the secret was out and we knew our teachers were lying.

We chalked up another lie two years later when Watts burnt down. The teachers had told us that slums were a dying social phenomenon, almost non-existent thanks to good old Home on the Range Roosevelt with the shiny teeth and now all of a sudden we were being informed that one out of every three people were poor and wasn't that a disgrace said Life Magazine with colour photos. "Absolutely astonishing," said many prominent sociologists, "We never would have guessed that there was poverty in our affluent middle class society."

Liars, liars caught in their lies, the ashes of Watts, blowing in their faces.

"The Eve of Destruction" was the number one song on the hit parade when I graduated in 1965 into the labour market, still following the road to making It that so many people were falling away from as Mr. Cord had predicted. Only they weren't falling behind or being pushed off the road, they were leaving voluntarily in droves and after three months in a shoe factory I grew my hair and joined them.

The sudden wind that blew up in 1963 came back permanently after Watts and grew stronger every year. We found a word for the feeling we had buried in us all our lives, a feeling we inherited, it was called Revolution. And we would never be silent again.

February 5, 1971   Friday

The flu that's been getting everyone lately, finally got to me this morning. Weak, watery eyes, right side of the brain paralysed. A cough that just won't cough up, a tender, heaving rib cage, bones feeling like all the marrow had been sucked out of them and I'm busted, disgusted, sitting in Dawson's library writing this in company with

146

Sharon O'Day who is reading my edited journal for the
first time.

This is my first attempt at concentrated work while
at school; formerly I have found it impossible to study here
because of the many distractions. There's one walking by
right now, a brown-skinned girl - yeah swing it honey.

Nothing special so far happening this week. Charly
lent me twenty-seven dollars to buy books with. My hair
is getting long, longer than I've worn it in years, down to
the shoulders, a cascade of split-ends whirling about my
ears. Goddamn this bad cough of mine.

"You've really got control over words," said Sharon
suddenly, her right hand curling up into a fist, "I can feel
it."

"Well," I said, smiling, "the few words I do know I
have pretty good control over."

"I'm REALLY surprised," she said, looking up at
me again, "You could have this published right now you
know?"

"Yeah well that's what my teacher says too," I replied, "but it's not serious."

"Yes, I'm really surprised," she exclaimed while
handing me back the journal.

Ah Sharon now you've made me self-conscious, thick
and heavy with words. The head is beginning to swell
again, but I guess I am good because Sharon is very careful about complimenting people. But if I were to publish
the goddamn thing, what would I call it?

I wanted to write more about my high school science
teacher, Mr. Cord, a very complex individual. A short
powerful man, pigeon-chested with an impressive head, a
classic face, regular and handsome. A bachelor in his early
forties when I knew him although I heard he got married a
couple of years later. He was vain, very careful about how
he looked. We could always tell when he was going to a
girl's class for he combed his hair before leaving the
room.

I was the only boy he had ever strapped, at least
that's what he told me. It was just another one of those
days when I hadn't done my homework. "I'm going to
teach you boy," he said with a red face, "the only way

147

you'll understand. Go down to the office and wait for me outside." "Right now?" "Yes right now! " he said scowling, "I don't intend to interrupt this class just for you."

Fifteen minutes I waited in the hallway outside the principal's office. A passing teacher stopped and asked me what I was doing out of class. "Waiting for Mr. Cord," I said. "Why?" he exclaimed. "Well, I'm not sure," I replied, "but I think he's going to strap me." The teacher mumbled something like son-of-a-bitch and continued on down the hall. Then I heard Mr. Cord's heavy   hard track shoes echoing down the corridor. He turned the corner, a thick bantam cock with diamond-hard-blue eyes, not an ounce of mercy in his face. "Follow me," he said holding open the main door, and leading me down a short passage which ended in another door that opened into a small office. "Wait here a minute," he said closing the door leaving me to myself. I sucked in a deep breath and looked around me. It was a bright April day with the sunshine lighting up the room like a 200 watt bulb. "Will it hurt much?" I wondered, but I knew I wouldn't cry, not for Cord. I wouldn't follow him back to the class room with red eyes.

He returned with a green book the size of a large office ledger under his arm carrying the foot-long, one-half-inch-thick leather strap folded up in his right hand. Other guys had told me of the ritual. The book had to be signed. "Do you have a pen?" he asked. No, I nodded. He gave me one opening the book on the table to the page I was to sign. There were hundreds of names in the book; how old it was I do not know. A guy had once told me that if I refused to sign the book, the teacher couldn't strap me. Not wishing to directly confront Cord but not willing to go to the slaughter too mildly, I said as I leaned over the book with the pen, "Sure is a lot of names in here, you know someone once told me that if I refused to sign this book, I couldn't be strapped." "Sign it! " he bellowed. "Alright don't worry," I said quickly, "I'm signing. That's just what I heard that's all." I stepped back and Cord taking the strap out of his pocket, said, "Well David you're the first boy I've ever strapped in all of my years of teaching. I'm giving you eight wacks on each hand this time and sixteen the next. And if you persist after that in mooning about, dreaming, I'm telling you boy, I'll have you expelled. Hold out your hand. Straighten your arm. Straight, I said! " He grabbed me by the elbow and locked my arm in a parallel to my shoulder. Then he backed up about five feet behind me and let fly with the first wack. "Now the other hand," he said after the first eight wacks. It hurt much more than I expected, the palms of my hands were blistered red, black-bruised in spots and stinging. His anger appears to have softened with the first eight blows because my left hand, the second hand was less abused.

I was looking at my hands when he approached me, he was obviously intending to say something but the dead pan expression on my face appears to have intimidated him. He blushed and turned his back on me. "That's all?" I said. He said nothing, nor did he move. I hesitated a few seconds. Should I leave before him or let him go first? Still no sign from him so I moved towards the door but my hands were too swollen to manage the door knob. I turned around, Cord was looking at me so I held up my hands in a comic gesture to explain the situation. A weak smile passed over his face, "O.K." he said softly. He walked behind me back down the hall to the class room and it was more than a week before he looked me in the face again.

February 6, 1971   Saturday

A month or so later Mr. Cord decided it was about time for me to have a second strapping. Obviously I hadn't learned my lesson yet, because my homework wasn't being handed in. "You'll never learn, will you Fennario," he said spitting out my last name in disgust. I stood by his desk stammering with excuses. "Go down to the office and wait for me." I hesitated. "Go! " he snarled, eyes narrowing, finger pointing to the door. Although not in the least disturbed by the idea of having swollen hands again for a few hours, this time I felt scared and nervous, very much shaken by my memories of the anguish both of us had gone through the last time.

149

The second strapping I felt would be an even more tense scene and one in which I wasn't sure I could control my emotions. I wasn't sure whether I'd succumb in tearful apologies or attack him in a fit of rage.

Standing in the hallway, thoughts flashing through my brain, images, memories, ideas at the speed of light. The sound of Cord's heavy footsteps coming down the corridor. Even before I saw his face I sensed that I wasn't going to be strapped just by the way he was walking. His face was red, his manner nervous and flustered, uncertain of himself as he turned the corner and moved over to where I was standing. Without looking at me he said almost as if he were talking to himself, "I don't want to have to go through with this again. It's horrible." "Mr. Cord," I said, "I know exactly how you feel. It's all so stupid. I'm not saying this because I'm afraid of being strapped, but you know what I mean. I promise you that from now on I'll have all my work done. It's not worth all this and I should have realized that before."

Between the office and the classroom we walked together talking like brothers, going to the root of things as only people under stress can do. At the classroom door we automatically reverted back to our old roles. The strange, spontaneous intimacy we had with each other that afternoon was never resumed and of course never spoken of in the months that followed. But something that wasn't in William Cord or David Fennario before that day had been added. Each of us had grown a little.

Got myself a little drunk and mellow Friday night on Normandy wine, sitting in the living room waxing poetic with poor Liz as a captive audience. Talking about my writing. "I like reading your stuff," said Liz, " 'cause it's easy and enjoyable - just like comic books."

She told me a story about when she was three-years-old and living with her family in a rooming house on Dorchester Boulevard, just opposite the Purity Ice Cream factory.

"My mother was putting me to bed one night and asked me if I wanted her to pull the blinds. 'No,' I said, 'I want to see the Purity Ice Cream sign.'" "Oh Liz," I said, hugging my knees, laughing, "You're a real country girl."

"Well, you know," she said, "I was only a baby and the sign had very pretty colours, red, green and blue, used to shine right in through the window and I liked to look at it before I fell asleep. My family still bugs me about it, always asking me if I remember the Purity Ice Cream sign."

Talking about Pat and Mary. "Well I phoned Pat the other day," I said, "and he sounded pissed off at me, so I guess we're still friends."

February 7, 1971   Sunday

The back of a coal miner and the hands of a poet. Sleeves rolled up, cigarette dangling out of my mouth, house painter's son on a Sunday winter's morning. "Ain't no use in talking to me, it's the same as talking to you." A voice that's but a warm reflexion of a hundred million working men on this continent whose very lives are today pregnant with revolution and poetry.

Down at my mother's this evening for supper. She's sitting at the dinner table with little Jean on her lap and Liz says, "Mrs. Fennario, that's the story of your life, eh?" My mother sighed and said, "Yes, don't send me flowers when I die Elizabeth, just put a diaper in my hand." I laughed and took out my pen and notebook, "Hey that's good Ma, I'm gonna put it down in my journal." Placing Jean on the floor my mother turned and said, "You're writing that journal David, but it would be nothing to mine if I was to write one."

After supper I played train with little Sarah and Jean, all the kitchen chairs lined up in a row with Sarah as the engineer. "All aboard-chug-chug get your tickets ready fer Toronto." "David stop playing with the kids," yelled my mother down the hallway, "and help the girls with the dishes."

Afterwards sitting around the kitchen table with the family telling them stories about my hitch-hiking trip down in the Southland back in 1963. "Never told you about the time I was nearly lynched down in Daytona Beach, Florida, did I Ma? Ah," I said, wagging my fore-

151

finger, "there's a lot of stories I never told you. Do you
want to hear this one?" "I want to hear it," said Virginia.
"Me too," said Sarah.

"Well you know," I began, "down there in the south
it's all segregation - black and white. The restaurants are
segregated and so are the beaches. 1963 if you'll remember
was quite a political year, involving civil rights and so on.
Remember they had that first big march on Washington?
John F. Kennedy was still in the White House. People
were demonstrating all over the Southland in those days
and they had one in Daytona Beach while I was there.
Coloured people all marching single file, hundred or so
of them holding signs, "All men are equal" and stuff like
that, walking up and down the boardwalk. A great mob
of Southern white boys were all standing around jeering
them, waving Dixie flags, yelling niggers and spitting,
going right strange. There was a carnival in town and all
the roughnecks who worked in the carny were down there
on the boardwalk, you know real bad actors with scars
and tattoes carrying knives and chains. There was about
forty or so cops stopping the white boys from doing
anything. I sympathized with the demonstrators and
wanted to show them some support but I was too afraid
of the mob. Then a middle-aged bald-headed man, an ordinary looking American tourist stepped in behind the
black people in their demonstration giving the southern
boys a defiant look as he did so. I felt ashamed of myself,
I figured hell, if he's got the guts to do it so do I and I
stepped in right beside him. "Good boy," he said slapping
me on the back. The white boys went crazy at the sight
of us joining the demonstration and the cops had to
bust up the mob and cart us away for our own protection.
The tourist they escorted back to the motel, but I was
given different treatment. You see the cops are about as
prejudiced as the mob and when they found out I was a
drifter sleeping on the beach they laid a beating on me
and then drove me out to the city limits telling me that
the next time they'd let the mob get me, lousy nigger lover
that I was. And that's how I left Daytona Beach."

They chewed that story over for awhile and I began
another one after my father placed a pint of beer in front

of me. "Another incident of a similar category happened to me on the same trip, but it's a funnier story to tell. I was hitch-hiking through Georgia and some dusty old cotton farmer in a battered up old Chevy pick-up truck dropped me off in a little honky-tonk town, the kind you see in the movies. Hot, sleepy, bugs and mosquitoes all over the place. A great place for a lynching scene. I was hungry and thirsty, in bad need of a cold soft-drink so I walked over to the nearest restaurant along side of the highway. But the waitress inside of the place didn't like the looks of me; you know I was kind of dusty and carrying a knapsack. 'You're not getting nothing in here boy,' she said, 'Why don't you go across the street?' All the truck drivers sitting at her counter broke out laughing as if what she said was something really funny. Well to hell with them I thought to myself, if my money's no good here, I'll go some place else. And I walked across the highway to the other restaurant. There was all black people inside sitting at the tables and they kind of looked up when I walked in. Not friendly looks either, mean looks like as if to say, 'Watch what you do in here man.' I sat down at the counter, slipped the knapsack off my shoulders and picked up the menu, all the time feeling pretty nervous 'cause of all those hard eyes burning me in the back. The black waitress was down at the other end of the counter talking with a girlfriend. I waited about ten minutes, tapping my fingers, waving the menu like a fan in front of my face. The waitress wasn't doing anything, just talking so finally I got pissed off. 'Hey!' I said. No response. 'Hey!' I said again knocking on the counter. She snapped her head round in my direction and said sharply. 'What are you doing in here, white boy. This isn't your place.' 'What do you mean what I am doing in here?' I said. 'I want a hamburger and a coke-a-Cola that's what I am doing in here. The other restaurant wouldn't serve me,' I said. 'Who do you have to be to get something to eat in this goddamn town.' The girl gave me a puzzled look for a second, than she chuckled a bit and said, 'Where you from boy?' 'Canada,' I said, 'Do I get a hamburger?' 'Give the boy a hamburger,' said somebody in the back and everyone was friendly after that. People came over and talked with me."

"What did they talk to you about?" asked Virginia.

"Well," I said, polishing off the beer in front of me, "they asked me questions. Questions about Canada, my family, where I was going and why. They wished me good luck on my trip. One guy even gave me a lift up the highway to a spot where there was more traffic. Ya see ya gotta understand when I walked into that place they must have figured I was there to insult them or something. But when they realized I walked in there in all innocence with no conceptions of black or white prejudice, they all just had a good laugh, treating me like I was somebody who had just fallen off the moon."

February 9, 1971   Tuesday

Yeah and on Monday afternoon I'm sitting in the library, a cigarette in my mouth and no matches in my pocket. I see a guy sitting a few tables away rolling some cigarettes so I get up and go over to him, up to his table recognizing him from close up as one of the hot shot student radicals on the campus, one of these guys actively going around in circles. "Ya got a match?" I said leaning over him. "Yes, sure," he replied grinning up at me. I'm lighting up the cigarette when he says, in the manner of a prominent social scientist questioning the common denominator, "What do you think of education?" I took a deep drag on my cigarette to prevent my lip from curling in anger and replied, "It's to train people for the industries." "Good, good," he said returning his attention to his book. The guy was just too much for me, so with a grand flourish I stepped back and said, "Well thank you. You learn something every day!" Well we all got our troubles.

Eight fingers and two thumbs, just try digesting a sandwich with your mind or having a transcendental shit.

154

February 11, 1971   Thursday

As for me I feel as if I am about to fade away, just
say good-bye and I'm leaving. There are poems I still
have to write if only I could unbend my twisted mind
and guess if there is some animal in this world called
happiness. What do you think? Well I think people who
are naive enough to believe that demonstrations can stop
super highways would be foolish enough to demonstrate
against a thunderstorm. What do you believe? What my
eight fingers and two thumbs tell me. I believe in atoms,
molecules, in the flesh.

February 12, 1971   Friday

Emile had a good story to tell me in French class
this morning while Madame Sonac was fixing up the projector. Actually we were trading stories and Emile came
up with a surprise winner about a drunken car accident
he had last year. I started the ball rolling talking about
Dawson's proposed Beer Bash coming up in two weeks.
"Ah, yes, Emile," I said, "you're only a baby but I can
remember the golden days of the ten-cent draughts when
a man with two bucks could fill up a table and get his
friends all gorgeously drunk." "Well, how old are you?"
he asked. "Old enough to remember dinosaurs on Ste.
Catherine Street sonny," I replied, squinting like an
octogenerian. He laughed and then said, "Yeah but
they still serve ten-cent beers in the St. Henri taverns."
"True, true," I exclaimed, "but not uptown." "I know
for sure they still serve ten-cent beers in St. Henri,"
Emile continued, "because one night last year I drunk
about a hundred of them and smashed my friend's car
into the back of a parked truck. No licence or I.D.'s on
me either when the cops came. They didn't ask me for
any papers, I was lucky, talked my way out of everything.
It's a good thing I was really drunk and seeing everything
in triplex because if I had only been half-way drunk seeing everything double I wouldn't have known which
cop to talk to. But seeing triple it was easy, I just talked
to the cop in the middle."

All the guys nearby laughing at Emile's story with Madame Sonac, having finally fixed the projector, hissing for silence. The curtain drops.

It rises again three or four hours later showing me sitting on the upstairs lounge floor giving Berny Artuso and Gary Firestone Dear Abby advice on how to deal with the feminine sex. "I don't know why I'm so good-hearted giving you guys all this valuable information free, when if I wrote a pamphlet on the subject I'd make a fortune selling it. Yeah I'm an old battle-scarred veteran of the war between the sexes, boys, and because I'm such a good-natured slob I'm gonna give ya a few tips on how to deal with the Feminine Mystique. Gary you tell me that you just finished spending four frustrating hours arguing with a pretty girl about almost everything under the sun right?" "Right," says Gary, "Oh the pain, the PAIN!" "Yeah well you know I understand that," I said smiling, "but Mother Fennario's gonna let you in on a little secret about women. They're always saying don't touch me but touch me anyhow. You got that? It's as simple as that, it's all a matter of timing - ya know ya gotta know when to be a little gross. The hand on the knee or the quick but sliding pat on the ass, but of course don't be dribbling at the mouth when you make the advance, even if you feel like it. And never, never be blunt or say something stupid like 'I got ten inches. Let's go fuck.' That's N.G. That never works. Joke about it. Be subtle, but give bold hints, tease her. Birds do it, bees do it. It's a very old game, Gary, and keep politics out of it. Back in my free-wheeling days when I was young and greasy I went to bed with Maoists, Trotskyites, Fascists, vegetarians, Christians, Zionists, Woman's Lib and one time almost made it with a Hare Krishna chick so don't let the girl's politics get to you, 'cause the arguments don't count worth a shit in a warm bed, with some good wine bouncing around inside of ya."

Friday night Charly and Sharon were down at our place drinking beer in the living room and by ten o'clock all of us were in the mood for dancing and decided that the Seven Steps would be the best place to do it in.

The joint was packed but not nearly as full as I've seen it in the summer, with crowds standing on the sidewalk waiting to get in. I'm here to testify that the man's can in the Seven Steps is about the size and shape of a fair size broom closet and contains only one throne and two urinals. Gangs of guys were all lined up waiting to piss when I walked in. Nearly everyone was having troubles pissing in the troughs - man but it's just hard to let go when two dozen strangers are packed all around you. Guys were standing in front of the urinals for five minutes and then moving away with glum faces, the whites of their eyes turning yellow. When I got up there, the same thing happened to me. Nothing would come out. "Niagara Falls, Niagara Falls," I kept repeating to myself but not a drop came out. Finally I gave up, zipped up and moved over to the throne where I could piss in privacy. A guy leaning on the throne door, with half-a-dozen other introverted guys behind him, said to me, "Are you next?" "Yeah," I said, "I'm shy too." And everyone had a good laugh.

The next morning, still only half-awake, I'm rapping with Liz in bed and she says, "Do you know David that I saw a ground hog yesterday?" "Where?" I exclaimed, "In the West End?" "Yes." "Ah, it must have been a rat." "No, it was a human ground hog! " I gave her a puzzled stare, then smiled and said, "Oh, you mean the old man across the street who sits on his front steps night and day in the warm weather." "Yes, exactly," she replied, "I saw him peek his head outside the door yesterday so I guess summer will be coming soon."

Saturday night Liz fell asleep on the sofa while I
sat back in the easy chair reading up on Roman history.
Towards ten o'clock I phoned up Robin and we talked
for awhile about Jean Yves and Sharon O'Day.

It was dark and cold outside, bitter death rattling
wind seeping in through the cracks of our old house, whispering old grandfather's tales.

Mike Smyth came down to our house in the wind,
in the night. "I told you I'd be coming over, Dave?"
he said smiling at the front door. "Yeah, but, Mike, on
such a night? Sweet Jesus, that's a hurricane going on
out there," I said lighting up a cigarette. "C'mon, Liz
is asleep. We'll go over to the Dominion Bar and have
ourselves a couple of beers."

Angus was sitting at one of the back tables when
we walked in. Angus Ryan, a noted West End style intellectual, a man about sixty-years-old. "Say, Angus,
what's happening?" "Sit down, sit down," he said
shaking hands with me. "Angus," I said, "This is Mike
Smyth, he's from a real old West End family." "An
aristocrat, eh?" said Angus as he leaned over the table
and shook hands with Mike. "You must have heard of
Neddy Jackson, Angus?" I said. "The Neddy Jackson,
one of the hardest guys to ever come out of the West
End. Well this is his son." "Yeah, I've heard the name,"
replied Angus. "Yeah," I continued, "I keep telling
Mike he ought to wear a sign warning ordinary mortals
of the fact that he's Neddy's son."

The go-go waitress, the blonde girl with the lungs,
brought over three fresh quarts of Labatt's 50, giving
us a dirty look because she only got a quarter tip. As
she bounded away from the table Angus said, "She's
not worried, she's young and strong but just because she's
got a nice ass doesn't make it right for her to treat us
this way. But it's not serious."

A few yards away Dubois the bouncer was playing
pool with a "Bell Boy" buzzer clipped onto his belt.
That's a sure sign that Dubois' involved in some kind of
operation, not that I would be so impolite as to ask
questions. Curiosity in the West End can be very bad for

the health. Hear, see and speak no evil.

I sat back, drank back, listened in on the argument
Angus was having with Mike on semantics, "Why are you
always using the words they, we and them. Why don't
you use the word I. I think this, I think that. Them and
they are your enemies!"

My attention kept drifting between the conversation
going on at our table, the pool game and the go-go waitress.

"What is time?" said Angus dramatically. "Define
time. We're fucked by time. It's absurd, it's a steal to be
cut off with sixty or seventy years. Just when you're beginning to understand the score, your body starts fucking
up on you."

An hour and two quarts later as I sat engrossed in a
surprisingly good French movie showing on the T.V. I
overheard Angus use the word procreate. "Procreate," I
said turning my head back towards them laughing, "Upper
Westmount procreates, the West End fucks," Old Angus
really appreciated that one, almost choking on a mouthful
of beer. "True, true," he gasped as all of us leaned back
laughing in the Dominion, in the night, in the wind.

February 15, 1971   Monday

Sitting with Sharon in the library early this afternoon
and we spoke of the early days on the scene as we lived
it back in the winter of 1965-66. That was a good year
before the media informed us that we were hippies. We
never would have guessed that we constituted a social
phenomenon. We were like weather vanes showing which
way the wind was blowing, finding pathways that other
people were later to follow. The Rolling Stones sang of
our anger, Bob Dylan of the agonies of living in desolation,
and the Beatles warmed up our hearts by telling us it was
gonna be alright.

Yesterday evening my mother told me that Jimmy
wrote home from army camp to let us know that the
food is lousy and the girls are ugly out in Nova Scotia.
"He must be lonely," my mother said, "because he phones
me every week collect. I had to tell him to stop phoning
so often because I can't afford it. But anyhow on Thurs-

day night he kept lingering on the line - not saying much
you know, just not wanting to let go. So finally I had to
say, 'Good-bye, Jimmy, I've got to let you go, be good.'
And he said, 'I have to be good, I can't be anything else
in this place.' "

February 16, 1971   <u>Tuesday</u>

During Sally's class yesterday the people were discussing group therapy and the subject brought to mind
an unorthodox, therapeutic experience I underwent as
a kid in elementary school. Just the memory of it made
me bust out laughing in class causing Sally to give me a
puzzled, worried look of concern since she hadn't said
anything that was meant to be funny. "The boy's cracking up" her face seemed to say; but, no, I was only remembering Bobby Frost and the eraser.
    Bobby Frost was one of those guys, you know, who
end up being sixteen-years-old in grade seven. He wasn't
stupid but he was a terrible bully, a guy everyone was
afraid of, and one week in particular he began picking
on me all the time. Pushing me down flights of stairs,
tripping me up in the school yard, using me as a dummy
for new wrestling holds he was in the process of learning -
the standard bully stuff. Consequently I spent an hour
one dull afternoon writing "Bobby Frost is a fuckin' son
of a bitch" on all sides of a large sponge eraser I had in
my possession. The teacher being out of the class tem-
porarily I turned around and showed the eraser to Gary
Bowden sitting behind me. He looked at it then threw it
over to Bobby shouting, "Hey Bobby catch this." My
poor heart did a somersault just thinking of what Frost
would do to me if he chanced to read what was on the
eraser. It was panic fear that sent me bouncing over to
where he was sitting. "Gimmee that! " I said snatching
the eraser out of his hand stunning the whole class with
my apparent boldness. Bobby tried to grab the eraser
back and I gave him a stiff punch in the chops just as the
teacher walked in. "I saw that David!" said Miss Denison.
"You leave Bobby alone and go right now down to the
principal." I was strapped but it was well worth it for

160

not only did I gain Bobby Frost's respect, I also got a reputation as a hard rock in the school.

As I was writing the above story down, sitting in Dawson's library, Helen came over to say hello. "I'm not growing a beard Helen," I said rubbing my cheeks, "I ran out of razor blades this morning." "I thought you looked different," she said smiling; and then scanning my face with narrowed eyes she exclaimed, "You know David I could never decide who you look like most, Charley Chaplin or Adolf Hitler?" What?

This afternoon I had the Free School drop outs working on a play about the Don Jail. The whole play takes place in cell number seven of corridor six, the plot being a dramatized version of an event that actually occurred to me while I was in the Don. Alister plays me, Flash Fennario, Sandy as Fatmouth Harris, Michael as Tonto, Jany as Mother and Warren as Greasy Rick.

The kids weren't too sure about Mother as a character because they only have the vaguest ideas about queers so when I told Jany to act natural (that is feminine) she said, "But I'll be dressed as a man!"

Oh yeah the real Mother was something else, her real name being Ernest Sutherland, a man in his fifties as queer as a three dollar bill. He was the quartermaster of Corridor 6, meaning that in exchange for cleaning up the tables and bringing the dirty dishes back to the screw he had the priviledge of sleeping in cell number 15 which was much more spacious than any of the other cells, a private suite with only one bed while all the rest of us were sleeping four to a cell the size of a large closet in two bunk beds so close together that I was able to do hand springs on them.

Mother's character was exactly as her nickname would imply, she mothered us. Gave us lectures, wrote letters home for us and to lawyers, listened to our problems and troubles patiently by the hour and on request would entertain us with stories of the good old days when she was a high stepping young filly, "My, boys," she'd say, "What a beautiful wardrobe I used to have in those days. Furs, evening gowns designed in Paris, the whole shot. But I'm too old for that kind of thing now, especially since the booze got to me; but I was a beautiful young girl in my youth."

Most of the quartermasters were middle-aged mothers of the Ernie Sutherland type and all of them had gained through their kindness the respect of even the lowest two-bit punks in the joint. Although we did kid Ernie good-naturedly at times. I remember Fatmouth Harris throwing a wet roll of toilet paper over at Ernie one day saying, "Hey Mother, here's a kotex for ya! " And Ernie picking it up saying, "But that's too small for an old hen like me, sweetheart."

February 17, 1971   Wednesday

D.R.S.O. - Dawson Radical Student Organization, a Maoist fronted movement which has kids handing our communiqués decorated with a shot gun carrying hab-itant, "Power to the Students." Get serious. Bitter, bit-ter words are spoken. Bomb scares. Black Evangeline, beady-eyed Maoists stomping through the hallways, secret desperate would-be martyrs determined to save us all at gunpoint. "I really don't wanna hear from ya." The sad life you're leading is reflected in your politics, in your black and white mentality void of all colour. Everything you have to say sounds like a muffled scream.

A bad day in a sad way with really nothing to write. "Say something brilliant Sharon so I can write it down in my journal."

Why was it such a rotten day? First of all I forgot to bring along my lunch money, then that student radical passing out Maoist literature in the cafeteria saying, "Here, get educated." But mark down inner conflict as the major cause of my misery today.

"Sometimes I wonder if you know you have a home at all David," Liz said to me tonight.

Are you ready? Are you sitting down because here it comes. I don't know any secrets about myself. (Say that in capitals.) I DON'T KNOW ANY SECRETS ABOUT MYSELF. Have I ever mentioned that I still wear the old vest I found abandoned in the closet of a rented room on

Ontario Street back in 1967? That I've used up one and a
half two-ounce bottles of Parker "Super Quink" ink since
I first started writing this journal in December 1969. That
I am now in the habit of drinking coffee for the first time
in my life. That I gave up drinking Coke-a-cola since all
the fillings started falling out of my teeth. That I'm up
to smoking nearly two packs of cigarettes a day and consequently three fingers on my right hand are nicotine
stained. That I weigh one hundred and thirty five pounds
and stand at five feet, ten and a half inches in my bare
feet. That my height is considered tall in the West End but
average size in Westmount. That I was named after my
Uncle David who drowned at the age of twelve in the Mac-
Donald College Swimming Pool. That I have a childish
phobia about stepping on manhole covers, that I sing out
loud to myself whenever I'm walking alone. That I used
to be a high school track-and-field star. That I wrote my
first poem about Robert Scott in the Antarctica at the
age of fourteen sitting in a grade nine geometry class. That
I never passed geometry. That I love brown-eyed girls
and dandelions are my favourite flowers? That it was me
and Terry Holdbrook who set fire to the shed in Willibrord
lane on Firecracker Night back in 1957. That I used to
catch pinheads in the river and that Danny Malone and I
once saw a bull frog as big as a basketball and no one in
East Verdun would believe us. That I couldn't or wouldn't
talk until I was four years old. That my earliest memory
is one of digging holes under a flight of tenement stairs.
That three has been my lucky number ever since I learnt
that the earth is the third planet from the sun. That I
was the only one to ever flunk Fine Arts in my high school.
That I drew smiling faces on the sun until a grade eight
teacher told me it was no longer done. That I wrote down
this long list of unconnected sentences only in order to
complete my writing quota for the day? And good night.

Y.ah, without a parachute, that's going to be the title of my book. Without A Parachute. In memory of Andrew Boyle.

Some kid was reading about the F.L.Q. manifesto in school yesterday as a joke to a group of twenty or more students sitting on the lounge floor stoned on grass and laughing.

Such is vanity, Paul Rose, for this you killed a man. The joke's on you, Paul, the people are laughing, they never asked you to be a martyr.

There're so many would-be martyrs around today, that maybe it's best we make jokes out of them, then perhaps they'd stop taking themselves too seriously. Murdering people and killing themselves for our sakes - what a bad joke, what an ignorant waste. We've had enough martyrs.

Thursday night I called on Patrick and Walli, Walli hugging me at the front door, "Is your ugly old man home, Walli?" I said glancing over her shoulder. Pat peeked his head around the corner. "Oh yeah there he is," I said blowing him a kiss.

Modesty forbids but I'll say it anyhow, I was brilliant that evening, sitting up on the edge of Walli's living room sofa spinning out stories in friendly competition with Patrick, a master bullshitter in his own right.

"You're gonna have to write a book about 63 Craig, Dave," he exclaimed. "You know, one of those monstrous novels like War and Peace with twelve major characters in it."

"Yeah," I replied, "63 Craig, down amongst the pawn shops in the heart of Chinatown. Soya sauce scented breezes up and down the streets on hot summer nights and the moon like a golden brown fortune cooky. Remember I was sleeping in the tool shed on the back gallery using a door on top of two truck tires as a bed?"

"Yeah," said Pat, "it was Eduardo's place before you started crashing there. Man! All the freaks that used to live there. Remember how we used to feed ourselves, shop-lifting, panhandling?"

"How about the Milk and Eggs Route, remember that? Me, Jesus, P.K. and Liberty used to go up to the luxury apartments around the Sherbrooke Street filling up suitcases with the stuff the milkman left in front of the apartment doors early in the morning. Milk, eggs, butter, eggnog, we'd bring it all back and feed the house. Well there was one morning I remember I didn't go with the guys because my intuition told me that the cops were getting wise to our little game. So I'm sitting on the back stairs of 63 Craig waiting for the guys to come home with breakfast when suddenly P.K. and Jesus bust into view running at top speed across the parking lot, the milk bottles in their suitcases clanking like crazy. "The cops are after us," they said as they panted up the backstairs. "They're chasing Liberty down Lagauchetiere Street." It was early Saturday morning. Chinatown was deserted and we could hear Liberty off in the distance-rattle-rattle-rattle, then there was a sudden silence and we knew he was caught. He was out of Bordeaux a month later with all his hair cropped off but still wearing that gold earring in his left ear. All the guys were wearing them around that time and having chicks pierce their ears for them."

"Remember the Welcome Café, a plate of rice and gravy for twenty five cents?"

"Yeah our staple diet, that and the stale loaves of bread we got from Superior Bakery on Clark Street for ten cents. So hard we used to have to massage them with a hammer before they could be eaten. And we couldn't understand why we weren't welcome at the Welcome Café. Four of us would walk in there, ya know, festooned with beads, weighed down with bells and the usual apparatus and call over to the waiter, "Hey, Buddha, one rice and gravy and four forks please." They didn't like us. Those Chinese really had it in for flower children. They said we were bad for the tourist trade and even sent a petition to Mayor Drapeau to get us out of their part of the city. They'd swear at us in Chinese all the time, ding-a-ling, ding-a-ling that's how it sounded.

"And then there was that hungry winter we spent on Coloniale Street, you know the place that was heated by a psychedelic coloured wood stove. We used to go out in convoys down back lanes salvaging wood for fuel and when back fences started getting scarce we resorted to tearing wood out of the walls and chopping up furniture. It was a bitter cold winter and us flower children were pretty well withered before its conclusion. Well one particularly sad and stormy January evening we were all sitting in the kitchen hovering around the hot stove listening to the noises our empty stomachs were making. It was too late and much too cold to try panhandling so Eddy, Kenny, me and Jacky Robinson decided there was nothing left for us to do except knock off Delta Pizza down the street.

"There were about twenty to twenty five people crashing at Coloniale in those days. Most of them were kids from the suburbs, vegetarian acidhead types, sons and daughters of doctors, lawyers and teachers who were pretty useless when it came down to surviving a Montreal winter on the streets. All of us backstreet boys had to do the major portion of hustling and conning required to feed the house and pay the rent. It was simply a case of if we didn't do it no one else would. Our compensation was the reputation we gained on the scene as latter day Robin Hoods, a highly informal community service organization you might say. But anyhow four o'clock in the morning found us outside Delta Pizza, Eddy and Kenny working on the door while Jacky and I stood watch across the street. The door took longer than we expected to crack open and twice we had to take a walk because of passing patrol cars, not to mention the fact that we were all freezing our balls off in the sub-zero weather. I was just about to yell out 'Let's call it quits' when Eddy signalled to us that the door was finally opened. Crash boom, a few expert kicks opened the cigarette machine and we were one hundred and twenty dollars richer than we had been a few minutes before. While we were piling the cigarette packs into a cardboard box Jacky yelled from the refrigerating room

he was messing around in and said, "Hey, guys, there's
enough meat in here to last us until spring." There were
long racks in the cold room with hundreds of pepperoni
sausages hanging from them. A half-hour later the four
of us were sliding large boxes full of meat and cigarettes
over the snow covered sidewalks to the house. We even
hit the front page that time, a puzzled little article in the
paper wanting to know who would rob a hundred and
fifty pounds of pepperoni. We all had heartburn for months."

It's a damn shame there was no tape recorder in
Pat's living room because the stories lose most of their
charm when written down. It was an evening none of us
will forget. Yeah and the boys finished the night whoop-
ing it up in the Pocket Rocket Tavern. Every beer drunk
had a story to go with it and Pat grew more eloquent with
every round.

February 21, 1971   Sunday

I called on Charly Friday night and he was sitting
in the living room with Sharon, just about ready to leave
for a party they had been invited to. Neither of them
wished to go, but both of them felt obligated. "Come
along with us," they said.

It was, as Charly warned me, an academic party
the first one I've actually ever been to. Budding young
social workers arguing politics with future literature professors; McGill M.A. graduates standing about being
brilliant making forced witticisms while sipping the straw-
berry punch the hostess was serving. "So these are the
people who are gonna save the world, eh Charly?"
"Don't wait around for them," he replied.

Us non-intellectuals parked ourselves in the small
front room beside the record player and proceeded to get
pleasantly high. Charly left for a while to mingle with
the intelligentsia leaving me alone to talk with Sharon.
"It's not my life, Sharon," I said referring to a nearby conversation going on about community projects in Point
St. Charles. "I don't wanna sound harsh or superior but I
feel I have the right to criticize these people, just from the

167

way tonight I've heard them patronizing the people in the Point in whose poverty they have a vested interest. Now it seems to me that when they're not talking of building bigger and better slums they're talking of their own personal disillusionment with everything and everybody in general. Big fuckin' deal, I don't wanna hear from them. If they wanna go down whimpering writing about their empty lives, sounding like they lived in a closet all their lives, jacking off to pass the time and then calling it art, that's their business but I don't have to listen."

February 22, 1971   Monday

Poetry was discussed in Sally's class today, iambic pentameter and all those other technical terms I failed to memorize for my high school exams. My mind cringes at the very sound of the word pentameter, it makes what comes so naturally to me sound like it would be too difficult to do.

February 23, 1971   Tuesday

A strange realistic dream last night of a fight with Willi on a flight of tenement stairs. The cause of the fight is vague in my mind but I know Willi was in the wrong; he was cracking up and just happened to decide in his insanity that I was the person he'd most like to kill. His cousin Big Boy, a massive guy well over six foot, stood calmly at the bottom of the stairs while Willi and I battled it out.

I beat Willi, sent him bleeding, rolling down the steps whimpering as he lay crouched up on the sidewalk spitting blood. Big Boy looked up at me. "I didn't want to fight him, Big Boy," I said. "You know Willi. You know me." He helped Willi up from the sidewalk and said, "It was a fair fight and none of my business". They walked off together down the street, Willi sobbing, cursing me, his black face twisted in rage. I sat down on the stairs puzzling over Willi's attack, lighting up a cigarette just as

Danny Gaynor, another one of Willi's cousins came walking slowly up the quiet street. A big heavy dude, a professional boxer.

"Willi send you to me Danny?" I asked as he stepped in front of me. "Yeah, Dave," he said, "he tells me that you laid a heavy beating on him for no reason." "It's not true, Danny," I replied, "I was going home to bed when Willi ran up real crazy like and jumped me on the stairs. Ask   Big Boy he was there." He shrugged his shoulders, "Guess it's alright then. Let's go for a beer."

We passed through a dump yard on the way to the bar, clowning around, climbing over the rubble heaps. Danny squeezed himself into a battered up baby carriage, rolling around, turning the wheels with his hands, laughing. The cops busted us for disturbing the peace and Danny has a warrant out on him for a serious charge. We were booked and placed in the number one station bull pen to await our trial. The usual booze derelicts with red pock-marked faces were sitting around on the steel benches. Three young boys, (the oldest one looked around eight-yeard-old) were sitting in the middle of the floor talking to one another. They had thick Scottish accents. "How long have you been in Canada?" I said to the oldest boy. "A week," he replied looking me slow in the face just like a grown man. (He looked and acted just like myself.) One of the younger boys had a tiny baby cradled in his arms and it was crying. "He's hungry," the kid said, "there's no milk left in the bottle." I was sitting back on the steel bench brooding over the situation when the alarm woke me up and a great blizzard was happening outside the window.

The dream was still haunting me when I walked into Dawson this morning, my hair white with snow. "Ever dream about prisons, Gary?" I asked while sitting with him in the library. Baby carriages, stairs, milk, dump yards, bull pens, black men and blood. Tell me your dreams and I'll know who you are.

Sharon, Nicky and myself sat at a sunshine table in Dawson's library this afternoon during a free period discussing the problems of English speaking Quebecers learning French.

"Well," I said, "I've always followed the policy of speaking English to Montreal cops and French to Toronto cops." Both of them laughed. "Yeah," I continued, "there's a story behind that, something really comical that once happened to me. Sharon do you remember Micky?

"Micky?" A light came into her eyes, a smile, "oh yeah, Micky? And Tress? Do you remember Tress?"

"Sure I knew them both well," I replied. "They escaped from a girl's detention home in T.O., both of them drifting into the 1966 scene here in Montreal where I first met them panhandling outside of the Café Prag."

Sharon smiled and said, "Tress was a very sweet person."

"Yeah, she was," I exclaimed, "but she could be really violent at times, real crazy violent."

"Is that true?" said Sharon. "She never impressed me that way."

"Well I oughta know," I said, "I slept with her. Back when she was thirteen she was put in a detention home for the criminally insane because she killed a girl in a street fight, kicked her head in, killed her on the sidewalk."

"Ugh."

"Yeah it's an ugly story but so is the Cabbage Town district of Toronto that she grew up in. I sat up all night with Tress one time in a tourist rooming house down on Jarvis Street listening to her life story. A part of it, an anecdote she told me, I've never forgotten.

"As I said, Tress was up on manslaughter and placed in a special home for girls, some old stone dungeon type place in Toronto where the inmates are given a long grey smock nearly down to the ankles and army boots to wear. Anyhow Tress told me that the first night she was there she kicked up a shit storm and for punishment they made her scrub a long hallway floor over and over again. So she's down on her hands and knees with the pail and scrub brush when a big ugly bull-dyke guard happened by and asked her roughly who she was. "Cinderella," she said looking up at the woman with that sweet little girl face of hers. And the bull-dyke couldn't help but bust out laughing."

"Beautiful, too much!"

"Yeah I like that story myself, but anyhow I've gotten a little side-tracked it seems, I was gonna tell the story of Serge, Suzanne, Micky and me in Toronto. You see, so like I'm sitting in the Prag with my partner Serge Leblanc over a cold cup of coffee wonderin' where our next meal is gonna come from when Micky comes busting into the joint telling us the story you've just related to us, Sharon, of how the both of you escaped down the backstairs of the Westmount cop shop.

" 'I gotta skip town,' Micky says to me, 'I'd rather die than go back to detention.'

"It's O.K. with Serge and myself, like we're starving in Montreal and we figure maybe we'll starve a little less in T.O. So the same afternoon found the four of us with our thumbs out standing on the 401."

"Four of you?" said Nicky. "Who's the fourth person?"

"Oh yeah," I said, "I forgot to introduce Suzanne, that sweet little thing from Quebec City, a fifteen-year-old runaway who couldn't speak a word of English. She had ambitions of becoming a hippy. It was a good year for runaways, 1966 the year of the Hippy.

"Anyhow to simplify the story let me just say we made it to Yorkville after a lot of the usual hassles with horny truck drivers trying to ball our chicks. Neither Serge nor Suzanne had ever been out of Notre Dame de Quebec, out of the Catholic womb, so Yorkville really freaked them out. The crowds, the games, the Freaks like Forty-Niner and Hungry Smith, heavy predators like the Vagabond bike gang, specializing in stalking down flower children. Junkies, speed freaks, whores, all the rest of Yorkville's paraphernalia, including the ever present undercover narcotics agents. The R.C.M.P. were quite amateurish back in those days and any self-respecting flower child could spot one from a block away. Most of them were big heavy dudes, like football players with overgrown crew cuts wearing very unconvincing beads and sandals. Guys like Spider and Crowbait, the Yorkville Regulars, used to play games with these plainclothes Narcs going around slapping them on the back saying, "Hey, Narc, bust anyone lately?" And the next night the horsemen would have a new agent, just as conspicuous as the one who had been exposed, standing out front of the Grab Bag picking his nose, trying to look hip."

"Another popular game in Yorkville was called Teasing the Tourists. Hordes of them used to cruise through the Village loaded down with cameras bug-eyed at what they were seeing and the guys used to put shows on for them. 'Hey!' we'd yell holding up some stoned-out freak by the collar, 'Ya wanna buy a hippy?'"

"Anyhow so there we were, Micky and me with two Quebecois babes-in-the-woods knocking around Yorkville two o'clock in the morning, mugging time, looking for a place to crash."

Nicky laughed and said, "Fuck! This isn't a story, it's a saga."

"Vikings wouldn't make it in Yorkville Nicky," I replied, "The Vagabonds wouldn't stand for any competition; and please no more interruptions I've got a class in ten minutes and I want to finish this story.

"So where was I? Oh yeah, so finally some kind-hearted dude informed us that maybe, just maybe, there might still be some floor space left in a crash pad down on dirty old St. Charles Street, known fondly to one and all as Cockroach Heaven. We went down there and you know it was the typical Happy Hippy Home trip of wall to wall people, eighteen people (I counted them) in a fair-size room heavy with the pungent odour of dirty socks, sex and grass. The room had a comfortable softwood floor and the four of us soon rolled off into Dreamland only to be rudely awakened early the next afternoon by a detective bellowing 'Alright everybody up and show your I.D.'s.'

"The irony of it all is that the cops had raided the wrong room, mistaking us for the people they really wanted who were living upstairs in Room 34. Our room number was 24.

" 'Goddamn it Sam! ' One of the cops said while checking out the number on the door, 'Number thirty-four is upstairs! '

"They went bouncing upstairs dropping our I.D.'s on the floor in their haste but naturally the occupants of number 34 were missing. Like nearly everyone else in the rooming house they had either escaped down the fire escape or out onto the roof.

"We were sorting out our I.D. cards and laughing when the cops came stomping back down the stairs with woe-begotten looks on their faces. We shouldn't have laughed. That was a mistake; a mistake that cost me thirty days because the sergeant detective had a lousy sense of humour. 'Alright you clowns! Big joke eh?' And motioning to one of the uniformed cops he said, 'Phone the station for a wagon we're taking this circus for a ride.'

"The sergeant detective proved impervious to a chorusing plea of mercy that wailed up in the room after his discussion, and in answer to a loudly voiced threat (our final card) of a sit down Gandhi-type strike he said, rubbing his hands together with a wicked grin on his face, 'Oh Goody! Then we can have the fun of rolling all you bastards down two flights of stairs.' He had a point there, we had forgotten about the stairs and the idea of the sit down was quickly dropped by all with the exception of one fanantical vegetarian-type hippy who went Gung Ho down the stairs ass over elbows. The rest of us walked and lined up single file into the paddy wagons, boys and girls together packed like sardines.

"Anyhow, now the plot thickens, so let me explain that we had a plan all figured out by the time we reached the station that all of us were going to make believe that we couldn't speak a word of English which would hassle the cops so much that they'd let us go with a minimum of questioning. It was a technique that had worked for me a number of occasions. All of us had false I.D.'s and each of the cards had typically French names embossed upon them - Nicole LeFleshe, Diane Beauchamp, Jacques Rivard and mine was Jean Baptiste LeVoleur, a card given to me by Le Pou, a pusher on the Mountain circuit, as a joke.

"The plan worked out great in the beginning even though my French is not really that fluent and Micky's was a weird combination of French swear words and broken English - 'Hi don' speak de good H-english cawlis, est-ti, tabernack.' Not a single cop in the whole station could speak French and consequently the detectives were on the verge of dismissing us in disgust when the sergeant happened upon my notebook with Tress's name and Toronto address inside. The cop's eyes flashed, I gulped, I knew what he was reading. 'Game over now,' I thought as he grabbed me by the collar, yanking me out of the chair, across the big room into his office. A few slaps in the face and I broke out into perfect English 'Alright-alright, lay off for Christ's sake.' I exclaimed. 'You're shaking up my brains so bad I couldn't tell you anything even if I wanted to.'

"Obviously Tress was very much wanted by the Toronto police force; they considered her to be a very dangerous person, a human time bomb. A photograph was shown to me of her. 'Yeah that's Tress,' I said, 'She left Montreal a few weeks ago and gave me that address. That's all I know.' 'Spill it all kid! ' he snarled leaning over me in a menacing fashion, 'or I'll bring you downstairs and you may never come up again! ' 'You'll just waste your time bruising your knuckles on my head Mister,' I said, ' 'cause what I just told you is all I really know. Honest.'

"The sergeant was an old timer, he knew when people were telling the truth or not. He had the hard diamond-hard eyes of an old cop but his face was not without feeling, you could sense that he was a man capable of brutal actions but not unless he felt the violence was justified. At least that's what I read into the lines he had about his eyes and mouth. He got up wearily from his desk and said quietly, 'Alright kid, I believe you, it's been a long day. I'm letting you off this time and go tell your friends we're bringing in a detective who can speak frog language.'

"Well young Suzanne nervously spilt the beans to the French-speaking detective and consequently Serge and I got thirty days in the Don Jail for vagrancy; but they never caught onto Micky, she was back out on the streets the next day. As for Suzanne she was escorted back to her parents in Quebec City and that's the last news I've heard of her - so I presume the short taste she had of the street life convinced her that growing up to be the wife of some work-a-day man wasn't such a dull idea after all.

"Did you ever see Micky again?" asked Sharon.

"Oh yeah, several times in the next two or three years. Last time I saw her in '68 she told me that Tress had been killed that summer on the 401 in a car accident."

"Yeah, Nicky, so now you know. Sharon and I used to be hippies."

February 26, 1971   Friday

Incidentally I actually had a fight with a kid on a flight of stairs similar to the one with Willi in my dream. An Indian kid from the neighbourhood, one of the best enemies I've ever had in my life. When I was about ten-years-old the both of us had a knock-down drag-out fight that I won much to his shame and amazement. He was especially humiliated because his father had watched the whole fight from across the street. The Indian kid never forgave me for disgracing him in front of his father and for the next two years he continued trying to beat me in a fight. I'd be walking home from school and I'd hear him coming for me from a block away yelling like a maniac, swinging his arms like pistons. "Ah no, here we go again," I'd think to myself as I went through the ritual of beating him down to the ground. He never gave up trying and after awhile I began to worry that one day he just might beat me. However the spring of the next year his family moved away from the block and that's the last I was to see of him for five or six years. Then one day I'm walking along Wellington Street with Wayne Young on the way to High School when some guy trotted up behind me, punching me right in the nose when I turned around. I was stunned, we looked at each other for a few seconds. He was dancing around, fists up, ready to fight, but I didn't know who the fuck the guy was so I just turned my back on him and continued walking alone the street with Wayne. The guy didn't bother coming after me and it wasn't until months later that it dawned on me that it was the Indian family finally getting his revenge. I felt proud, I mean anyone can have friends, but very few people are fortunate enough to have a good enemy.

175

Talking with Berny in the cafeteria for a short while about women and philosophy.

"Ah ya always have to play games with girls at the beginning, if you want to get to know them, ball them," he said.

"Well so what's so wrong with that?" I exclaimed, "Birds do it, bees do it, that's life."

"I met a girl at the Mustache the other night," he said, "She gave me her phone number after we had been talking only a few minutes. (Berny's a very good looking dude.) So I phoned her up the other night and I played the game, I didn't want to but I did, I had to."

"We all do as far as I know Berny," I said, "but once you've made love with the girl then there's no longer any need of the games."

"Yeah well so what?" he replied. "You get to sleep with her and then what?"

"So by putting your hands all over a person, a stranger, a young woman you get to know her well and there's one less stranger in the world."

"Big deal! So you know them," he mumbled.

"Well what the fuck else do you want out of life Berny!" I exclaimed. "Tell me, I'm curious."

"I want God, I want Infinity," he said half-seriously.

"Don't make me puke Berny, giving me that God, Infinity shit!" I exclaimed, "You are God, you are Infinity. You're just chasing yourself in circles!"

We both laughed and lit up our cigarettes.

"Hey that was good Berny," I said, "I'm gonna put it in my journal."

March 1, 1971   Monday

Yes it's March, a word that is full of promises. Today I saw the first signs of spring coming to the West End. A kid kicking a garbage can down the middle of Coursol Street People stepping gingerly along the sidewalks, dodging the ice falling from the roofs. Old Irish ladies gossiping on their front stairs with brooms in their hands, taking inventory of who's died and who's been born since the first snow fall. The windows of the Fulford Street tavern are wide open for the first time in five months. The whores in Rockhead's Paradise are blossoming forth in mini-skirts and Dubois the bouncer is back to wearing short-sleeve shirts showing off his 16 inch biceps. Black kids boogalooing down St. Antoine Street singing, "He jumped so high, he touched the sky and didn't get back 'til a quarter to five, walking the dog." Electric west wind blowing in April warming up the sidewalks and this cold heart of mine, tongue slipping into songs, fingers dancing and clapping down St. Antoine Street - just wanna show you how to walk the dog.

Saturday night Pat and Moe, Charly and ourselves were up at Jacky's place on Cote St. Luc for his birthday party. Jacky's been off speed for a month now and consequently all his natural awesome energy has returned to him, a powerhouse pounding on my guitar so long and hard that it was as hot as a radiator when he handed it back to me. Charly says that Jacky is a classic case of hyper-activeness. "Ninety-five per cent of the people grow out of it," he said, "but I think Jacky is one of those five per cents."

Charly and ourselves stayed on until two o'clock drinking beer and listening to Jacky's stories. An old time favourite of mine is the story about how he broke into a Salvation Army Girl's detention to see Danny the little butch broad. Unlike most butches Danny (Diane) is a very sweet looking girl, very petite and easily mistaken for a thirteen or fourteen year old boy.

"We were having a party down on Argyle Street, remember all the sharp chicks we used to get down there Dave? Well that night I was very drunk and feeling very lonely even with all those good looking chicks around because Diane was in detention. You know we were working things out together. I reached the point with Diane where I could hold her hand and kiss her, something she never let any other guy do or even try. So all those sharp chicks were around but I just wanted Diane. I decided I just got to see her so I go booming out of the house without putting on my boots and beat it down to the Sally Ann around two o'clock in the morning. I walked around the building yelling her name but there was no response, no answer, so I started climbing up the drain pipe to the second floor where the dormitories are. The windows were open and I stuck my head in one. 'Diane,' I whispered and then a little louder, 'Diane!' No answer so I pulled myself onto the ledge and crawled in nearly falling on some girl in bed who started screaming, 'A-a-a-a-hh there's a man in the room!' Big fuckin' racket, freaking out, big confusion, all the girls are screaming now and Diane comes running over to me in the dark and says, 'Jacky is that you?' She grabs my arm and pulls me over to her bed and says 'Hide under there!' Anyhow so the bull-dyke guards came in with flashlights but I'm glued to the springs under Danny's bed so they don't spot me. They think the girls are just playing a joke on them and they give the dumb blonde chick shit for getting them out of bed because of a bad dream. Danny whispers to me to stick and stay and as soon as the guards are out of sight she goes over to talk with Dumbo who's the only uncool chick in the joint. Danny says to her, 'Supposing the man was to come back, would you scream?' 'Yes,' she says, 'But supposing that man was my friend would you scream?' 'No,' 'Supposing I was to tell you that that friend was in here now would you scream?' 'No.' 'Well,' says Danny pointing to me under the bed, 'There he is' 'A-a-a-a-h-h' screams Dumbo, 'There's a man in the room!' And all the confusion comes back again only louder. And Danny comes running over to me, 'Get out Jacky,' she says, 'or they gonna give me life or something.' I'm up on my feet hopping. The girls are screaming. Some of them laughing, one or two whistling. 'Jump out of the window.' 'It's two floors down Danny. Fuck that,' I says, 'I'm using the door.' I ran out of the dorm into the corridor and fat old ladies in white nightgowns are running up in my direction and they're yelling for the watchman. I cut down another hallway; it's a deadend. Nothing else for me to do so I boot open an office door and jump out the window down twenty-thirty feet to the sidewalk in my stocking feet. I bruised my knees and elbows and limped on home as fast as I could. Danny told me later that the Sally Ann officers told her they knew it was me but they couldn't prove nothing."

I was over at Stu's on Monday night rapping with him and a friend of his, Kevin. Stu got me to tell stories and I told him about the Rape of Fennario.

"I was raped once by a Cree Indian girl named Angel. That sounds poetic but it's true. You've lived in Toronto Stu so you know how thick the thieves are there, whole streets of rooming houses just jampacked full of rounders and B and E artists around the Jarvis Street area. Well about five years ago I was invited by Steady Eddy to a party being held in a house down on Gloucester Street. (That's when Eddy was still living with his wife.) Some really bad actors were at this party, Dirty Ed, Cy the bootlegger, Al the Pal, Angel, and a psychopathetic ex-boxer named Duke, a real maniac when he was drinking. Once he pulled Steady Eddy by the beard for four blocks along Yonge Street. He was jealous 'cause he couldn't grow any hair on his own face. Duke had a thing going with Angel as sort of an unofficial pimp. There was a hole in her apartment door from the last non-paying guest Duke found in bed with Angel. He was drinking Pepsi-Cola that evening. 'I nearly killed a guy last week,' he said in explanation.

"So I'm sitting there not feeling too great sipping my beer when Angel comes over sits down on my knee announcing with a caressing kiss that she has the hots for me. Angel has the hots for me. Angel was a sweet looking girl but I wanted no part of her. I like my face the way it is and inbetween wrestling Angel away from me I keep shooting nervous glances in Duke's direction to see how he was taking it. His face had stiffened but he was still drinking Pepsi-Cola.

"Steady Eddy has a lousy sense of humour and he thought the whole situation was very comical. He gets up all of a sudden with his wife and says, 'Dave, we're going to a restaurant. See you later.' 'Wait a minute,' I said picking up my jacket, Angel hanging on me like a leech, 'I'm going with you.' But he was already gone down the stairs. 'You're not going,' Angel exclaimed twisting her legs around me. 'Gotta go baby, gotta go.' 'No no no -

give me a kiss first.' I pecked her on the mouth but
she grabbed my hair forcing my face down to her and
French kissed me. A lot of hassles went on between us
but she wouldn't let go her strangle hold and finally I
found myself sitting up on the edge of her bed feeling
like a nervous virgin.

"She took off my jacket and I put it back on only
to discover that she had taken off my boots and socks in
the meanwhile. And so it went on but she was quicker
than me and as soon as I was naked she grabbed me
under the armpits and dragged me under the covers. The
hall light was shining in through the hole in the blood-
stained door and believe me poor Angel got nothing but
a very quick one indeed. She was still in a prone position
when I rolled off her, snatched my clothes and boots
and stepped out into the hall dressing myself as I rushed
down the stairs. 'Hey Fennario where are ya going?' said
Steady Eddy walking in the front door with his wife.
'This is the last party I'm every going to with you Greenfield,' I said shaking my fist in his face as I pushed by
him. Eddy told me later he had the best laugh of his life
that night of the Rape of Fennario. As for me I'm just
happy that Big Duke stuck to Pepsi-Cola.

March 7, 1971   Sunday

Yes now let's put everything in order. Liz came
home from Murray's around three-thirty today with a
purse full of change. I took two dollars and went up on
the Main to take in some fifty-cent movies. It was the
usual one-dimensional fare of cheap western and horror
flicks but the popcorn was good.

What's a poor boy gonna do? Our lives are so limited. Well we do what we can with the words that we
have. We get along wondering where the hell we're
going, sleeping, eating, shitting another day away. Why
does it take so long? How much more will we suffer before raising our fists in revolution? I wait, I speak, I
retain my hope and sanity.

Every tribe had a man with words, a man like me
who could speak of the changes. Of the wind, the blood,

the birth and why. The first winter I can remember, the first West Wind blowing in April, untied my tongue and I gave words to the songs.

March 8, 1971   Monday

Saturday morning I lost a ten dollar bill on my way over to Poncho's to get some bacon and eggs. I didn't miss it until I was on my way home when I fished in my pocket and found only a dollar bill. My heart sank into my cowboy boots thinking of how badly Liz would take the loss. That ten bucks was our grocery money for the week-end. In what I felt could only be a futile attempt I returned to Poncho's and informed him of my loss. "What number was on the bill?" he said. "I don't know," I replied, "I don't read my money." "Well," he said, "because a little boy just left a few minutes ago after buying fifteen packs of hockey card chewing gum with a ten dollar bill." "It was probably mine," I exclaimed. "Let me see the bill." He pulled a crisp fresh purple Queen out of the cash register. "Naw! " I said somberly, "mine was old and wrinkled." "Sorry," Poncho said as I walked round-shouldered out of the store back home to face the music. I was just going up to my front stairs when I heard little Jimmy the kid who helps Poncho in the store calling my name. I stopped and he came run-ning up to me on the sidewalk eyes big with excitement telling me that my ten bucks had been found by a little girl who just walked into the store. Judy was the girl's name and fifty cents with a big kiss on the cheek was her reward and Jimmy got a quarter just for being so happy that I was happy.

So that's the way Saturday began and it ended with Liz and me sitting in the Guy Cinema watching Jane Eyre, a movie we both appreciated.

Yesterday evening I went up to the Westmount
Library carrying ten heavy books on subjects ranging
from British Music Halls to the Cold War in a tattered
A & P shopping bag. Great crowds of people were milling about Ste. Catherine Street outside the Forum, lining
up at the gates in anticipation of the "Fight of the
Century" between Cassius Clay and Joe Frazer. Dozens
of pigeon-proud black dudes from the West End were
strutting around dressed up in their best strides with all
their hearts and money bet on Muhammed Ali.

I got a seat on the 105 bus beside a very stiff middle-
aged woman who was reading a book on how to win
friends easily. I suppose a sarcastic remark would be in
order, but actually I found myself admiring the woman's
courage. Imagine openly announcing how lonely you are
on a public bus. It takes a lot of guts, or something.

After returning my books I walked over to Betty
Ann's and stayed to watch the late news on T.V. Ali
knocked down in the fifteenth round and Joe Frazer
wins by an acclamation. The great Casey has struck out.
Gloom in Mudville. They'll be wearing sack cloth and
ashes down in the West End.

Liz is downstairs and crying, fed up and tired from
working, while I'm writing this. Everyday she asks me if
there's any mail in the hopes that my government loan
has come through. My mythical grant. It started off as a
dream, then a wish and now it's a myth. The Great Government Grant.

Hard to tell, hard to tell how I'm feeling. Think of
all the places I've slept in during my life. Back sheds,
railway stations, by the sides of highways, on a soft mattress of pine needles in the midst of a Carolina piney woods,
on the white sands of Daytona Beach where the Atlantic
Ocean demonstrated to me that tide was not only a box

of soap. In cells, in bullpens, Station 53 in Toronto, Station Number One in Montreal, Cell number 7, in corridor 6 of the Don Jail, the main cell of Daytona Beach's City Jail. Missions in Toronto, Sudbury, Jacksonville, Florida, Washington, D.C., Norfolk, Virginia. Yeah Norfolk, tattoo parlors, John Wayne movies standup bar saloons whores and sailors - yes I've been to Norfolk. It took me a whole afternoon just to bum one dime for bus fare out of town.

The Good Shepherd Mission in Toronto down on Insane Tracy Street lined with Philadelphia red brick houses and polluted with kids all with ambitions of growing up to be better thieves than their absentee daddies, kids so tough they were mugging mission bums in broad daylight for cigarettes and donuts, throwing stones at us as we stood in the grub line outside the Mission yard door. Yeah somebody ought to write a country'n western song about Tracy Street. The closest thing I can remember in Montreal comparable to Tracy Street was the Diamond Court in Griffintown behind the Dow Brewery. A pest hole of crime until it was torn down seven or eight years ago, breeding in its lifetime whole generations of Jack the Rippers.

Hotel Providence on the Bowery. Chicken coop wire for a ceiling and walls of bristol board so thin I could hear the guy in the next cubicle puffing on his cigarette.

The William Slowne Y.M.C.A. Hotel in New York City and me a very young and green sixteen-year-old. There were so many queers in the joint that I couldn't bend over a water fountain without being goosed. I'd walk into an empty shower room and by the time I turned on the water, the place would be packed with spectators. Yeah I was a great hit.

The Y.M.C.A. on Franklin Avenue in Richmond, Virginia, just down the way from Robert E. Lee's old house. White pillared houses, magnolia trees, Scarlett O'Haras by the gross and big, long ugly deep southern fried cockroaches that were absolutely fearless.

A cheap hotel in Washington, D.C., on E. Street. I forgot the name, but I'm sure the managers still haven't forgotten David Fennario, Montreal, Quebec, Canada

183

found in an unsegregated bed with the black girl the next morning by a cleaning woman in defiance of the No Visitor (particularly not black ones) rules of the house.

I suppose if I would have gone to her room as she first suggested I really would have got cleaned out. A broken bloody pile of ragged bones found somewhere in a ghetto alley but as it was she was very good to me. She fingered out the few dollars change I had in my wallet of course but all my big bills were hidden in my boots anyhow. Besides she was forced to rob some of my money because I never offered her any. I was too embarrassed to because I didn't come onto her like she was a whore (which she was) but as a young and pretty girl I had managed to charm into my bed; offering her money would have only destroyed the little fantasy we were both living in that evening. Me drunk and Caroline all doped up on snow, snuggled up together all night. Black hands on my pillow.

March 16, 1971   Tuesday

I hate banks. Two of them refused to cash my government cheque even thought I showed them my Dawson College I.D. card with photo and signature on it. "Do you have any friends, or an account in another bank?" the clerk said. I snarled, snatched the cheque out of his hand, murder in my heart as I went stomping out through the Nihon Plaza onto Ste. Catherine Street. I went storming into the nearest bank, a big eyed cute little blonde watching me fling open the glass door. "Oh she'll cash it," I thought to myself, checking out the love lights in her eyes. "Honey," I said sweetly, placing my cheque and I.D. on the counter before her, "I don't suppose it's possible for you to cash this cheque?" I got a knock out smile along with the cash.

Money in my jeans walking along Ste. Catherine Street back to Dawson humming a little song I made up about how much I hate banks.

I never had a bank account, I never had the money to spare. It just rolls and flows. Besides on principle I hate banks, I don't like what they're liable to do with my money.

184

My Aunt Simund has photographs taken of my father
just a few weeks after he returned from overseas. One of
them is a family group picture. My father's shirt is hanging from his shoulders like a rag he is so thin, his mouth's
tight and hard, his eyes like those of a tormented animal.
Shell-shocked. He was wounded three times. My mother
said that for months after he came home he'd wake up
in the middle of the night from terrible nightmares.
"Give me a fag, mate? Give me a fag." He never joined
the Legion, never talks about the war and would have
thrown out all his medals long time ago if my mother hadn't
stored them away.

He was five years overseas without having seen or
touched his wife or the young daughter born to her seven
months after he had shipped out to England in September,
1940. He came back home in June 1945 to a big Welcome Home Daddy banner criss-crossed with maple leaves
hanging from the gallery. All the kids in the block banging pots and pans and throwing streamers. My father
walked up to the gateway with my mother, yelling at the
kids to fuck off and asking my mother what all the noise
was about. She broke down in tears.

Wartime Verdun was a community of women of
war brides without husbands. "Red Sails in the Sunset,"
"Blue Birds Over the White Cliffs of Dover." A one-armed
veteran of the First World War delivered the telegrams
that informed the women of Verdun who was wounded,
dead or missing. "We hated to see that one-armed man
come up our street," my mother says, "He lost a son himself."

Yesterday Sally had us writing compositions on three
subjects, snakes, mothers and darkness as seen by an eight-
year old boy or girl. I always thought of snakes as being
some form of erotic rat. Nobody I knew was afraid of

185

them although little girls used to pretend to be so that
little boys would chase them. There were no snakes in
the neighbourhood but thousands of them could be found
on Nun's Island, easy for quick backstreet boys to grab
as they lay sunning themselves on the hot rocks. We'd
rent boats at Leblonde's Wharf in East Verdun and row
over to the island, filling up sacks full of snakes and letting them loose in the back alleys. Peter O'Neil used to
nail them on his back fence as targets for knive throwing
contests but I just used to play with them until my
mother found them and threw them out. I guess I was
one of the more sensitive boys because I never could kill
anything other than the odd cockroach or two and even
then I'd whisper an apology.

Once a bunch of us carried two shopping bags full
of snakes uptown and let them loose in a department
store basement. We waited until the salesladies were
looking the other way and then we dumped the snakes on
the floor, a baker's dozen of them sparkling gold under
the neon lights slithering away into dark corners and
under the counters. We split the scene once little old
ladies began convulsing, screaming out blue murder. Big
mystery back in the fifties, all sorts of speculations were
made by the press. My mother sitting at the supper table
weeks afterwards saying, "Oh Jim, they found another
snake in Eatons."

Mother, big heavy arms, kitchens, cast iron frying
pans. Sometimes strange, mysterious sitting by herself in
a dark room looking out the window. She was the person
in the house until the man came home for supper. The
voice and the heart, she cooked, sewed, dressed us in the
morning for school, hit us for ripping our clothes or
running out in front of cars. Told us what was right or
wrong and worried about our health. Talking with her
friends in the kitchen about their husbands and the
troubles. "The war changed Jim," my mom would say,
"He came back a stranger to me."

A sweet memory also of my mother sitting on my
father's knee kissing him and the strange brightness about
my old man's eyes when he gave me and my older sister
a quarter each to go to the movies. "Take your time,"
he said.

Also the night she threw an ash tray at my old man's head, missing him by a thin inch. Later on we lay in bed listening to the noises in the other room "Mommy's getting a spanking," Peggy Anne told me, "for being drunk."

Darkness. I like the darkness outside in the night but not in my room. The curtains would turn into monsters, kidnappers whispering in the closet. Little bugs flying in the air. One sinister-looking shed back of the tenements on Third Avenue was reputed to have a skeleton living in it. One day two older boys, Butchy Denis and Arty Leonard, locked me up in that shed and my screaming brought half the neighbourhood out on their back galleries.

Liz was sitting back on the couch reading Jane Eyre while I was writing and suddenly she says, "David," "Yeah?" "What does physiognomy mean?" "Well, it means general physical appearance." "Oh!" she said smiling. "Well what did you think it meant?" I asked. "I-uh-well," she said with a faint blush on her cheeks, "A cock?" I laughed. She blushed a little redder and then began laughing herself. "How was I supposed to know?" I asked her to read out the paragraph that contained the questionable word. I quote: - "He had been looking for two minutes at the fire, and I had been looking the same amount of time at him, when, turning, suddenly, he caught my gaze fastened on his physiognomy. "Hell, Liz," I said laughing, "That's Jane Eyre you're reading, not Fanny Hill."

March 19,1971   Friday

Somehow I've managed to fuck up my right shoulder again, shooting pain in my muscle whenever I move my arm too quickly. I checked it out with the school nurse this morning and she told me to apply heat. "A hot water bottle would be good," she said.

Agony, agony, biblical pain, righteous anger. I was not born to move my arms in pain goddamn it!

Misery, bad news and trouble as I sit here in the library with two pages to write in my journal and not a drop of inspiration to aid me. Two virgin white sheets and not a sperm of an idea. I suppose I'll revert back to a former subject and continue my account of the places I've slept in. Once in a small clothes closet folded up like a jack knife. I walked around the next day for hours hunched over like a cripple.

Once in a double bed with two pretty French girls, unfortunately both sisters and the attempts I made at emulating Casanova were all in vain. A most frustrating evening with two birds in the bed but none in my arms.

I've slept in deserted houses, lumber yards, wretched cars by the sides of many different highways. On buses, trains, the floor of the Prag coffee house and beside the bed of Elizabeth Black, one of the most beautiful girls in Montreal. Alas she was faithful, and I had to comfort myself with fantasies. And Elizabeth, if you ever read this, I have to confess that yes I did sneak a peek the next morning while you were putting on your bra. Can I ever forget the time I slept over at your parents' house while your mother and father were on vacation and the door bell ringing next morning causing you to rush me out on the back escape with just my jeans on. Cote des Neiges was quite scandalized by my appearance, barefoot and half-naked standing in the nearest telephone booth I could find asking you over the line to sneak my boots and shirt and jacket out on the stairs so I could go back downtown.

March 20, 1971   Saturday

Friday evening I was walking around uptown asking myself, will I meet someone I know tonight? All strangers coming and going, same old story and the same old song. Well I sat down on a bench in the C.N. station and took it all in for a while. The train announcements. "Train for Ottawa, Sudbury, North Bay, Sault Ste. Marie leaving at track five." Other people just as much alive as I am. They have places to come and go from carrying dreams, ambitions and sorrows around in their suitcases. I'm always asking myself, why are we so separate? People, other people outside scurrying about, each with a secret that hasn't been told to me. I am familiar with the physics of the

universe. Egg sperm womb. Growth, the seasons, the
decline. Men have words and the word has made him
human. I see and understand remembering the words.
Remembering my inheritance, my birthright, the propel-
ling revolutions, the people. Sticks and stones can't break
all our bones and names can be misleading.

March 22, 1971   Monday

    Jay dropped in on me while I was upstairs in my
study writing in my journal. He's living with his girl
Lisa now in a basement apartment on Monkland Boulevard.
    I interrupted the nervous small talk going on between
us by saying, "Jay, do you think we'll ever make a decent
living?" He laughed, "Damned if I know Dave, but, short
of a working-class revolution, I very much doubt it." "I
feel the same way, Jay." I said looking out the window.
"Goddamn it! It's not like I want the whole world, I just
want to make a decent living - you know enough to
afford an old car, a T.V. set, a flat in Verdun and three-
and-a-half kids." "You dreamer you," says Jay socking
me in the shoulder. "Yeah but just imagine if we had
the wealth and leisure time owing to us. Man! O Happy
Day! A rainbow in every lunch bucket and mosaic sidewalks to dance upon."

March 23, 1971   Tuesday

    Charly came over and invited me out for a beer. "Well
I guess I can finish up my writing quota later," I said. "Let's
go."
    The place was quiet, a few guys leaning over the pool
table while Crazy Leroi was showing off a new dance
step to his latest girlfriend. One old dude talking to himself at a back table was suffering from what Charly said was
the Dostoyevsky syndrome.
    "What will it be Dave? A large or a small one?" "Make
it a large one I guess."

Charly told me of a teacher he had in grade nine, "A really weird guy with a deformed hand that he always had covered with a black glove. The first day of class he walks in and says, 'Will all the girls kindly cross their legs please.' They did so. 'Good,' he said, 'Now that the gates to hell have been closed, we shall proceed.' "

Charly talked about the houseboat he lived in for two years, a little seven-by-seven foot boat moored on Seattle Bay. The bohemian student. "Happiest days of my life," Charly said. Young girls, lazy afternoons, medical students, 1966-67, good years for me too.

March 25, 1971   Thursday

"Never No More Blues" by Jimmy Rodgers going through my head this morning, Rodgers the singing brakeman dead of T.B. in the early 1930's.

"Portland Maine is just the same as Sunny Tennessee
Any old place I hang my hat is home sweet home to
me." He wrote songs about trains mostly, hobo songs,
songs of farewell.

"Whether I'm right or wrong
I know you're gonna miss me when I'm gone
You're sure gonna cry when I tell
that I ain't coming home no more."

He had a raspy, nasal voice that could sound as hard as a high-ball express rattling down the rails, so quick to pass, leaving behind a long silence.

"I'm gonna be a rounder 'til the police shoots me
down."

And he could sound tender and moving, like a train whistle moaning in the night.

"I had a dream last night
I dreamt my good gal had gone
when I woke up this morning
—she really hadn't done me wrong."

Jimmy's life's ambition was to own a guitar completely covered with mother-of-pearl. He died owning one and Hank Snow bought it at an auction some years back. He says it's one of his proudest possessions and I believe him because Snow idolized Rodgers to the point of naming one of his sons Jimmy Rodgers Snow.

Hank himself grew up in a Nova Scotia fishing village; he gave up going out on the Grand Banks in the fishing boats after nearly drowning a couple of times in storms and in the course of events he became one of country 'n western's greatest and best known performers. Unfortunately like most artists in that field of music he lost his gut-feelings once the money started rolling in. His only good songs were those he was singing back in the early fifties as a relatively unknown performer. It's the same for Johnny Cash, all his best songs were composed back in the fifties before he reached stardom.

Then of course there is the incomparable Hank Williams, the only country 'n western star in my opinion of the same rank as Jimmy Rodgers.

He died at the age of thirty from an O.D. of speed in the back seat of a car that was speeding him on his way to a New Year's Eve concert. New Year's Eve, 1952.

"No one could sing that sad and live for long," my Uncle Art said about Williams the day after his death as the family sat down for New Year's Day dinner. Thousands of families from all over North America felt like they had lost a friend.

"Luke the Drifter" he liked to call himself, "I'm so lonesome I could die." Straight from the backwoods of Alabama, out making a living at the age of eight shining shoes and bringing home his first pay, thirty-five cents, saying, "Ma put the kettle on, we're all gonna have some gumbo soup."

He first learnt to play guitar from a blind street musician, Ti-tot, a black man, and unlike most poor whites from his background, Williams was colour-blind. Matter of fact years later as a singing star he threw a head waiter through the plateglass window of a deluxe restaurant for refusing to serve a black friend of his, a fellow showman. "I don't care if tomorrow never comes."

Towards the remaining years of his life as a performer, Hank's managers used to lock him up in a hotel room the night before a concert to keep him away from the booze. There's stories reported of Hank Williams drunk on stage

191

pulling fat wads of money out of his pockets and stomping
on it while screaming obscenities at the roaring crowds who
loved him even in his insanity. "I'm gonna jump in the
river and lord I'm only coming up twice."

Jimmy Rodgers and Hank Williams are the working
man's T.S. Eliot and Ezra Pound.

March 26, 1971   Friday

I'm sitting in the library at nine-thirty this morning
with Nicky perched upon my table thumbing through the
poems I'm gonna hand in to Sally this afternoon. "You
write a lot about birth don't you Dave?" said Nicky. "Well
I guess it's because I never got over it," I replied.

Then Berny came by and I showed him my most
recent poem, the one I dedicated to Patrick O'Neil. "It
should be longer," he said and I agreed. He then asked me
to explain the significance of the line, "Every time a
woman laughs, a death is forgiven."

Yes I remember only too well what inspired that
line, it was the death of Sharon Baily at the age of eighteen
from cancer. A bruise on her knee that wouldn't go away,
she consulted a doctor and in three months she was dead.

I never knew her well but her sister was in my class
back in Verdun High School. Sharon was a prefect, a
Latin student, and one of the most beautiful and popular
girls in the school. She had a sunny open smile for even
the most wretched individual in the place, myself.

She graduated in June of 1964 and died that fall.
My Aunt Helene the family harbinger of bad news, told
my mother of Sharon's death during the Christmas holidays. I didn't smile for months afterwards moping about
the uptown streets at night like a regular Edgar Allan Poe.
I had trouble sleeping, visions of Sharon would come to me.
Visions of Sharon crying alone at night in her hospital
bed knowing she was dying. Sharon rotting in the grave
because of a bruise on her knee. A bruise. How sad the
doctor must have felt when he first discovered that the
insides of her lovely young body were totally corrupted
with cancer. Oh he must have cried and washed his face
to hide his grief from her.

I didn't cry. The sons of coal miners never cry, the winters are so long and cruel the tears would never stop. A young woman's death is not to be celebrated. Wakes are only held for those who die old with families to remember them. A young woman dying is an outrage, a war, an obscene cruelty. Death is our enemy, the only enemy.

So for months I grieved for the girl, living dreaming thinking only of how all things must pass and die, to the point that I became a confirmed hypochondriac constantly worrying about my own health. The sleepless nights, the sad friendless days. Then one evening on my way home from work on the subway, a beautiful girl in the same car as myself began laughing and as I looked at her face my grief for Sharon began to fade from my mind. "Every time a woman laughs, a death is forgiven."

March 29, 1971   Monday

Today, at least this morning, I was feeling like Jim Casey the Preacher in Steinbeck's Grapes of Wrath. Monday morning, Jonathan, Mike, Nicky and myself sitting on the hallway floor opposite Madame Sonac's class room. "If everyone's feeling the same way Mike," I said, "and everyone is, why don't we do something about it?" Yes we're all serving life, doing our time down on Rockefeller's plantation.

Eat your heart away. April is coming and everything on four legs in the West End seems to be in heat. Even the air in the neighbourhood has a salty taste to it. Bedlam twenty-four hours a day, and Lord have mercy, it happens every March just like clock work.

March 30, 1971   Tuesday

What can I recall of my early life prior to entering elementary school?

We used to play in the lanes, on the roofs and in the back sheds of the West End. Everyone who went to school

193

was so much older than me. My sister Peggy Ann was
very old and her best friend was Shirrel Smart who liked
to kiss me. "You don't mind when I kiss you, do you
David?" "Nope," and it's true I did like it. Soft wet lips
on my mouth and she had golden hair and wild eyes like
an Indian.

Her father was a taxi driver, he drove a Studebaker
the colour of a cherry popsicle, a very funny car with
wide windows. My father used to grumble at the supper
table about Jack Smart, saying that he had a big mouth
and one day the cops would catch him in his rackets and
he'd go to jail. I knew all about jails from the pictures
in the comic books. Jails were where they put criminals,
tough guys with beady pigeyes and fat mean faces criss-
crossed with scars. Jack Smart didn't look like that, he
had a raspy grumbling voice always laughing up from his
belly whenever we did somersaults on the sidewalk for
him. "Hey, Mr. Smart! Gimme a dime, look at this!
Gimme a dime," and he had black hair and quick shining
eyes like his daughter but he didn't look like the bad
guys in the Superman comic books even if the police
did come to his house sometimes. And then one day they
took Jack Smart away to jail charging him with dealing
in pornographic literature.

Shirrel Smart showed my sister and me a pack of cards
her father was supposed to have given her and each one of
the cards had a photograph of naked men and women on
it. One of the cards showed a man and a woman taking
a bath and laughing amongst the bubbles and another one
showed a man with a cock like a sword sticking up from
his belly. "Don't tell anyone you've seen these pictures
David," Shirrel said. "Nope," and I didn't, but I was puzzled by the big deal they made over the photos, giggling,
asking me if I knew what the people were doing.

I remember Mrs. Reilly who lived upstairs, a saintly
old woman that all the young mothers on the block consulted in times of domestic troubles. One day I fell back-
wards off a kitchen chair cutting my head open against the
edge of a foot cabinet as I fell. My mother in tears rushed
me upstairs to Mrs. Reilly. "Calm down Peggy," I remember
she said laying me down on the sofa with a damp tea bag

194

applied to the lump on my head, "Come into the kitchen and I'll make you some toast and tea."

About a year or so later (I may have been four years old) I can remember Mrs. Reilly's wake, half the neighbourhood gathered in her living room drinking, crying, milling about and my mother saying, "Look up in the sky tonight David and you'll see a new big star in heaven belonging to Mrs. Reilly." Nearly everybody gave me a dime and Mr. Kelly punched a hole in the hallway wall he was so full of grief.

The Kellys also lived upstairs from us, right above us, Annie and Bill Kelly, both of them weighing over two hundred pounds with a big family of freckle-faced sons, the terror of the block, Sonny, Billy, Jerry, etc., etc. Everytime Billy and Ann Kelly would have a fight the plaster on our ceiling would fall down. "Goddamn those Kellys!" my father would say, "I wish the hell they'd fight out on their back gallery."

The Kellys were Irish from Liverpool, "I'm from Liverpool!" Bill Kelly would shout in the taverns and everybody knew he was tough. So were his sons, especially Sonny Kelly with flaming red hair and fat freckles over every square inch of his body. He used to hang me by my ankles head first over his third story gallery yelling to the boys down on the street, "Hey look at Davy the bravest little kid on the block. I was terrified everytime he did it but I pretended to like it because I was proud that Sonny liked me so much.

We used to stand around watching Annie Kelly wash her front stairs because she never wore any panties. Great huge ass, each buttock the size of a four year kid. I called the Kellys aunt and uncle because they were my parents' best friends.

Danny Malone, Larry Omer and Robert Taylor were my best friends. Danny was my special, special friend and he had eyes just like his mother Blanche Malone who was a very pretty woman. I liked to look at Mrs. Malone and I liked to listen to her musical voice which was just like my Aunt Jessy's. Blanche Malone and my mother were also friends and Mr. Malone once punched a grocery boy in the head for running over some kid on the sidewalk with his bicycle.

Larry was the baby of his family and everybody said that Rita Omer spoiled him. (He grew up to be a cop.) Mrs. Omer was an Irish woman from Griffintown and she never missed a Sunday mass, unlike Annie Kelly who only went once a year and that was to the Easter mass. "She has to go to that one," my mother said, "or else the church would dismiss her and she'd never get to heaven."

And I couldn't understand how come there were catholics and protestants and how come they went to different shcools. "Catholic, catholic ring the bell, protestant, protestant go to hell." I was protestant and my father said it was good that I was protestant. Robert Taylor was protestant but I liked Danny much more and he was catholic. I didn't like to think about the differences, it was hard enough fighting with French kids without worrying about Catholics.

The summer my mother had Jimmy, Virginia and I stayed for a month with my Aunt Mary and Uncle Frank out in Ile Perrotte in an old country house with a rain barrel and a vegetable garden in the back. My grandparents lived there too, my grandpa Kerr working as a security guard in the Ste. Anne de Bellevue hospital. I used to help him shine his shoes in the morning and brass his buttons. "That's a good lad," he always said even when I put brown polish on his black shoes.

One morning my aunt Mary was giving me hell for getting dirty in the backyard when all of a sudden, out of nowhere I said to her, "I hate catholics." "Who told you to say that?" she snapped. "Catholics are stupid, they wore running shoes in the war. My father told me." "That's not true!" my hot-tempered aunt exclaimed and turning to my grandmother she said, "It's just like Jim to teach his son something like that. We can't let the boy grow up hating Catholics." Both of them lost their tempers with me because I wouldn't listen to reason and continued repeating over and over exactly what my father had told me. My grandpa finally stepped out of the kitchen, annoyed by the noise, and told the women to lay off. "Leave the lad alone for God's sake," he said, "he doesn't even know what he's saying. He'll find out for himself."

The first day of kindergarten I was the only kid in class who didn't cry after the mothers went away. Not only that, but I walked home myself and found the front door locked. My mother had gone with Jimmy in the baby carriage to take me from school but I had left right after class had been dismissed. I sat on the front steps for over an hour until finally I saw my mother coming up the block. "There you are David!" she said laughing, "and I was afraid you might have got lost."

I used to watch the older boys playing pitch-penny on the street outside of Rainey's (René's) candy store. Sonny Kelly would always hand me over a nickel if he won a good game. "You're my good luck charm Davy" he'd say tossing me up in the air. Bryan Cleary was a favourite with the pre-school kids on the block also, but everyone's favourite was Cammy. The neighbourhood, mothers and fathers, everyone loved him.

We'd sit at the bus stop nearby on a flight of stairs waiting for him to come home from work. "Cammy Cammy Cammy!" we'd yell running up to him as he stepped off the bus, pulling at his jacket, hugging his legs. "Put me on your shoulders Cammy, put me on your shoulders." Once Cammy picked me up so I could pull a white blossom off old Gibo's dogwood tree. "He won't live long," the people said, "He's too good."

Then there was the old railroad man who walked like a duck. "Quack Quack Quack" we used to say as he waddled by us in all his overalls and brakeman's hat on, going home for supper. My mother heard me doing it one day and she ran up and slapped me saying, "I'm very sorry Mr. Tucker." "That's alright Peggy," he replied, "your boy don't mean no harm." He had been injured years ago in a bad train wreck.

Mr. Omer was a brakeman too and Larry used to run around the streets with a railroad cap on his head. "Patsy, Patsy ore-e-ay, Patsy Patsy ore-ee-ay Patsy Patsy ore-ee-ay workin' on the railroad." "Get outta the way I'm a train!"

A bunch of us climbed up a back fire escape onto a roof one summer's day looking at the mountain and arguing amongst ourselves as to how long it would take us to walk up to the cross. I said five days, Robert Taylor said one, but Danny Malone said we'd never make it and Danny had a way of saying things that made people be-

lieve him. One time he told me he thought he'd like to
be a priest. "But you laugh too much Danny," I said.
"Yes but I love Mary and Jesus," he replied.

My sister Peggy Ann told us one day while we were
playing baseball in the backlane that the sun is a lot bigger than the earth. "It only looks so small because it's so
far away, 93 million miles away," she said. How far is a
million? What's bigger than a million? A billion a trillion
a zillion, a zillion billion million. The cross on the mountain looked smaller than the sun so I guessed that the sun
was closer to us than the mountain and my sister Peggy
Ann used to get very angry about all the questions Danny
and I would ask of her. "Find out yourself," she'd say.

I liked the warm summer nights when we played
hide 'n seek (hangoseek we pronounced it) using a lamp
post as a base. "In free!" "You're it!" "All in, a bottle
of gin, you don't come in, you got it!" We had songs to
pick sides with and my favourite was "Engine Engine number nine going down Chicago line, if the train falls off the
track, do you want your money back? Yes. Y-E-S spells
yes." (Or "No, N-O spells no," and you are not it.)

We used to do most of our singing in the streets or
on the swings and see-saws in Campbell's park. We'd
stand up on the swings if fat old Pop wasn't looking and
yell out "Red white and blue, my father is a Jew, my
mother came from I-ire-land, red white and blue."

When we were fighting with the French gang from up
the street we used to yell "French peasoup makes me
puke up and down my belly boot!" and if we won the
fight we'd sing "We won the war in 1954" even if it wasn't
1954 because it was the only year that rhymed with the
song.

Larry had an uncle who was a cop with the Verdun
Police Force. He was a good-natured man and never stopped the people from building bonfires on Firecracker Day
(Victoria Day)' One hot summer afternoon Larry's uncle
pulled up in his patrol car in front of the Omer's house
beeping his horn and when Rita Omer came downstairs
to talk with her brother he began shooting at her with a
water pistol through the opened car window. "Goddamn
it. Paddy when are you ever going to grow up!" she
yelled as she ran back into the house fetching a pail of
water which she threw at him just as he was stepping

out of the car. He had to sit on her front steps for a half
hour in the sun until his uniform dried.

I had been out of touch with the guys I grew up
with for four or more years when one day back in 1966 I
literally walked into Danny Malone on Ste. Catherine
Street during a heavy snow storm. I was hurrying along
the sidewalk in the teeth of a fierce wind with my head
bowed to protect my face from the driving sleet when I
bumped into someone. Someone tall and wearing a uniform because my nose was pressed against the top brass
button of an overcoat. "Cop," I thought to myself, and I
stepped back a bit to let him go by when he grabbed my
arm and said, "David are you blind or drunk? Don't you
know who it is?" "Sweet Mother of God!" I said wiping
the snow from my face, "Danny Malone? We laughed and
hugged each other. Passersby must have been quite intrigued by the sight of a long-haired weirdo hugging a guy in
an Air Force uniform. I suggested to Danny that we talk
about the news we had for each other over a coffee at the
Prag. Danny hesitated, "I can't go there with you David,"
he said, "I'll feel foolish sitting with all those beatniks in
my uniform." I laughed and tapping one of Danny's
brass buttons I said, "Ah Danny the Prag's not like you
think it is and besides fuck 'em anyhow if they don't
like you." "Oh alright Dave," he said pulling the same
smile I remember him using as a kid, "Let's go." I knew
he would come with me because even when we were kids
I was the only one who could talk Danny Malone into anything he didn't like. That's why we had been best friends
because I could talk with him in a way no one else could.

Danny was shy for the first five minutes in the Prag,
rather awkwardly taking off his hat as he stepped in the
door, but once we had settled ourselves at a comfortable
table his natural high spirits began to return, especially
after the waitress laughed at one of his jokes. Besides having a fine ringing voice like his mother's, Danny is a very
good looking young man standing six foot four in his air
force boots. Within a half-hour we had the two prettiest
girls in the Prag that evening over at our table flirting
with us. "Why didn't you tell me about this beatnik life
before Dave?" Danny said winking at me when one of the
girls bent over in her mini-skirt to pick up a quarter she
had dropped on the floor, "Yeah how sweet it is."

While we were charming the girls, the two boys we had stolen them from were sulking at a back table shooting us evil glances. Finally one of them came up and bent over one of the girls saying, "We're late if we want to go over to Raymond's to turn on." The girl gave him a nod, looked at her friend and then both of them looked at us. "What a night to be caught without money," I thought to myself. With no offers coming from us the girls reluctantly packed up and left after giving us each a good-bye hug and kiss while their boyfriends stood close by smouldering in jealousy. "Win some lose some," said Danny smiling at me as he leaned back in the chair stretching his arms over his head. Then picking up his hat from the table straightening out its brim he said, "Hey Dave where's the nearest tavern around here?"

The Nova Rex Tavern was still serving ten-cent draughts in those days and we ordered a whole table full of them and every beer we drank had a story to go with it.

We didn't see each other for over two years after that evening. Then one night I was sitting drunk with Teddy Mingo, another boyhood friend of mine, in the Rialto Bar. Teddy was treating me to the beer in the hopes of cheering me up because Liz was in the hospital at that time being doctored for the knife wound she had received from a crazy woman on Dorchester Boulevard a few nights before. So we were sitting there both feeling pretty high when Teddy mentioned that he had met Danny Malone while visiting the St. Jean Air Force Base. "Jesus it would be good to walk and talk with Malone again," I said. "I've got his phone number, you can phone him at the base if you want to." Teddy replied. "Naw," I said, "I'm too drunk. My tongue feels about three inches thick."

It took Teddy more than an hour of convincing but finally I rang up Danny from the bar telephone booth and had a short, mostly incoherent conversation with him. "How come you're so drunk Dave? he said and I told him about Liz. "Look Dave," he explained, ,'I have to go now, I'm on call but give me your address and I'll pay you a visit the next time I'm in Montreal! "

A couple of months later one hot humid summer night Danny and Larry Omer came rapping at my door while Elizabeth and I were in bed. Long tall Danny standing in the shabby neon lit hallway beside Larry, both of them looking very sad. Ah poor Dave living down here 'longside of Chinatown with all the whores, thieves and stew bums. And his girl, so young sitting up in bed staring at us with great brown eyes.

"It's O.K. Dave? We're not disturbing you?" "Naw, naw," I replied slipping on my cowboy boots, "I got paid today - c'mon we'll go out and I'll treat the two of ya to a beer."

I suggested the Swiss Hut and Larry drove us up there in his car. We were just settling down in one of the booths before three quarts of beer when Larry said, "Do you come here often?" "Not really," I replied, "the guys around here are just not my kind of people." Danny glanced at me with a frown and said, "Who are your kind of people?"

I smiled at his words even though he was frowning. "That's just like Casey," I thought to myself, "he couldn't lie to himself or anyone else even if his life depended on it."

"You and Larry, you're my kind of people," I explained.

Danny leaned back in his seat with a grunt, a slight smile playing about his eyes. He had once told me, "Dave you nearly always come up with the right answers to my questions and I guess that's why we were so close as kids." I'm used to the silence, I'm used to having to speak for more than myself.

"Yeah but we don't smoke dope," grumbled Larry.

"Neither do I, " I replied. "Although I've tried it enough to know I don't like the effects. As for the hard stuff, speed, acid and junk I wouldn't even think of trying it."

They continued to measure me with questions throughout the rest of the evening, trying to pinpoint me and only discovering that I was basically still the same strange kid they used to play with in the alleyways of East Verdun.

"By the way Larry," I said as we were driving back to Hotel de Ville Street," I never asked you what you're doing for a living. Are you still with the C.N.R.?"

"No," he replied, "I'm working for the government."

That was a vague answer but I let it pass figuring his answer to mean that some relative of his had landed him some easy, good-paying desk job in the Civil Service.

I haven't seen Danny Malone since that spring evening in 1968 but I was to meet Larry three or four more times on the street in the next couple of years. Once outside Eaton's one night while Liz and I were walking home from a movie theatre. Larry was dressed up in a navy blue suit, we shook hands and I asked him where he was going. "I'm on my way to work Dave," he said. "Oh, you're on the graveyard shift eh?" "Yeah," he said smiling, "Catch you later, I gotta go."

I took down his phone number I believe, I'm not sure, but anyhow I was to meet him only a couple of weeks later at the St. Jean Baptiste parade. The year the separatists stormed the reviewing stand on the steps of the Montreal Library in a vain attempt to get their hands on Pierre Elliot Trudeau. According to the newspaper report Pierre never even turned a hair when an empty pop bottle whizzed by within a few inches of his head causing a general scramble for shelter amongst the less courageous dignitaries in his company. A platoon of motorcycle cops finally succeeded in driving the rioters out of the immediate vicinity of the reviewing stand and into the depths of Lafontaine Park. Some of the rioters, a few with bruised faces and one with a bloody handkerchief held to his nose, came storming down the sidewalk past where I was standing with a bunch of hippy friends in front of the New Penelope. "What's happening?" we murmured. "Trouble happening somewhere?" Separatists - rioting - library. Snatches of conversation, rumours.

There were maybe a hundred or so street people congregated around where I was viewing the parade just west of Park Avenue. We had been anticipating Mayor Drapeau's appearance in the parade all evening because he was giving us a particularly hard time that summer and we all planned to do a massive thumbs down demonstration on him when he passed by.

I was standing on top of a public wastepaper basket alongside of Greasy Don from Ontario, both of us hanging onto the pole that basket was attached to for balance, really grooving on the sweet long-legged majorettes passing by, when I happened to glance behind me and chanced to see Larry Omer pushing his way through the dense crowd on the sidewalk.

"Hey, Larry! " I yelled "Larry! " as I jumped down from the basket over towards him. "Wait a sec! How ya doing?"

He extended his hand in greeting but kept answering my questions with nervous tight-lipped monosyllables and twisting his head around as if he were looking for someone.

"He's nervous," I thought "Perhaps he's uneasy being surrounded by so many freaky-looking people. Then I looked around and saw that nearly all the freaks were staring at us. "Lord Jesus," I thought, "they think I'm talking to a cop. They think Larry's a cop." And Larry does look like a cop, a heavy six-footer with a hard, stern face, dressed in a shiny blue suit.

"Hey Larry," I said laughing grabbing him by the arms, "Ya wanna hear something funny?" "What Dave?" he said somberly. "All these guys are staring at us because they think you're a cop. They think I'm talking to a cop."

"Dave," he said slowly in a voice thick with sadness, "I am a cop." He pulled his I.D. card and badge out of his pocket, "See?"

"Yeah, I'm sorry, I mean you know it means nothing to me."

"It's alright Dave," he said while snarling at the freaks, "but I gotta go - these bug-eyed goofs are getting on my nerves. See ya around."

Over a year later I was getting on a Verdun bus on my way uptown back from visiting my mother. While dropping my fare in the box I glanced down the back of the bus and saw Larry sitting by himself on one of the side seats. He was staring right at me without recognizing me because I was wearing my cap. I smiled and Larry frowned; he doesn't like hippies. I walked towards him down the aisle, still smiling, and the closer I got the more hostile his face became, his mouth tightening with anger as he tilted back his head glaring at me. When I got within punching distance I pulled off my cap and folded my hair behind my ears. Instantly his face lapsed into a moving gentleness. "Dave," he said softly, a confused blush slightly reddening his cheeks as I extended my hand. We had been nursed and mothered by the same streets, sharing common joys and sorrows and in our hearts we were like brothers regardless of the adult roles society had hammered us into.

I slipped down beside him on the seat determined to speak what was on my mind before our conversation became molded by the usual conventional questions and answers. "Larry," I said, "I know what being a cop can sometimes do to a man and I only hope you remain the same Larry Omer I knew and loved as a kid on the street."

He grunted, cleared his throat and said, "It's only a job to me, Dave. I work thirty-seven and a half hours a week with a lot of fringe benefits."

"You must have seen a lot of terrible things Larry, in the last three years," I replied. "Number ten station is in a rough district."

"Dave," he said quietly, "I've seen about everything I guess there is to see. Some things so ugly I wouldn't even talk to you about them. Murders, suicides, rape - none of that stuff bothers me any more, althought I still get shook up whenever we come upon a case where some poor kid's lying dead on the floor because his asshole parents didn't have enough sense to lock their medicine cabinets. Ugly, ugly - ugly people. It would break your heart Dave, you'd throw up your guts at the sight - at the sight of some of the garbage people I've had to deal with, day after day, over and over and over again. It gets so you wonder if there's any people left in the world that are not sick."

He told me he worked for awhile as an undercover detective hanging out in the downtown west side taverns where all the rounders drink.

"This loud-mouth goof was sitting a few tables away from mine bragging to all the guys he was sitting with about all the scores he had pulled off, all the cops he had punched out and all the girls he had screwed. Just the sound of the goof's voice drove me up the wall but he hadn't done anything I could hold him on that would stick in court. If I wasn't a cop I probably would have just got up and beaten the living shit out of the goof right on the spot.

"Anyhow I got a break that evening, the big mouth got into a fight, just a small scuffle but he pulled out a gun and palced it on the table, not to use it, you understand, just to show what a big man he was. Man he made me happy because now I could bust the son of a bitch ard maybe get him the pen. But I couldn't just get up and snatch the guy, what with all his friends sitting there. I could have called the station for help; you know I'm no hero but I didn't want to give the goof the satisfaction of putting on a tough guy act, a hero who needs more than one cop to pick him up. I had a gun on me but I never use it.

"So what I did was invite myself over to his table. I sat down with him and began bugging him about his big mouth. 'You're all mouth and no guts,' I said. The guy got really hot and said, 'Come on goof, let's take a walk outside.' When we got out into the alleyway the bastard pulled his gun on me. I had my fists up and I said, 'What's the matter big man? Where I come from we use these!' Well the goof put his gun away and I knocked him cold with one shot to the face before he even had a chance to get his hand back out of his pocket. Then I dragged him by his jacket out onto Sainte Catherine Street and called a car."

Larry's the kind of cop who takes his job seriously. He really believes his job is to safeguard people and justice. Consequently I doubt whether he'll remain for long on the force, for good cops are generally always the first guys to get the axe.

<u>April 2, 1971</u>   <u>Friday</u>

Richard Cooper, my creative writing teacher, liked the story I handed in to him enough to have me read it out in class. "It's really very good, the dialogue in particular," he said, "is marvellous. So natural, lively and flowing." "Thank you," I mumbled, both pleased and surpised by his words since I expected he would be much more critical of my work than Sally has been.

Sally asked me to see her after her lecture yesterday afternoon. We walked together up to her office and I felt more relaxed with her than I expected to be, perhaps because I sensed that, having read my journal she would understand my behaviour no matter how I acted. She was very cautious with me, very careful that she would not hurt my feelings, approaching each subject she, wished to discuss with me by first referring to my own wishes.

Primarily we spoke of my journal which she feels is worthy of publication. In particular she said my dialogues were consistently real. "Your sentences keep me very busy David," she said. "They're, uh, always exploding unexpectedly."

She proposed that I have Dawson print five hundred or so copies of my journal which I am to have copy-righted and placed in various bookstores on sale.

"I like the idea of perhaps making some extra bread Sally," I exclaimed, "but the writing is so personal. You know, I wouldn't like the idea of my family reading it."

But, think of it, David. Holding something you've created and sweated over in your hands!"

"True, true," I replied nervously tapping my thigh, one leg curled defensively under the other. "She's so careful with me," I thought, "and shy."

Again after referring to my preferences we began discussing my poetry which she feels does not compare with my journal.

"They're too simple . . . thin, based on a single theme in general," she explained. "Your phrasing is good, your phrasing is always good," and she quoted, " 'And who's to tell of the West End boys that died without speaking, if I did not measure the beauty of their steps with my words.' " Her favourite poems of mine were, "Concerning the Immortality of Dandelions", "Poets are Liars", and "For Christiane", all of which she felt had more depth than the others.

Sally told me that she does not share my optimism about the future. "I have a rather dreary attitude towards human nature," she said. She also thought my political views were rather simplistic, narrow and limited in scope. "Your writing, your insight, falters," she said, "whenever you delve into political theory."

Our hour-and-a-half conversation terminated with Sally saying that she would like to become friends with me. "I like you," she said, "at least I like what I've seen of you in

your writing." Then she lent me a pile of books which she
insisted I read - all heavy stuff that I quickly filed away in
my locker, out of sight, out of mind.

Strange, but the areas in which Sally believes I'm limited
are precisely those in which I feel she is limited.

April 4, 1971   Sunday

Tricky old Fennario. Charly and Sharon wrestling
with each other on the sofa, Liz in the kitchen cooking
up some herring, Tim Hardin album on the record player
and everybody drinking Spanish wine. Then Jay phoned
up to invite us over to his new apartment on Monkland
Boulevard and we drove over there in Charly's old Volkswagen. "I'm gonna miss this old car," I said punching
the hood. "Me too," replied Charly. His father's buying
him a new one when he graduates. "I don't know how
people can have the heart to keep a car just for one year
and then trade it in."

Jay was all ready for us with a fridge stocked full of beer,
wine and vodka. It's a cute little flat he has, very compact,
almost like a doll's house.

"Man, I'm telling ya Jay," I said, "It's funny but
nearly all my friends live either on top floors or in basements."

Jay has always been a good audience for me and consequently I get loose with a number of good stories including one about Jacky Robinson and me in the Unemployment Insurance building.

"This happened quite a few years ago when I was
living with Jacky down on Coloniale Street. We were
getting tired of sitting around waiting for something good
to happen and in a moment of weakness we decided we'd
go downtown and look for a job. We stayed up all that
night so we wouldn't sleep in and eight o'clock the next
morning we were in front of the Unemployment Manpower Building on Dorchester Blvd. when the security guard
unlocked the door. Jacky had never been in the place before. Our hair was all slicked down with about two pounds
of vaseline and we were wearing our best pairs of jeans and

the whitest shirts we could find, which were not too white.

"There was a tremendous line-up of people at the Manpower counters that morning. There was maybe forty guys and dolls ahead of us, all of them looking pretty grim. We weren't feeling none too good ourselves, especially since neither of us had been up so early in the morning since elementary school. So both of us were feeling pretty low-down and mean, particularly Jacky whose scowling face and brisk barking voice quickly gained the attention of the security guard and the stern looks he was continually giving us seemed to say 'Aha we got a couple of shit disturbers down at the slave market this morning'.

"What with all the people in front of us I figured I had time for a cigarette. However the bureaucratic wheels were rolling at an incredible speed that morning and I still had a good size butt smouldering between my fingers when it came my turn at the counter. The woman dealt with me as she had done with all the other poor slobs. She took my card, got my file, stamped a date, handed me a white form and mumbled some banality like 'Give us a call sometime. Next.'

"I stepped out of line to allow Jacky to belly up to the counter. It took the clerk quite some time to decipher Jacky's social security number because his card was so beat-up and faded.

" 'Why don't you take better care of your identification card! ' she snapped, using the chilly, officious tone of voice favoured by devout bureaucrats in dealing with humble working men desperate for jobs.

" 'Why don't you shove it up your fucken cunt bitch! ' barked Jacky. I grabbed his arm, he pushed my hand away. The clerk was obviously used to having people cringe before her every whim, consequently Jacky's short, pungent reply stunned her into disbelief.

" 'Qu-est que - what did you say?'
" 'I said——'
" 'He said he'd like to see his file madame,' I exclaimed, interrupting Jacky with a poke in the ribs.

"The woman's chin was very much up in the air as she huffed away in the direction of the filing cabinets.

" 'You have no file,' she said on returning. Then taking out a blue form from under the counter she said, 'Where did you work last?'

" ' I never worked, I'm a thief,' Jacky said. 'I only want my card stamped so my girlfriend will think I'm looking for a job and quit hassling me.'

"The woman's mouth slammed shut with a sharp click as she pushed a white form over to Jacky. 'Bonjour. Next,' she said.

"Jacky didn't move. 'Monsieur,' the woman said in a voice that could cut diamonds, 'You are blocking up the line.'

"Jacky turned and faced the long line of people waiting behind him.

" 'Why do you bother waiting?' he said addressing them. Then snatching the pile of white forms the woman had been giving out to everyone from off the counter he passed down the line giving everyone a form.

" 'Here-here-here-here,' he said. 'This is all you're gonna get. Good-bye you can go home now.'

"From the corner of my eye I could see that the security guard was on the phone. Jacky was starting back to the counter to get more white forms when I grabbed his arm and said, 'Guard's on the phone Jacky. The cops will be coming.' 'Yeah, yeah, yeah,' he said pushing my hand away. I shrugged my shoulders as he passed by me and double-stepped out of the joint on my own.

"Jacky got out of the place before the police came, he was walking across the street to where I was standing just as the patrol car pulled up at the office door.

" 'Jacky you're nuts,' I said hugging him as he stepped on the sidewalk.

" 'What the fuck,' he replied, 'I couldn't leave the place without giving all those poor bastards a white form.' "

Both Liz and Sharon fell asleep sitting up on the couch by midnight but Jay, Charly and myself stayed up close to three in the morning telling jokes and stories and playing on a couple of harmonicas until the last drop of liquor in the fridge had been drunk.

Jacky had himself entered in the Royal Victoria Hospital last Thursday and the next night he underwent two minor operations, one for a hernia and one for a broken nose a kid busted for him last year on St. Antoine Street. We went up to visit him Saturday walking through the main hospital entrance about six-thirty that evening. We approached the information desk and I asked for the ward and room number in which John William Robinson had been placed. Then as the man began flipping through a wheel of file cards I thought, "Lord Jesus, I hope Jacky didn't enter himself under one of his aliases. Boudain? Sebastain? Baker? Lewis?" The man turned towards me, "Did you say Robertson or Robinson?" "Rob-in-son" I replied. He hesitated and then pulled out a card, "1045 on the tenth floor," he said looking up at me, John William Robinson." "Thank you."

A long neon-lit vinyl corridor led to a double row of elevators and a white marble statue of a matronly Queen Victoria with two children scampering about her knees. I patted one of the kids on its ass and the marble was smooth and surprisingly, warm, like suede to the touch.

The statue was truly a relic, a left-over piece of junk from the defunct British Empire. It brought up all sorts of associations to my mind. Kipling, "Lest we forget," the Diamond Jubilee and the White Man's burden. Young British officers, Oxford bred, with swagger sticks leading their men over the top in Flanders. Cavalrymen with spurs on their boots but no horses. No chivalry, no more honour or glory, just mud, rattling machine guns, poison gas, barbed wire and trenches. "Good bye to all that." Victoria Regina. Big Bertha yawns from seventy miles away and the shells fall in the boulevards of Paris. Zeppelins flew over Glasgow, my grandmother saw them. The innocence was gone.

The slums of London, Birmingham, Liverpool, Manchester and Glasgow had so stunted the working men that the required height for army recruits had to be lowered to five feet two inches. England paid dearly for her empire.

Jack the Ripper frequented her Majesty's capital back in the eighties slicing up whores in the East End of London.

You must have heard of him, Your Majesty, perhaps the screams of his victims may have even penetrated Buckingham Palace on the outskirts of the City. He butchered nine whores each of them found with their wombs cut out lying beside them on the street. "I'm down on whores," he wrote in explanation to the newspaper and he included a poem to correct the speculations that had been made about his identity:

"I'm not a doc
I'm not a Yid
Nor yet a foreign skipper,
I am your own true loving friend,
Yours truly, Jack the Ripper."

Beneath the pomp, the splendour of the triumphs and the jubilees, the vain-glorious poetry, the proud eloquence and scholarly histories, the plush bourgeois homes, the mahogany tables, lace curtains, bay windows, the genteel ladies, their perfumed hands, there was MURDER.

Vampires sucking profits out of their stunted human cattle corralled in the numerous slums of the nation. Jack the Ripper knew his friends well, Your Majesty, the vampire class of whom you are the living symbol. He was the British Empire, he was the consequence. Anyhow, I've never been able to look at statues or pictures of Queen Victoria without thinking of Jack the Ripper.

A long ride up the elevator shaft in company with two old ladies took us to the tenth floor, top floor, 1045. Franky saw us first, her black eyes widening with surprise. "Dave? It's Dave?" said Jacky lifting his head from the pillow. I moved over to his side and shook his hand, "Hi man, good ta see ya." "Look at him, Liz," I said turning towards her, "Jacky Robinson in a hospital. Sleeping Ugly!" Elizabeth leaned over and gave him a kiss. "Hey Jacky," I exclaimed, "now that the family jewels are back in shape you'll be able to wear tight pants again and thrill all the girls on Ste. Catherine Street."

I pulled up some chairs for Liz and myself and we sat down at the head of Jacky's bed. There were three other patients in the same room as him, one of them with a broken arm was propped up in his bed reading Atlas Shrugged by Ayn Rand. He looked the type.

"Roll up the bed, Franky," Jacky said, "so I can look at Dave." It was hard for him to talk because his nose was masked over with a thick wad of gauze and bandages. "I wouldn't be here if I could walk," he announced after the nurse told him to put out his cigarette.

"I came up to see him early this afternoon," Franky said, "he was just coming out of the ether and he asks me to roll up the bed. Then he raised himself by his elbows, wriggled over to the side of the bed, stepped out and stood on the floor. He was shaky but he still stood. 'Are you proud of me Honey?' he says, 'Sure I am Jacky,' I answered. 'Well,' he says, 'Go and tell the nurse I'm standing because she said I wouldn't be able to.' "

Yeah, Jacky's always digging his own grave and climbing out of it.

April 10, 1971   Saturday

I met Danny Boy from Dawson uptown yesterday night and I invited him down to a couple of beers at the Empire Tavern. At the table he began a story about how he first met his girl Nancy in high school. While listening to his words I proceeded to scan the tavern, checking out the people when, with a jerk, I recognized old Joe Coté sitting just a table away from us. It was good to see him because Claude the waiter hadn't seen him since Christmas and we were worried that he might have died. Old Joe Coté, nearly eighty now, a little more pale, his legs a bit more unsteady and his cough a little more persistent but his voice is still full of piss and vinegar. His eyes filled with tears when I came over and surprised him with a hug and handshake. "Hey Dave! " he exclaimed. "Claude told me you've been asking for me, est-ti. Sit down, sit down - bring your friend over."

First things first, I asked him where he had been the last five months. "I been drinking at home most of the time," he said. "The legs are bad, hard to walk since that damn car, THAT DAMNED CAR, hit me on St. Antoine."

When he found out that Danny Boy was joining the Navy he warmed right up to him and began telling us about the ships he sailed on as a cook in the first and second world wars. "Good ships. Good ships, Dave, to England, Africa, Singapore and good times. I made a lot of money gambling and selling food on the Black Market."

I paid for a couple of rounds of beer and Joe got hot at me for including a beat-up looking guy that was sitting with us after he told me not to. "Dave, Dave," he said wagging a fore finger, "You have no respect for an old man. I told you not to buy him any beer. He's no good, no good, est-ti. I've been buying him beer all afternoon. He's had six quarts." I shrugged my shoulders picked up Joe's pint bottle and poured him a glass. It was good to see the old man again. "I'll never forget you Dave," he said in parting, "I'll never forget you." I shook hands with Danny outside the tavern and walked home by myself. The curtains on the front window were open so I knew Liz was worried about me being late.

April 12, 1971   Monday

I was down to my mother's yesterday afternoon with Easter eggs for Jean, Kelly Ann, Dawn and Sarah. Jimmy was home on leave for the Easter holidays. After supper we drank beer with my mother and father at the kitchen table. I hardly had a word to say myself and to-wards midnight my father said, "There's a big bust coming for sure. If I were both your ages and knew what I know now from my experiences, I'd go and jump in the river tonight." The big bust he went on to explain is coming in the form of a massive war. "It's the only thing that brings people together. If they were to drop a bomb in Canada, overnight everyone would be for war and stop quibbling amongst themselves. Only trouble is, it would probably be a very big bomb."

"What about a revolution?" I asked.

"Oh that will all be forgotten about if a war happens."

I went home on the bus by myself wondering what was going to happen and how.

I went uptown this afternoon with the fifty bucks
that Harry Rossman lent me and bought thirty-six dollars
worth of books at the Classics bookstore. Stuff by Pirenne,
Marx, Engels, Kerouac and so on. I was like a hungry man
wide-eyed in a grocery store after having found fifty bucks
on the street.

There is so much crap between fancy art covers passing for political science nowadays. Whole shelves of books
with pretentious titles internationally advertised as panaceas
for all the social evils under the sun. Books on poverty,
crime, pollution, unemployment, avant garde education,
social psychology, all of them beautifully designed and
wrapped but with nothing but a lot of hot air holding the
two covers apart.

Bearded "exis" post graduates were milling about
the Herman Hesse section dressed in red hunting jackets
with construction boots on their feet and packages of
rolling tobacco sticking out of their shirt pockets. Rolling
tobacco is a funny thing. University students are quick to
demonstrate that they can roll their own but the ordinary
working man would rather be caught with his pants down
than pull out a pack of tobacco at a tavern table and
thereby advertise his poverty.

On the way home I saw two construction workers on
St. Antoine Street with long hair hanging below their hard
hats and my head lifted a little higher as I remembered
reading in Life and Work in the Middle Ages that only free-
men were allowed to wear their hair long. Cropped hair has
always been a badge of slavery and I hope what I saw today
is a good omen for the future.

Upon this most, most auspicious day walking into the
student's building on Belair Street and discovering, oh sweet
Jesus, that my five hundred government dollars in the form
of a cheque has finally arrived in the mail. "Oh yeah!" I
said when the secretary informed me that yes my loan has

been received. Roll the drums the fantasy ship has finally reached port and the first thing Liz says she wants is a bed. We've been sleeping on the narrow pullout sofa for months since I threw the old boxspring out.

April 16, 1971   Friday

Believe it. I am writing the following while sitting in the living room chair at ten to six this snowy April morning. I haven't been to sleep yet for reasons I'm about to explain.

First off I went down to the Salvation Army Store on Notre Dame Street yesterday evening with Liz, where we ordered a bed and two coffee tables from Pat's Mom, Mrs. O'Neil, who works there. Good woman that she is, she was kind enough to help us in our selection, pointing out the best bargains to us.

Liz, very much pleased at the idea of having a real bed for the first time in two years was chit-chatting little-girl-happy hanging on my arm all the way back home from Notre Dame Street.

"You'll see David what a difference a coffee table will make in the house."

"Uh huh."

"Oh it'll be so good now that I won't have to place people's coffees on a chair now."

"Yeah, one minute, I wanna stop off at Turcot's and pick up a deck of weeds."

Liz told me when she got home that the Academy Awards were being handed out on T.V. that evening and she wanted to go up and watch the show at her mother's.

"It comes on so late though," she said. "It finishes at twelve thirty and I wouldn't want to walk home at that hour from uptown."

She pondered over the problem for awhile and then said, "I could sleep at my mother's overnight?"

"Does she have room?"

"Oh sure she has plenty of room."

"Well, then why not?" I replied.

She left around eight-thirty and I settled down to my Medieval history books, the whys, wherefores, and how comes of Charlemagne. Towards eleven o'clock I got a little hungry and ordered a small all-dressed special from Athen's Restaurant. A pizza smothered with onions, mushrooms, cheese, salami, pepperoni and bacon - Greek style and very heavy on the stomach.

By one thirty the words on the page began jumping around too quickly for me to read them so I called it quits and rolled into bed. Two-thirty, three-thirty, four-thirty and still I couldn't fall asleep, tossing and turning with all the week's events passing through my head. Finally I gave up and turned on the light. "Oh well it's been a long time since I've seen the sun come up," I thought. "Maybe I'll go out and take a walk in the dawn air." But glancing out the front window I settled down on the bed with a pillow propped against the wall to rest my back and began reading more about the Middle Ages.

Then it happened, a sudden light rapping at the door. I couldn't believe it. Then it happened a bit louder and the rapping gradually became a pounding. "One minute," I said, figuring maybe it was Liz coming home, lonely because in the last four years there have been only three nights that we didn't sleep together. Pulling on my jeans I hopped over to the front door and looking through the door window I saw a wild looking face staring bluntly at me. "Who is that?" I wondered. "Is it Jacky drunk?" I squinted my eyes, no, but his face looked kind of familiar so I walked into the porch to get a closer look at the guy. His eyes had an insane brilliance about them and his black greasy hair was sticking out in tufts all over his head, and I figured he must have been in a fight because the skin about his mouth was smeared with dried blood.

He signalled at me to open the porch door. I clicked open the lock and asked him what he wanted. "Let me in," he said, "I wanna talk to George." I could smell the guy and he stunk of cheap wine, its aroma perfumed the whole porch. "There's no one by that name living here man," I replied. "You got the wong house." "No man, I got the right house. George lives here and I wanna talk to him."

"Look," I said with a tense smile, "believe me this is the wrong house this is 2282."

"Now, don't start giving me hassles man," he replied, "George lives here. GEORGE I WANNA TALK TO YOU MOTHER FUCKER."

"You got the wrong house I tell ya, nobody by that name lives here."

"No man, no, George lives here PRICK," he said. "This is the right place and I'm coming in." He began wedging the door open with his hands and feet. I checked his advance by moving in front of him.

"You're drunk. Go on home."

"Let me in." he snarled, "better let me in man," opening the door wider with his hands. I threw a quick straight arm to his chest just as he was squeezing his shoulder by the door and he stumbled back into the outside porch. "Motherfucker," he hissed, glaring at me through the window as I slammed the door.

"Get out of here before I call the cops," I said shaking my fist at him before I turned back into the house.

"Open the door! " he yelled. "Open the door motherfucker! "

He continued to pound on the door so I phoned the cops; then I went into the kitchen and armed myself with a king size coke bottle just in case the maniac broke in before they got here.

He was kicking the door when the patrol car finally pulled up at the curb and two cops, both of them over six foot walked casually over to my front steps. I watched all the action from my living room window.

"Hey you," the biggest cop said and the dude turned his attention towards them. "Yeah?" he said, leaning out of the outside porch door.

"What are you doing knocking on people's doors, making all this noise. It's not nice."

"Yeah?" the cop said, "Well cut down on the noise. There's been some complaints."

"Hell no," I thought, "they're not gonna bust him. They're gonna leave him here." And I moved out into the porch behind the crazy dude who was now standing on the front stairs and yelled, "I don't know this guy. I never seen him before. He comes pounding on my door saying he lives here and I'm the only one who lives here in this house." The cops only stared at me without comment but the crazy dude turned his head slightly and hissed, "I'll be back man and you're gonna have trouble. You've got trouble now. I'll be back."

Then he stepped down on the sidewalk and the cop said, "C'mon I want to see you." and shone a flashlight in the dude's eyes, "What happened to your face?"

"I just want to talk to George," the guy exclaimed. "He knows me."

I went back to the living room window carefully locking the porch and house doors behind me. (I don't wanna live here anymore. What if Liz had been alone in the house?)

"I used to be an amateur boxer," I heard the dude say, "I've won prizes. Are you guys gonna drive me home? It's cold out here."

The cops were sitting in the car checking out the guy's I.D. over the radio as he stood close by with his right arm resting on the roof of the car. His I.D. must have checked out positively wanted because the cop looked up at the guy and told him to get into the car. "No. I don't want to!" he exclaimed. The cop moved out of the car and stepped in front of the guy. "Get in the car," he said softly, almost like he was pleading.

"No!"

The cop grabbed his arm but the dude wrestled him off.

"GEORGE I'M IN FRONT OF THE CAR. I'M STILL HERE, GEORGE."

Then the cop folded him up with a couple of belly punches that collapsed him into the back seat and off they went. I took a hot bath to relax myself and then sat down in the easy chair to write this out.

April 18, 1971   Sunday

I went up to the Atwater Library Friday afternoon to check out some new sources for my Spartacus essay and I met Old John in the reading room. Old John from Ribkoff's dress factory days. They fired him a couple of months after I left the company and he's been on unemployment insurance ever since and that was a good year and a half ago."

"My money runs out in three months," he said, "and then I guess I'll go on welfare, if I can. I'm over fifty and if

you young guys can't find jobs, what's the chances for a
man of my age?"

Yeah, Old John. He was the head of Ribkoff's unofficial grievance committee, the only man with the guts
to stand up to any of Joe Ribkoff's flunky managers whenever the work load and over time got to be too heavy. "Go
tell old John, go tell Old John and tell him to speak to the
boss."

Old John, his life wasted away as a "boy" in the
sweatshops. It's a bitch.

April 19, 1971   Monday

"It's a joke, it's a laugh Jonathan (John from the
wrong side of Outremont). You really don't think anyone takes CEGEP's seriously do you? We're the slum
proletariat of the academic world, man - maybe some of us
will graduate and land a job but not too many. The government's letting us amuse ourselves while keeping us off
the labour market, off the streets. Guess it's cheaper
this way."

A round-shouldered Monday morning remembering
Friday night, Jay, Jacky, Charly and me drunk in Charly's
living room singing, "I think it's gonna rain all day."
Charly singing for the first time that I can remember in a
kind of childish slightly off-key tenor.

Saturday is a blur in my mind. Oh yeah, the Sally
Ann guys delivered our bed to the house eight-thirty in
the morning waking us up and Liz so happy about not
having to sleep on the pull out sofa anymore. "I feel
more like a human being now," she said.

Sunday, the end of the week panic - gotta get my
work done sweating over my Spartacus essay upstairs in
my little cubby-hole study. O sweet Jesus and all alone by
myself shadow boxing with my inherited nightmares.
Sucking down the panic tension, shuttling the loom of
my mind back and forth, a thread here and there in assorted colours, weaving my ideas. Coughing up sentences
and chopping them down into paragraphs. A word, a word,
a word . . . what belongs there? Does it sing on the tongue?

In April, of April, within April and the mysteries and the promises at my finger tips.

On Sunday night I went with Mike and Liz up to the New Byzantium Restaurant on the Main for a special meal of Greek food.

I had my first taste of lamb and as I pronged the first chunk of mutton into my mouth I said, "I sort of feel like a cannibal,Liz."

We wandered about the old neighbourhood we used to live in until the sun went down. Coloniale, DeBullion, Laval streets and St. Louis Square where Liz used to play as a little girl. "The fountain used to work then," she said, "and we used to paddle around in the water. My cat once climbed up on the roof of that old Synagogue on Coloniale Street and the caretaker wouldn't help me get it back down again. It was up there for weeks yowling its head off at nights. I guess it lived off the pigeons but anyhow my sister Elsy ended up giving a Portugese boy twenty-five cents to go up on the roof and get the cat. He climbed up and got it and the poor thing was ragged, bony and dirty and the boy's arms were all scratched."

We dropped in for a beer at the Maidenhead on the way home. Straight middle-aged businessmen were sitting at the bar having silly conversations with the pretty waitresses who flashed bright show-biz smiles off and on just to keep the customers satisfied.

We were at a table watching Ed Sullivan on the colour T.V. when a long red-haired fellow walked into the place with a girl. "I think I went to elementary school with that guy," i said turning to Liz.

Yes his hair was less of a fiery red than I remembered it, but I was positive that it was Gary. I remembered him as a quiet soft-spoken kid, always sitting in the back of the class and always in trouble with the teachers for day-dreaming. When he sat down at the empty table next to us I tapped him on the back. "Excuse me, but are you from Verdun? Did you go to Bannantyne School?"

"Yes," he said. "You're Dave, uh, Dave . . ."

"Fennario, that's right! " I exclaimed while extending my hand. "Haven't seen you for over ten years . . . so what's been happening?"

The Northern Electric plant as an assembly worker, that's what's been happening with Gary the last five years. He also told me he was attending school at night and has ambitions of buying a farm.

"Yeah, I remember that even when you were a kid, Gary, you were always talking about the good life in the country."

"Well, you know Dave," he replied, "I lived on a farm as a kid before we moved to the big city."

We spoke of our boyhood friends and the old Verdun names were like poetry to me. Stucky, Brewer, Quinn, Snow, Mingo, O'Neill, Russel, Holdbrook, Featherstone, Waterfall, Horn, Frost. Of the days when we used to rob bread and sweet cakes out of the bakery just down the street from Bannantyne School. "Wow," Gary said, "remember the day we stampeded the horses in the stables and Danny Malone came within inches of being trampled all over." Yeah they still had horses pulling bread wagons in East Verdun back in the fifties and yes those wild horses nearly did run over Danny who was the last one to scramble under the barbed-wire fence that day.

"Remember Dale Eden?" I asked and he nodded. "She was so cute remember? Freckles, sunshine blue eyes, little turned up nose, toffee-brown hair and a saucy kind of bouncing walk. I used to follow her home from school every day, at a discreet distance of course. I can see her now cutting through the laneway behind the Bell Telephone building over to her home on Third Avenue and my little boy's heart doing double trip flips at the sight of her."

"Oh David," said Liz smiling, "you must have been such a sweet little boy"; and she blew me a kiss.

"Well some guys like cars and hockey games," I replied. "Me, I've always liked women. Love to hear them talk, love to see them walk. Love it! "

Liz gave me one of her - you're getting drunk and

it's time to go home Fennario smiles and said, "It's ten o'clock Dave."

"Uh huh, Gary," I said standing up and extending my hand. "It's been like poetry to see you again and I hope we meet soon."

"Sooner than that," he replied grasping my hand.

April 25, 1971   Sunday

There's a quiet and shy girl at Dawson who has the same mannerisms and look about her as Elizabeth. Her name is Cathy and she reminds me of how Elizabeth looked and acted back in her middle teens. From the first time I saw Cathy in one of my classes I haven't been able to keep my eyes away from her. I began making myself known to her, using the same approach as I did when I was making Elizabeth's acquaintance and soon we were on a hello and good-bye basis. Then one afternoon I saw her walking through the lobby and I held out my arms and she came over so naturally to me and I said, "Cathy, darling if I was eighteen years old I'd run away with you for sure, even if you do walk like a milkman."

"I told Liz I wanted her to meet Cathy and she took the day off from work on Friday and went into school with me. She enjoyed Madame Sonac's French class and afterwards we went with Sharon and sat in the cafeteria. Nicky the Fool came over and then Gary Firestone. I left the group talking amongst themselves and went upstairs to the library looking for Cathy. She was sitting at a table by a window going over her homework.

"Work work work!" I said as I walked up to her. "Cathy you're always working."

She smiled, "Yes I guess so."

I bent my knees until my head was at a level with the table and then looking up at her I said, "Cathy are you ready for the acid test?"

"What do you mean?"

"Acid test. Now I'll be able to prove to you that you really look like my girl Liz because she's in school with me today. She's downstairs in the cafeteria. Come on down."

"O.K.," she said slapping her books closed.

Liz blushed when she saw us approaching the table.

"Well, what do you think Liz? Cathy?"

"I don't know," said Liz with a weak smile.

"I'm not sure," said Cathy.

"Nicky, Gary, Sharon, what do you think?"

All of them replied no, they didn't think there was
a strong resemblance between them, except for Gary,
who said yes they do have the same strange look about
them. They most definitely do.

I told two stories while we were all sitting together in
the cafeteria. Nicky was talking about the river and I
said, "Yeah the river. You know one time a friend of mine,
Danny Malone and I saw a frog in the bullrushes about -
yea big - no kidding, as big as a basket ball and nobody in
East Verdun would believe us any more than you guys
believe me now. Man it was a monster. We jumped
back about six feet when we first spied it, eyes as big
as silver dollars staring right at us. We waited a little while to
see if the frog would move and it did - k-plunk-k-plunk, one
little hop at a time. It had to take breaks inbetween hops
it was so big and fat. Well we decided that anything that
moves that slow, you know, couldn't be too dangerous so
we stepped slowly up to the frog and touched it and everytime I touched its back it would bounce one hop away
-k-plunk-k-plunk. Until finally it splashed into the water
and took off across the river like a nuclear sub. There's
monsters in that river believe me.

"I believe you," said Nicky. "Who knows what the
pollution is breeding?"

"Yeah the river is really getting dirty," I replied.
"Even when I was a kid and we used to go swimming
just below the old power dam in LaSalle, pieces of shit
were always floating by along with a lot of other garbage.
I once drank a coke bottle full of river water on a bet with
Arty Leonard for a pack of chewing gum. I waited until
all the crap in the bottle settled down in the bottom and
then I slugged the stuff down. It was the colour of piss
and tasted like it. The gang of kids that were with me
that day were all expecting me to drop dead at any second
and as I think back I wonder how come I didn't. 'You're
a dead man, Dave,' they said. 'It'll kill ya for sure. It's

gonna creep up on ya, all those bugs and worms and germs are gonna eat ya up before supper time.'

"But man I was laughing. I jsut sat back there chewing on Arty's gum and I never got as much as a stomach ache. Guess it takes more than a little dirty water to kill a back-street boy.

"Yeah my first love was a dogwood tree but I forgot all about her once I saw the river, and then I knew what true love was.

"No kidding, there was this dogwood tree in the district that I grew up in, one of the few that I have ever seen in the city. Every spring it would break out in white blossoms that would perfume the whole block and I was young, you know, and I had never seen anything so pretty as that tree all decked out with feather-white flowers like a beautiful June bride. I couldn't resist her. I used to sneak into old Geebou's yard at night and sit in the branches, talking to my sweetheart and dreaming things that four-year-old boys dream about.

"Yeah it was a beautiful romance but a tragic one, a regular Romeo and Juliet, because the tree was growing in old Geebou's yard and he was not only a landlord, but also the meanest old man in the neighbourhood. He had three sons just as mean as him and all of them built like Neanderthal men. They referred to me as that crazy kid out there hugging the tree again,' and Boom they'd storm down into the yard and kick my ass over the fence. But love is love and I always came back even after they installed a flood light and put a roll of barbed wire around my sweetheart's trunk."

All the guys laughed but Liz and Cathy only smiled.

April 26, 1971   **Monday**

My birthday. Oh no, the door bell just rang.

224

April 27, 1971   Tuesday

It was Charly at the door and an hour later Jacky and
Franky came over. We listened to records in between Indian
wrestling on the living room floor and then I announced
that since it was my birthday I was going to treat everyone
to a beer at the Dominion Bar. "Great idea," waves of
enthusiasm.

Five quarts of Labatt's fifty all around the table and
the new go-go waitress was a delight to look at.

"Dig the lungs on that girl," said Jacky dodging the
punch that Franky shot at him.

"Sock 'em Franky!" said Liz laughing.

"I just can't help myself."

Then Jacky told us of the lover's quarrel he had with
Franky on Easter morning. "Oh it was a dandy, but Franky
ought to know better than mouth off at me before I've
had my morning coffee. We were sitting at the breakfast
table, she was bitching away, so I picked up the five pound
bag of sugar and threw it at her saying, 'Take that sweets.'"

"Yes and I threw it back at him," said Franky, "but I
forgot there was a bag of brown sugar in the cupboard and
he dumped that on my head along with a cold cup of coffee.
Ugh, my hair was all matted and sticky and we really went
to it wrestling on the floor."

"Yeah and you kept trying to kick me in the balls," said
Jacky, "and I just had the operation."

"That's not true. I was only kicking you in the leg."

Spence Robinson and Willi the drummer from the
neighbourhood joined us in our second round of beer and
it turned out to be as pleasant a birthday party as any I
can remember.

April 29, 1971   Thursday

We were invited up to Robin's wedding reception
last Friday evening. Liz got all dressed up in her new
clothes, I changed my shirt and after a few beers we went
out on St. Antoine Street and flagged down a cab.

The cab driver started off a political discussion which lasted all the way to Ste. Famille Street. He was a middle-aged fellow, a Hungarian with a lot of relevant things to say.

Among a lot of other things he mentioned that prior to the Medicare programme his wife underwent a serious operation that had put him back fifteen hundred dollars in the hole.

"She had the operation in a private hospital," he said, "and I've been paying off the bill for the last ten years, mailing the doctor fifteen dollars a month. Well last year my wife went into the same hospital for another operation, only this time it was paid for by Medicare and the doctor, the specialist who operated on my wife ten years before, called me into his office and began giving me shit about how long it was taking me to pay the bill. He went on and on talking to me like I was a dog and finally I threw a quarter on his desk and said, 'Mister are you hungry? There's a quarter, go and buy a loaf of bread'. He shut right up and I walked out."

Robin wasn't home, a friend of hers, Macky, let us in and sat us down in the living room, pouring us each a glass of Muscatel wine. I asked Macky where Robin was and she said, "She just left her mother's house and should be here any minute now."

A small group of people were gathered in the living room with us, none of them known to us nor did they pay us the slightest bit of attention. "Well I hope the scenery improves," I whispered to Liz.

Towards nine o'clock Robin walked in the front door with her two older brothers, Gared and her sister-in-law, Dale Eden. Robin was dressed in a long white gown that was very becoming and I gave her a great hug of congratulations when she walked into the living room.

I introduced myself to Dale Eden, still as pretty as she was as a little girl. "Oh yes," she said smiling, "I remember you." "But you never knew I was madly in love with you in grade three, did you?" I said. "And that I used to follow you home from school?" She blushed. "Oh David," she said, "Why didn't you tell me?"

I sat down on the arm of the easy chair she was sitting in and we spoke of the past, of people we knew in

226

common and her own children, a boy and a girl.

"I lived in a fantasy world as a kid," she said, "a lot of people may have thought I was stuck up but actually I was just a very lonely and strange little girl."

"You grew up fast," I said.

"Yes, too fast," she replied. "I'll be twenty-five this year and I have a son that is eight years old."

More and more people kept arriving and by ten o'clock it was a full house with every chair occupied and about fifteen people sitting on the floor.

Meanwhile Gared was introducing me to everyone as a very special friend and a guy who is gonna have a fantastic book published in the immediate future. Liz was kind of peeved by his behaviour.

"Ah he means well Liz," I said. "He's had a couple of drinks and he's proud for me that's all."

We left the house towards eleven-thirty because I was getting stupid from the champagne and Liz had to go into work the next morning.

May 3, 1971   Monday

I was walking through McGill campus on the way home Friday afternoon and I decided to check around for Elaine. An acquaintance of hers was standing on the Union steps and I asked him if he knew Elaine's whereabouts. "You might find her in the library," he said. "Last time I saw her she told me she was working on a paper."

I took his advice and tripped on over there; in there moving about from section to section trying to find her. Long girls, short girls, some pretty, some not so pretty. "Hello, no you're not Elaine Rivard but perhaps you know her. No? O.K. Thank you."

Then I saw her standing by the library exit counters talking to a group of girls. I approached her from behind, placed my arm around her shoulder and when she turned her head I kissed her on the cheek.

"Oh Dave, it's you!" she said giving me a big laughing hug.

"Come on I'll buy you a coffee," I said. "I've got some news to tell you."

On the way over to the Student Lounge Elaine introduced me to her friend Essy, "We've met before," she said, "I remember you."

"In a good or bad way?"

"Good," she said smiling.

After we had settled down I told Elaine that I was being published this fall and that Robin had been married last week.

"Wonderful! "

"You're in the book, Elaine, so I'll give you a free copy," I said. "Is it O.K. if I use your real name?"

"Just as long as I'm not pulling down my pants in your book David I don't care."

I laughed. "Listen Elaine," I said, "I don't even mention those purple bloomers you used to wear when you were a high school girl, a nervous virgin tripping about the Prag."

We got into a discussion on what is good or bad literature and Essy said that I looked like an author. (How about that!) She said she could easily imagine me sitting with Ernest Hemingway and the rest of guys in a Parisian bistro back in the nineteen twenties.

"Essy, you sure have got an imagination," I said; and then striking an assumed literary pose I exclaimed, "Hey Erny, uh, it's about dis joint and duh wine. Ah, is dere any place in dis fuckin' city where a man can get a cold glass of beer? And who is dis goof Picasso anyhow. He can't even draw a straight line."

While we were talking Elaine kept glancing through the lounge windows, checking out a gang of students who were playing baseball in the field. Finally she said, "I think I'll go out there and ask them if I can bat for awhile, it might help my hangover."

I walked out on the field with her and the guys thought Elaine was a joke when she asked them if she could play for awhile. One of the students handed her the bat with a condescending smile as all the other guys moved in closer from the out field towards where she was standing. Of course they couldn't realize that the slender, black-eyed girl facing them had arms of steel.

CRA-AK and the ball went sailing away over their heads rolling to a standstill a good forty yards from where they were staring with their mouths wide open.

The next pitch had three of the guys shuffling back into the outfield and I heard one of the dudes say as he passed by me, "Who is that chick? She's really good."

Cra-ak. The second one looked like it was gonna end up on Pine Avenue.

"You're too much Elaine! " I yelled.

"Oh well, I was a little rusty at the beginning," she said. "It's been a long time."

CRA-AK, CRA-AK, CRA-AK. She had the guys red-faced and puffing all over the field for a half-hour. Then she said, while leaning on the bat, "I'm out of shape Dave, my arm is getting sore."

Then she thanked the guys for letting her play and I swear, for a few seconds I thought they were gonna ask her for an autograph.

May 7, 1971   Friday

Let me remove my disguise prematurely. I am every man. I am the boy who sat in the back of the classroom that the teachers can never remember, who never asked questions and never answered any, who threw snowballs at the girls on the way home from school and lost his books, who skinned his knees playing two-chase-the-bunch and Red Rover - Red Rover on the streets.

I'm the soldier who went silently to war and came home with nightmares, who did not smile at the photographer in the trenches, who got his medals from the government in the mail.

I am the good worker in the plant, in the factory and the office, the face in the crowd, the man in the line, the man on the subway, the man that magazine subscriptions are sold to who has two and a half kids, an old car and a T.V. he can't afford to have repaired. I am the face that has been stepped on for four thousand years. I am the April voice of a renaissance that is to come.